DEVILS WALKING

DEVILS

WALKING

Klan Murders along the Mississippi in the 1960s

STANLEY NELSON

Foreword by GREG ILES
Afterword by HANK KLIBANOFF

Louisiana State University Press Baton Rouge

Published by Louisiana State University Press
Copyright © 2016 by Louisiana State University Press
All rights reserved
Manufactured in the United States of America
First printing

Designer: Michelle A. Neustrom
Typeface: Sentinel
Printer and binder: McNaughton & Gunn, Inc.

Cold-case and Klan material adapted from Stanley Nelson's articles in the *Concordia Sentinel*
is reproduced with permission of the *Concordia Sentinel*.

Library of Congress Cataloging-in-Publication Data

Names: Nelson, Stanley, 1955 —author.
Title: Devils Walking : Klan Murders Along the Mississippi in the 1960s / Stanley Nelson ;
    foreword by Greg Iles ; afterword by Hank Klibanoff.
Description: Baton Rouge : Louisiana State University Press, [2016] | Includes bibliographical
    references and index.
Identifiers: LCCN 2016012820| ISBN 978-0-8071-6407-5 (cloth : alk. paper) | ISBN 978-0-
    8071-6408-2 (pdf) | ISBN 978-0-8071-6409-9 (epub) | ISBN 978-0-8071-6410-5 (mobi)
Subjects: LCSH: African Americans—Violence against—Mississippi—History—20th century. |
    Ku Klux Klan (1915–)—History—20th century. | Murder—Mississippi—History—20th cen-
    tury. | Murder—Investigation—Mississippi—History—20th century. | Ku Klux Klan (1915–)
    —Interviews. | Witnesses—Mississippi—Interviews. | Interviews—Mississippi. | Racism—
    Mississippi—History—20th century. | Corruption—Mississippi—History—20th century. |
    Mississippi—Race relations—History—20th century.
Classification: LCC E185.93.M6 N38 2016 | DDC 322.4/2097620904—dc23 LC record avail-
    able at https://lccn.loc.gov/2016012820

The paper in this book meets the guidelines for permanence and durability of the Committee
on Production Guidelines for Book Longevity of the Council on Library Resources. ∞

May they never be forgotten:

Henry Hezekiah Dee

Joseph Edwards

Earl Hodges

Wharlest Jackson

Charles Moore

Frank Morris

Clifton Walker

Ben Chester White

And to the memory of:

Sam Hanna

John Pfeifer

Billy Bob Williams

They were "devils a-walkin' [the] earth a-seekin' what [they] could devour."

—Charlie Davenport, ex-slave
    Natchez, Mississippi
    Late 1930s, describing the Ku Klux Klan

CONTENTS

ILLUSTRATIONS

following page 49

FBI AGENTS

Paul Lancaster, who taped two interviews with Frank Morris

John Pfeifer, whose investigations led to the convictions of Sheriff Cross
    and Deputy DeLaughter

Billy Bob Williams, who followed KKK members in Natchez

LAW ENFORCEMENT

Ferriday police chief Bob Warren

Noah Cross in Ferriday, circa 1940

Natchez police chief J. T. Robinson with detectives Charlie Bahin and
    Frank Rickard

Noah Cross taking the oath for his eighth term in July 1972

Vidalia police chief J. L. "Bud" Spinks

Noah Cross with Frank DeLaughter after their release from federal prison

SILVER DOLLAR GROUP MURDER SUSPECTS

Raleigh J. "Red" Glover, head of the Silver Dollar Group

Kenneth Norman Head

Homer T. "Buck" Horton

Elden "Junkman" Hester

Tommie Lee Jones

E. D. Morace

Ernest B. Parker

Coonie Poissot

James L. Scarborough

Sonny Taylor

James Ford Seale

Myron Wayne "Jack" Seale

following page 114

VICTIMS

Joseph Edwards, who disappeared in 1964

Earl Hodges in front of his shop, circa 1950s

Frank Morris and workers in front of his shoe shop, circa 1950s

Morris's bedroom in the back of his shoe shop after the 1964 arson

Rubble of Morris's shoe shop

George Metcalfe's car following the bombing in 1965

Wharlest Jackson, the Silver Dollar Group's final target

Jackson's pickup following the bombing in 1967

Blasting cap leg wire used in the bombing of Jackson's car

Henry Hezekiah Dee, killed by Klansmen in 1964

Charles Moore, killed by Klansmen

Thelma Collins, Canadian filmmaker David Ridgen, and Thomas Moore

OTHER

Curt Hewitt, manager of the mob-run Morville Lounge

E. L. McDaniel, grand dragon of the United Klans of America and later an
    FBI informant

Silver dollar given to Klansman Earcel Boyd

Earcel Boyd, who preached in black churches while a member of the
    Silver Dollar Group

Ernest Avants, following his arrest in the beating of two civil rights
    workers

Father August Thompson, who prayed with Frank Morris

James Goss, whose complaint led to Joseph Edwards's disappearance

L. C. Murray, one of three Silver Dollar Group Klansmen still living in
    2015

Stanley Nelson interviewing Klansman Arthur Leonard Spencer in 2010

FOREWORD

I DEDICATED my novel *Natchez Burning* thus: "To Stanley Nelson, a humble hero." I don't use that term lightly. Heroes abound in novels, but in the real world they are rare indeed. For most of us, it takes all our resources merely to lead a decent life and get the bills paid. But there is a special minority of persons who go beyond that—sometimes far beyond, into the realm of true heroism.

I'm not talking about lightning acts of courage in battle. Such bravery certainly qualifies as heroism and often costs soldiers their health or even their lives. But it's the willingness to sacrifice oneself in a just cause that ennobles bravery. And no cause was ever more just than the one to which Stanley Nelson has thus far given eight years of his life. Nor was any cause ever more selflessly pursued by a man who seemed to have no personal stake in it than Stanley's investigation into the Silver Dollar Group murders in Mississippi and Louisiana in the 1960s. This selfless dedication is what prompted me to model a character after Stanley Nelson.

Stanley is a gifted reporter, but he doesn't work for the *New York Times* or the *Washington Post*. He works for the *Concordia Sentinel*, a newspaper with 4,700 subscribers, based in Ferriday, Louisiana, a tiny farming town only a few miles from the Mississippi River. He has no pool of researchers or stringers on whom to call, no fat expense budget to exploit in his investigations, no battery of attorneys to protect him. Yet despite this lack of material resources, Stanley Nelson took up a group of civil rights cases so cold they could have chilled an industrial deep freeze and made them so hot that the FBI felt the burn. That's right—the chief law enforcement agency of the federal government had to scramble to play catch-up behind this one-man investigative juggernaut.

What does it take to accomplish such a feat? Empathy, for one thing. The ability to understand what it means to have lost a son, a brother, or a parent to cruel and senseless murder. Stanley Nelson put himself in the shoes—and the hearts—of people who for decades had no real recourse to the law because the lawmen in their town were among their loved ones' killers. But empathy alone wasn't enough. Several FBI agents in the 1960s deeply felt the suffering of those victimized families. To solve their cases, however, required the ability to inspire trust in African Americans who had been given damned little reason to trust whites since the time of slavery. Stanley has this gift, and he has used it with great effect. Finally, success required determination—the stubbornness and stick-to-your-guns fortitude that make rural southerners the kind of foot soldiers military officers love. Stanley also has that quality in spades.

Few people in his hometown thanked him for it. People don't like writers dredging up the past in New England or New York, but in Louisiana and Mississippi, turning over old stones can get you killed in a hurry. At the very least, it brands you a "race traitor" to more than a few people you see every day on the street or in the next pew at church. But no matter what the naysayers did or threatened to do, Stanley plodded doggedly forward. He followed every lead, no matter where it led, and confronted every witness and suspect he could corner, no matter how dangerous the encounter. His ultimate quarry was the most violent splinter cell of the Ku Klux Klan ever birthed in America, the Silver Dollar Group, yet he never once let fear slow him down. Even so, the most remarkable thing about Stanley's work was what drove him onward year after year, something so simple that I didn't quite see it for a long time. You see, Stanley's motive and his object were always one and the same.

Justice.

Stanley didn't go on this seemingly quixotic quest to gain money, or fame, or any kind of advancement. He did it because he couldn't bear the spiritual imbalance created in his hometown—and in America—by murder victims being abandoned by the justice system, and by their families being condemned to perpetual pain and grief. Stanley saw a wrong that needed righting, and since the authorities charged with redressing it had made clear that they had no real intention of doing so, he stepped into the breach and went to work.

What most inspires me about Stanley's solitary crusade is that the murder victims he sought to do right by were not celebrated leaders of the civil rights movement. They were just regular folks—a shoe repairman, a factory worker, a busboy—who wanted to improve the quality of life for their friends and neighbors. They were the salt of the earth, though they were not the color of salt, and Ferriday and Natchez were lesser places after they were gone. But thanks to Stanley's work, a hidden circle of American survivors bound only by shared losses to violent racism has seen the veil that concealed the killers of their loved ones lifted, and truth exposed in all its clarifying light.

Thanks to one dedicated reporter, the secrets of the Silver Dollar Group have been plumbed, and their evil set down between the covers of this book for you to try to understand. Some readers may shudder during this harrowing journey, but the path to truth and enlightenment is seldom easy. If Stanley could stand to listen to shattered relatives and cold-blooded killers tell him their long-held stories, then surely we can bear to read and learn from the secret history revealed as a result of his labors. Take comfort in the fact that the tale you are about to read is ultimately uplifting: Stanley Nelson raised his pen against the sword of hatred, and as a result, one bend of the Mississippi River looks a lot less dark than it once did.

Stanley Nelson gives me hope for the South, and for America.

— Greg Iles
November 23, 2015
Natchez, Mississippi

PREFACE

MY FIRST STORY on the Frank Morris arson murder was published on the front page of the *Concordia Sentinel* in Ferriday, Louisiana, on February 28, 2007. My boss, Lesley Hanna-Capdepon, had learned the day before that the Federal Bureau of Investigation (FBI) was taking a second look at a number of civil rights–era murders, including that of a Ferriday man, Morris. I had never heard of Morris, although I was born in Ferriday in 1955, a time when his shoe shop was thriving. His business served the town's black and white communities well for many years. Ferriday was a poor town, and most people there did not have closets filled with shoes. Parents depended on Morris to keep their children's shoes in good repair for as long as possible. Nevertheless, in 1964, Klansmen torched his business. Morris attempted to escape the conflagration through the front door, but his assailants forced him at gunpoint back inside the shop. By the time he emerged from the rear, he was naked, bleeding, and dying. His life ended four days later.

I grew up sixteen miles away in Catahoula Parish. My parents worked and shopped in Ferriday. On numerous occasions, my brother and I tagged along for haircuts and trips to the grocery store. My daddy was a farmer and plumber. In 1950 Mama was a graduate of Ferriday High, where Concordia Parish sheriff Noah Cross's wife, Iola, taught English. Like hundreds of other students, Mama loved Miss Iola, who was also a poet. Sometimes she'd read her poems at the end of class. My mother's younger schoolmate Jerry Lee Lewis wasn't a music legend yet, though she remembers that at almost every recess and lunch hour he'd play the piano in the school auditorium.

Later, Mama worked as a nurse at the Concordia Parish Health Unit. In 1961, during a local drive encouraging residents to get their polio booster, she was pictured in the *Concordia Sentinel* several times, giving shots to the mayor, the publisher of the newspaper, local businessmen, and others. I did a double take when I found her on page 8 of the April 14, 1961, issue, giving a shot to Concordia Parish sheriff's deputy Frank DeLaughter. A brutal man, he served time, along with Sheriff Cross, in federal prison in the 1970s. The deputy, I would learn in the years ahead, was a suspect in the Frank Morris arson and at least one other unsolved cold-case murder. I would also learn that the FBI considered Sheriff Cross and some of his deputies among the most corrupt in the South.

A press release from the Department of Justice in 2007 announced that the department had partnered with the National Association for the Advancement of Colored People (NAACP), the National Urban League, and the Southern Poverty Law Center (SPLC) "to investigate several aging unsolved violent crimes from the Civil Rights era." The announcement came in the wake of the FBI's arrest of James Ford Seale, a seventy-one-year-old former Klansman who, with others, had savagely beaten and killed two black Mississippi teens in 1964. FBI director Robert Mueller pledged that the bureau would "do everything we can to close those cases and to close this dark chapter in our nation's history." From the SPLC, I received by fax 150 pages of heavily redacted FBI documents concerning the Morris case. I read them quickly and wrote a story two hours later. I was fascinated by the murder case but figured this story would be the only one.

A few days later, Rosa Williams called. She had been twelve years old when her grandfather, Frank Morris, was murdered in 1964. Someone had sent a copy of the paper to her in Las Vegas, where she had moved years after the arson. She thanked me for writing about the murder, explaining that she had always wanted to know who killed her grandfather and why. For decades she prayed for justice and for truth, but she bore her frustration and pain silently, rarely mentioning it to anyone. Rosa told me that she had learned more about the case from the *Sentinel* story (764 words) than she had in the previous forty-three years. Never had any law enforcement agency—federal, state, or local—talked to her about the killing. Her grandfather had been forgotten. She was grateful Morris's name was on the FBI list, and she was hungry for answers.

My thoughts turned to an autumn night in my youth in the early 1970s when, after a football game, I came upon a gruesome scene on the highway. An intoxicated man had plowed his car into a Volkswagen Beetle, killing a young family, including a six-year-old girl. The child and her parents were trapped inside the flaming car. No one could get them out. It was awful. I thought about Frank Morris and wondered: What kind of man would purposely set another on fire? What had the moment been like for Morris when he confronted his killers? What led those men to commit such a heinous act? I put myself in Rosa Williams's shoes. How would I feel had that been my grandfather? Despite the racial divide, why wasn't Ferriday or nearby Natchez, or the state of Louisiana for that matter, outraged by this crime? Why hasn't anyone done anything about it? Who else has been forgotten?

I called Rosa. I promised her I would do everything within my limited power to find out who killed her grandfather and why. Careful not to promise success, I pledged that I would stay in touch and share my findings. No longer would she be alone in the dark.

I would go on to write 190 articles over seven years. There would be other cold cases, including some in Mississippi that had a Concordia connection. Not everyone was happy about my reporting. There were nasty calls and ugly letters and e-mails. The newspaper office was broken into. Two straight mornings before dawn, while I was making my daily walk, a pickup emerged from the distance and flushed me off the road. Through the years, I interviewed aging Klansmen and witnesses in many places, including cornfields, cemeteries, churchyards, hospitals, and hotel rooms. I was cursed often but received decently by most.

The 150 pages from the SPLC fueled a number of initial stories, and one led to another. The Sam Hanna family, owners of the *Concordia Sentinel,* a 4,700-circulation weekly founded after the Civil War by a former slave, gave me the green light to pursue the story. They stood behind me from beginning to end. In addition to following these investigations, I had to take care of my regular duties as editor, covering the school board, parish government, and town council, as well as writing about crime, court, and everything else, including a local history column.

I soon realized that Frank Morris's story was much bigger than Ferriday. I also recognized there was not a moment to waste. In the 1960s, Klan murderers on the loose were a formidable enemy. Although the few aging suspects still around in 2007 did not seem as intimidating as they had been during their prime, some remained dangerous.

Some well-meaning people tried to set me straight by insisting that justice for old Klansmen like James Ford Seale was no business for a newspaper reporter. They said that the matter should be left to God. I countered that before God gives judgment, we are morally forbidden from supporting killers, even through our silence or apathy. I reminded them of Proverbs 28:17: "A man who is laden with the guilt of human blood will be a fugitive until death; let no one support him."

The biggest foe of the FBI's cold-case initiative by 2007 was not a violent racist bully in the prime of his life but an embittered, dying old man—a fugitive until death—chained to the sins of his past. He was still in reach, but his days were numbered. He was counted among the Klan devils who had walked the earth since Reconstruction. In Concordia Parish, Louisiana, and nearby Natchez, Mississippi, and environs, the most secretive Klan group ever known had arisen—the Silver Dollar Group—led by a psychopath who outwitted the FBI. This man and his murdering associates, some of whom wore badges, had devoured all in their path and escaped with a swagger into the darkness of the decades to follow.

Fifty years later, with death offering the escape route for the fugitive murderer, *time* emerged as the new enemy of justice.

ACKNOWLEDGMENTS

MANY PEOPLE helped me during the writing and research of this book and during the investigations into the long-ago murders.

I am grateful to Lesley Hanna-Capdepon and Sam Hanna Jr. of the *Concordia Sentinel* for their support and commitment to justice for all, and to co-workers Tracey Bruce, Barbara Jackson, and Heather Kaplan Card for their assistance.

I thank Julia Dobbins, Denise Jackson Ford, Keith Hodges, Wharlest Jackson Jr., Thomas Moore, and Deborah Jackson Sylvester for sharing stories of their loved ones and recalling the tragedies that forever altered their lives. Special thanks go to Rosa Williams, the granddaughter of Frank Morris. Her life exemplifies grace, faith, love, and dignity.

Those who provided important contributions to my research and investigations include Chris Allen (FBI), Bill Atkins, Jim Barnett, Paul Benoist, Johnny Blunschi, Leland Boyd, Sonny Boyd, William Brown, Brad Burget, Tony Byrne, the late Woodie Davis, Antonne Duncan, the late Ted Gardner (FBI agent retired), Kirby King, Paul Lancaster (FBI agent retired), Norma Leake, the late Rev. Robert Lee Jr., the late Robert Lee III, Robert "Buck" Lewis, Johnny Loomis, Mary Manhein, Tron McCoy, David Opperman, Robin Person, the late John Pfeifer (FBI agent retired), Donna Robinson, Joe Shapiro, J. L. Spinks, Father August Thompson, Carl Ray Thompson, former U.S. attorney Donald Washington, the late Billy Bob Williams (FBI agent retired), and David Whatley.

I thank the Center for Investigative Reporting and the great journalists with whom it was my honor to work: John Fleming, Ben Greenberg, Peter Klein, Hank Klibanoff, Jerry Mitchell, Pete Nicks, David Paperny, David Ridgen, and Robert Rosenthal.

I am grateful to the LSU Manship School of Mass Communications, including Jay Shelledy (for too many things to mention); LSU deans Jack Hamilton, Ralph Izard, and Jerry Ceppos, as well as Bob Mann and many others at the Manship School; and especially the Student Cold Case Team, including Matthew Albright, Matt Barnidge, S. Rene Barrow, Chelsea Brasted, Gordon Brillon, Ryan Buxton, Zachary Carline, Brett Christensen, Jake Clapp, Ward Collin, Sydni Dunn, Tessalon Felician, Andrea Gallo, Joshua Jackson, David LaPlante, Sarah Lawson, Minjie Li, Katie Macdonald, Justin McAcy, Olivia McClure, Willborn Nobles III, Briana Piche, Patrick Rideau, Paromita Saha, Matthew Schaeffer, Morgan Searles, Brian Sibille, Jay Stafford, Robert Stewart, Kevin Thibodeaux, Jennifer Vance, Ben Wallace, Drew White, Amy Whitehead, Marylee Williams, and Xerxes Wilson.

My thanks also to the Syracuse College of Law Cold Case Justice Initiative and its cofounders, Paula Johnson and Janis McDonald, who work tirelessly for justice and peace for many families, and to CCJI's many volunteer law students.

These *Concordia Sentinel* interns did outstanding work during their summers in Concordia Parish, Natchez, and southwest Mississippi: Kellie Gentry and Jared Lovett, University of Alabama; Tori Stilwell, University of North Carolina; and Matt Barnidge and Ian Stanford, LSU Manship School.

Thanks to Teach for America, especially Zach Bell, Emily Coady, Taylor Pettit, Bryan Tomlinson, and Mark Young.

I also thank LSU Press editor Rand Dotson and the entire LSU Press team, especially Catherine Kadair, as well as freelance copyeditor Julia Ridley Smith, who found a book in my cluttered manuscript.

And, finally, I am grateful to Greg Iles for challenging white southerners to face the horrific racial injustices of our past and present with open minds and especially open hearts.

DEVILS WALKING

Locations of Silver Dollar Group murders. In the cases of Henry Dee and Charles Moore, locations are site of abduction; both were drowned in the old river at Davis Island in Warren County, Mississippi. (Map by Mary Lee Eggart)

1

WHY FRANK?

AT MIDNIGHT on Thursday, December 10, 1964, Ferriday's two youngest police officers parked the town's lone patrol car, a brand-new white Pontiac, on the southeast corner of the town's main intersection, where US 65 and US 84 converge. George Sewell, a twenty-three-year-old Concordia Parish native, had been on the force for a year. His partner, Mississippi-born Timothy Loftin, was a year older but had been a town cop for only two months. Dressed in their uniforms—white shirts and blue trousers—the two officers were restless this night, fifteen days before Christmas.[1] Weeknight duty was busiest during the period from 10 p.m. until an hour or so after midnight, when the factories across the Mississippi River in nearby Natchez changed shifts. Many plant workers stopped at the bars in town or along the ten-mile strip of watering holes between Ferriday and Vidalia.

A short time before midnight, twenty-three-year-old Kenneth Walsworth, a friend of the young, untrained officers, finished work at the Holsum Bread bakery in Natchez and cruised into Ferriday. As he often did, Walsworth parked beside the Pontiac and climbed into the backseat of the patrol car. Loftin was behind the wheel; Sewell was riding shotgun.[2] As they talked on this damp, cloudy evening, the temperature dipped into the high forties. On the southwest corner of the crossroads was Cecil Beatty's Gulf Station. There, almost every evening after supper, Concordia Parish Sheriff's Office deputies, some of them Klansmen, leaned on the fenders of their patrol cars while talking and watching traffic. By dark, some of the deputies went home, while others stayed out most of the night drinking and playing poker.[3]

On the northwest corner of the intersection, the lounge at the King Hotel closed for the night. Opened in January 1927, three decades after a railroad company founded the town, the hotel had suffered a disastrous opening year when the Great Flood of the Mississippi River submerged Ferriday and the lower floor of the three-story building. Once the damage was repaired, the King became a showpiece. But by 1964, after several changes in ownership, it had become infamous for prostitution and gambling. Pickups with cattle racks on the beds and gun racks in the cabs lined the dirt parking lot, and the place had become a favorite hangout for alcoholics, roughnecks, truck drivers, loggers, cowboys, factory workers, and the local unit of the Original Knights of the Ku Klux Klan.[4]

The Concordia Parish Original Knights unit was organized in 1962, and Mississippi's first Original Knights chapter was born in 1963. In Louisiana and the Magnolia State, the United Klans of America, responsible for a series of bombings in McComb, Mississippi, during the summer of 1964, was gaining strength. The White Knights, spawned by the Original Knights but limited to Mississippi, killed three civil rights workers in Philadelphia, Mississippi, that same summer. This case drew national attention and resulted in the opening of an FBI field office in Jackson, the first since World War II.[5] Meanwhile, a secret, deadly Klan cell known as the Silver Dollar Group came to life in Vidalia, Concordia Parish's county seat, located on the banks of the Mississippi River opposite Natchez.

At the King Hotel, the manager, a Klan leader and recruiter, kept a lookout for potential members. (The nearby plants, where thousands of men worked side by side seven days a week, had also become major recruiting grounds.[6]) From the dirty, dark lounge, the Klan staged some of its late-night raids of violence and intimidation against blacks and civil rights workers. Klan allegiances and alliances came and went, but as the civil rights movement grew and ignited violent white opposition to racial integration, there would be scores of beatings and arsons and at least five murders in 1964 alone attributed to the Silver Dollar Group.[7]

Shortly before 1 a.m. on December 10, two waitresses walked out of the King Hotel lounge, climbed into a dark green sedan, and headed for Vidalia. One of the young officers suggested following the girls to see what they were up to. It was not an uncommon thing for Sewell and Loftin to do, although the mayor and police chief forbade them from leaving the town limits in the patrol car for anything less than an emergency.[8]

Four blocks along the main drag south of the King Hotel, the Pontiac cruised by the shoe shop on the east side of the street. Fifty-one-year-old Frank Morris was in bed in a back room, while his grandson and lone full-time employee slept in a shanty located within five feet of the rear of the shop.[9] For almost thirty years, Morris had nurtured a loyal white and black clientele, a rare accomplishment for a black man in a southern town during the era.

A block to the south, the cook at Haney's Big House chatted with a customer, while a drunk slept it off on a bench. Though quiet on this particular night, the nightclub was often crowded and loud. Legendary in the region, and well known by African American singers who followed the Chitlin' Circuit, Haney's featured performers like B. B. King (before he was famous). Gamblers from as far away as Memphis played poker in a back room.[10] As a child, Jerry Lee Lewis, the Ferriday-born rock 'n' roll legend, occasionally would sneak into the club and hide under a table until the owner, Will Haney, would find him and gently kick him out. Lewis loved the music, the dancing, and the atmosphere in a town known for its violence and craziness.[11]

Attendants at service stations would remember nothing that stood out that December night.[12] By the time the Pontiac passed the sawmill on the south end of town and turned east toward Vidalia, the sedan had raced out of sight. The officers traversed the strip from Ferriday and back a couple of times before giving up on finding the women.[13] Rounding the curve at the lumberyard heading back into town, the officers spotted a red glow a few blocks up the street. In front of the shoe shop, chunks of cinder blocks and shards of glass littered the street. "Lord, this was no fire, this was an explosion," Sewell thought as he took in the scene. The shop was fully engulfed by flames.[14] As they drove past, the officers witnessed Frank Morris, now a human torch, emerge from the rear.[15]

Loftin parked in a vacant car lot between the shop and the Billups Service Station, a half block up the street. Morris was naked and bleeding. Smoke floated from his head. Straps of his tee shirt and undershorts clung to his body. One officer removed the flaming straps; the other patted Morris's head to put out the fire. Morris's skin peeled and drifted to the ground. Walsworth thought Morris was praying as he mumbled, "Oh, Lord! Oh, Lord!" He complained of being cold. One of the officers steadied Morris, whose flesh felt hard and crusty. Morris was strangely calm, as though, Walsworth thought, he knew "he was in his last days."[16]

They led Morris to the backseat of the Pontiac. Sewell, Loftin, and Walsworth squeezed into the front. As they quizzed Morris, Loftin floored the accelerator and headed to the newly opened Concordia Parish Hospital a mile away. Morris said that after being awakened by breaking glass, he encountered two white men outside the front of his shop. One poured gasoline from a can. As Morris reached the front door, the other man pointed a single-barreled shotgun at Morris and threatened to blow off his head, commanding, "Get back in that shop, nigger!" Morris said there might have been a third man in a car outside in the alley on the north side of the shop.[17]

At the hospital, one of the officers led Morris to the entrance of the emergency room, then raced back to the Pontiac to return to the crime scene. Morris made his way—alone—into the emergency room, where a nurse recognized him. He reeked of gasoline, his body a mass of charred flesh. "I've been burned," he said. "Someone threw something in my shop and blowed it up." He was inexplicably alert, following the nurse's every direction. She noticed the skin of one of his index fingers was missing; the bone protruded.[18] Dr. Charles Colvin admitted Morris at 1:45 a.m., thirty minutes after the fire was reported. He had suffered third-degree burns covering all but the soles of his feet and spent the next four days on his back inside Room 101.[19]

Before dawn, FBI agent Paul Lancaster was awakened by a phone call from Louisiana division headquarters in New Orleans. He was the senior resident agent at the Alexandria office, fifty miles west of Ferriday. The caller instructed him to race to the hospital to interview a Negro man who was gravely injured in a fire. Lancaster routinely carried a portable IBM dictaphone in his bureau car so that while traveling he could dictate notes for the steno pool in New Orleans. When he arrived at the hospital, Ferriday police chief Bob Warren and fire chief Nolan Mouelle greeted Lancaster. The first glimpse of the injured man told Lancaster death would come soon, and he hoped that Frank Morris could identify his attackers by name. The agent realized that this was the first time in the history of civil rights–era murders that a victim had lived long enough to be able to name his attackers to law enforcement. He also knew that the Ferriday police were incapable of solving the arson and that the sheriff's office, which considered the FBI the enemy, would never investigate or assist in the probe. If anything, deputies would obstruct it. They often notified Klansmen about bureau activities. One deputy in particular, the hulking Frank DeLaughter, who once said he thought no more of killing a man than a rabbit, was known to make harassing phone calls to the wives of FBI agents. But if Lancaster could record Morris's voice naming his killers, prosecutors could use the recording as legal evidence in court.[20]

Surprised that visitors walked in and out of Morris's room at will, Lancaster left the hospital with one request for the attending physician: Get Morris to identify his attackers.[21] Once the police and firemen left, a steady stream of visitors came by Morris's room. The Rev. August Thompson, who pastored at the St. Charles Church for the Colored, was at the post office in Ferriday on Thursday morning when he learned about the tragedy. He rushed to the hospital, where the sight of his friend nearly made him faint.[22] As Thompson greeted attendants in the room, Morris recognized the voice.

"Father, is that you?"

"Yes, Frank."

"Father, I'm cold!"

Once alone with Morris, Thompson comforted the dying man. He stood beside the bed and prayed. When he asked what had happened, Morris didn't respond. Church business required Thompson to go to New Orleans, and after a few minutes, he told Morris he had to leave.

"You coming back, Father?"

"Yes, Frank, I will be back."[23]

Another visitor was James White Sr., Morris's best friend. Some people thought the two were brothers. Ten months earlier, Klansmen, convinced that White was a black Muslim hoarding weapons, had launched a plan to kidnap and beat him. Used to harassment, White was always prepared. As gunfire erupted in his yard, White aimed and fired his shotgun, hitting one of the fleeing Klansmen in the face. White imagined the many scenarios his friend might have faced hours earlier, but his efforts to find out who was responsible failed. Morris would only lament, "I just can't believe it!"[24]

The Rev. Robert Lee Jr. came by. His wife, Lavinia, had attended high school with Morris in Natchez. During the last years of his life, Morris hosted a Sunday morning gospel music show on the Ferriday radio station KFNV, and he often dedicated a special song to Lavinia, who had a son in Vietnam. She loved to hear the Consolers sing, "Waiting for My Child to Come Home." Morris knew it gave spiritual strength to Lavinia and other mothers whose sons were in the jungles of Vietnam. He also knew the song had special meaning for black mothers, who prayed for their sons' safe return from the streets of Ferriday or from the hands of wicked cops: "Lord my child is somewhere in some lonely jail; Lord, with no one there to post his bail."[25]

Alone in the room with his wife's old schoolmate, Reverend Lee asked, "Frank, who did this to you?" Morris answered, "Two white friends." He would say no more. Lee left Room 101 convinced that Morris knew his assailants. But were the words—"two white friends"—generic? Morris told many visitors he didn't know he had a white enemy. Did his statement conceal that he knew who masterminded the arson but not the identities of the arsonists? Until his death at age one hundred in 2014, Pastor Lee was haunted by the evil attack. "I never want to see a sight like that again," he said repeatedly of his dying friend.[26]

Similarly unnerved by the sight, Ferriday's mayor L. W. "Woodie" Davis, who had known Morris for years, pleaded for the names of the attackers. Before his death in 2011 at ninety-three, Davis said he had made a mistake by talking with Morris in the presence of police officers. He was convinced that had he gone in alone, Morris would have whispered names of his killers. "It's one of the greatest regrets of my life," Davis said.[27]

One by one they came: black friends, white acquaintances, and relatives. Morris's father, Sullivan, who had taught his son the shoe repair business, could not for the life of him understand the cruelty. Many believed Morris was so traumatized that he failed to fully understand the severity of his injuries.[28] Morris had been given a grain of morphine the first day and a half grain the next before being wheeled to the operating room for a tracheotomy. A smoky-smelling mucous was regularly sucked from his throat.

Father Thompson arrived for his second visit shortly after Morris's surgery. With him was Father John Gayer, who ministered to Ferriday's white Catholic congregation at St. Patrick's and had previously headed up the now-inactive local NAACP. Thompson sensed Morris was near death. His eyes darted around the room, but he seemed unable to focus. Like everyone else, the priests wanted to know who had attacked him. Thompson asked Morris to move his hand or a finger if the priests correctly named the persons responsible. Gayer tried to reassure him, and each time a name was called out, the two priests studied Morris's hands, but they never moved. A short time after the priests left, Morris lapsed into a coma.[29]

Inside his topcoat, Thompson was carrying a Kodak thirty-five-millimeter camera. He snapped four shots of Morris to preserve a record for the world of what hate had done to a decent man. Thompson was inspired by the power of the 1955 photograph of the tortured body of fourteen-year-old Emmett Till, who had been killed by two white men in Money, Mississippi, for allegedly whistling at one of the men's wives. Unlike Emmett Till, however, Frank Morris was still alive.[30] And unlike in the Till case, the pictures of Morris were not published. Thompson kept them secret for fifty years.

Morris's face appears childlike, swollen and charred, almost as if it's covered with a mask. He is on his back, and his body is swollen, too, though much of it is hidden by a chrome frame onto which a sheet is laid to conceal his wounds from visitors. A black woman in a white dress rests her forearms on the chrome bed railing. (Her face is not in the picture; possibly it is Morris's stepmother.[31]) He is hairless from head to toe, and his lips appear bleached. A Ferriday woman whose husband saw Morris after the fire reported that the Klan had "burned him white."[32]

Dr. Colvin could do nothing to save Morris and told him that he was going to die. Before Morris went into a coma, he urged Morris to tell someone, anyone, who had attacked him. "Just tell at least one person." Repeatedly, Morris said he didn't know the men. When Colvin arrived at the hospital a few minutes after Morris, he had observed bloody footprints leading from the parking lot to the emergency room. He never got over it.[33]

Six years later, Colvin was one of five passengers to perish after a twin-engine Bonanza collided with a Cessna. The Cessna's pilot, the lone survivor of the crash, was the notorious Klansman James Ford Seale of Franklin County, Mississippi, who was convicted in 2007 for the 1964 murders of Henry Hezekiah Dee and Charles Moore. Seale died in federal prison in 2011. Had he been convicted in 1964 following the murders, Dr. Colvin and those who died with him would have lived longer lives. Rumors followed in the wake of the crash. Did the Klan fear Morris had identified his killers in the presence of the doctor? Such is the trail of carnage when justice lags.[34]

On the same day that Morris was attacked, Dr. Martin Luther King accepted the Nobel Peace Prize in Oslo, Norway. With the South on his mind, Dr. King told an international audience, "I accept this award today with an abiding faith in America and an audacious faith in the future of mankind." Four days later, at 7:30 p.m., on Monday, December 14, 1964, Frank Morris died. Not once had he identified his attackers by name, even though every friend or acquaintance who visited him in the hospital walked away convinced that he knew his assailants. Agent Lancaster had pleaded with Morris to make an identification. "If he had told me, we would have gone after those sons of bitches," Lancaster lamented in 2009.[35]

ALMOST A HALF CENTURY LATER, King's faith seemed renewed when new probes were launched into the murder of Frank Morris and others. In 2007, the *Concordia Sentinel* became part of that investigation, as would many others in the days to follow. The newspaper's search would widen to include related murder cases across the river, as it flushed out old Klansmen from the flatlands of Louisiana and the hills and hollows of Mississippi. Aging and battle-scarred FBI agents—ignored by today's bureau—shared their experiences and offered advice on how to finish the job they had begun so many years earlier. Elderly widows, black and white, voiced thoughts they couldn't say out loud during segregation.

It did not take long to figure out that the epicenter of Klan violence in the 1960s had been an area that stretched from Concordia Parish sixty miles eastward to Brookhaven and McComb, Mississippi. Concordia's shoreline along the Mississippi River is seventy-five miles, the second longest in the state. Between the river and Interstate 55 are seven southwest Mississippi counties, including Jefferson, Adams, and Wilkinson, which border the river opposite Concordia. To their east are the counties of Franklin, Lincoln, Amite, and Pike. John Doar, assistant attorney general for the Civil Rights Division of the U.S. Department of Justice, had branded Ferriday an "outlaw country" in 1965 and urged civil rights workers to get out. This region of the nation, Doar advised, was still "part of the American frontier, riddled with bewildering rural patterns of secrecy and silence, almost designed to make the work of any investigative agency difficult, if not impossible."[36] After announcing its cold-case initiative to reinvestigate civil rights–era murders, no case drew more attention from the FBI than Morris's. Cynthia Deitle, head of the bureau's Civil Rights Cold Case Unit in 2011, called the arson murder "one of the most horrific and troubling" of all. She vowed, "We will solve this crime. The FBI will not rest until we uncover the truth."[37]

No one has prayed more for that truth than Father Thompson. The *Concordia Sentinel* in 2007 quoted a question that had lived in Thompson's head since 1964. His two words became the theme of the newspaper's multiyear investigation into the murder of Ferriday's beloved shoe repairman: "Why Frank?"[38]

2

THE KINGPIN, BIG FRANK DELAW, AND THE KLAN

IN 1964, WHEN THE Ku Klux Klan was at the peak of its power, the Concordia Parish Sheriff's Office was the organization's best friend. Noah Webster Cross had been sheriff for more than two decades. Some local people knew him as a man who told funny stories, cried at weddings and funerals, drove sick people to the hospital, and would give the shirt off his back to those in need. Yet the criminal underground thrived during his tenure. Cross let crime against poor people, especially African Americans, rage uncontrollably. For years, he watched without empathy or outrage as the vice interests beat and stole from the underclass that spent money in their lounges and roadhouses. He displayed no compassion for the women who worked as prostitutes in the underbelly of the parish's long nights.

While his supporters faithfully went to the polls every four years to vote for Cross, others felt fear and shame. Preachers tried to defeat him and failed. Trained law enforcement officers opposed him and lost. So disreputable was he that a federal judge in 1971 labeled Cross "an unfit man to hold office as Sheriff of any parish in this state, or any other public office for that matter."[1] When a federal prosecutor asked the sheriff why he didn't enforce the laws against gambling and prostitution, Cross replied, "If you are in politics, you have got to overlook a lot if you are figuring on staying there a long time."[2] The unwritten custom, he said, was that if "you don't get any kick about it you let it go."[3]

Even as a child, Cross lived for politics. The son of a railroad worker and farmer in the community of Monterey, located at the toe of a big bend in the Black River, Cross was born on October 3, 1908, when Theodore Roosevelt was president. Like most boys growing up in a rural backwoods community, he loved to hunt and fish. Concordia's long history of lawlessness suited him fine—he was known as one of the biggest outlaws around. Everyone knew he killed deer out of season and fished illegally.

After graduating from Ferriday High School in 1925, Cross briefly attended Louisiana Tech in Ruston until he was suspended following a hazing incident. Standing an inch over six feet, he liked to drink whiskey and was not averse to fighting. Back at home, he was working as a truck driver when he threw his hat into the political ring in 1939, taking on Sheriff Eugene Campbell, who had held the office since Cross was born. Although Campbell pulled out a narrow victory, Cross believed the election was stolen. Rather than protest, though, the political novice counted the experience as a lesson learned. When Campbell died the next year, his widow was appointed to complete his term. Upon her death, Cross won the next election in 1940 and took office the following year.[4] (Although he held the office for a long time, he would not realize his goal of serving longer than Campbell's thirty-two years, the longest in Concordia's history.)

Enforcing the law was never a priority for Cross, but he was sometimes forced to act. He was shot in the foot when trying to stop a brawl at a bar known as the Bloody Bucket on the outskirts of Ferriday. When Cross was reelected in 1944, gambling and prostitution remained firmly entrenched. Four years later, as World War II veterans returned home, married, and looked toward building a family life, Cross lost his bid for a third term to James Hartwell Love, a teetotaler, former railroad worker, and wildlife and fisheries agent who campaigned on a platform of law and order. Love pointed out in his political ads that he was the "sober" candidate.[5] One of Love's first acts as sheriff was to put an end to a horrific ordeal involving four black youths who had been jailed for the murder of a black child in 1945. Studying the circumstances, Love learned that the boys had been accused of being in a gang of Ferriday hoodlums. Yet there appeared to be no evidence that such a gang existed or that the boys were involved in the child's death. The four were released from the parish jail in 1949, and their cases dropped. At the time of their arrests, the oldest boy was thirteen. The youngest, age ten when arrested, was fourteen on his release; he had spent almost one-third of his life in jail. (A year later, Cross faced legal problems himself. He was indicted for the alleged misuse of public funds during his previous term of office, but the charges were never brought to trial.)[6]

Sheriff Love also went after the vice interests, and by April 1951 the parish grand jury convened to investigate illegal gambling. The courtroom in Vidalia was packed when the grand jury reported that it was "evident that slot machines and other gambling devices are openly operated and run throughout" the parish and had been for a long time. The panel requested the devices be removed. Despite threats of political reprisal, Love dutifully gave notice to all gambling operators to shut down their operations. Gambling promoters complained that the parish couldn't survive without the gambling industry. But the preachers disagreed. They said gambling offered the parish "a false premise that citizens . . . are not willing to pay just and fair taxes for essential governmental services, and that the present set-up gives gambling interests a disproportionate voice in the affairs of the government." Concordia, they claimed, had "built up an undesirable reputation" as a community of "immoral and lawless people."[7]

CONCORDIA'S GAMBLING addiction, and the prostitution that came with it, was as old as the parish. These vices had traveled across the Mississippi from Natchez, the first settlement on the big river and the hub of European civilization in the area in the eighteenth and nineteenth centuries. The city was born below the bluffs at a place known as under-the-hill. There, flatboatmen delivering goods from the Ohio River Valley drank, fought, and bought sex at the taverns and brothels that sprang up to meet the demand. Natchez under-the-hill was at times a violent, dangerous place to visit. When the Orleans Territory was established following the Louisiana Purchase in 1803, gambling and prostitution jumped the river into the new parish of Concordia, whose name came from the word *concord,* meaning amity. The parish seat, Vidalia, was founded in 1798 by Captain José Vidal, who served the Spanish military administration in Natchez and later Concordia for three decades until the region became American. Ferriday was founded in 1903 as a terminal for the Texas and Pacific Railroad, and local sawmills employed hundreds of men and manufactured lumber for sales across the country. Located on an old plantation that bordered Lake Concordia, the rough-and-tumble town was known for the vices that made Natchez under-the-hill famous.[8]

Slot machines arrived during Gov. Huey Long's administration in the 1930s and were everywhere—in grocery stores, gas stations, and restaurants. Ferriday was said to be the only town in the United States with a slot machine in the post office. There were fights most every weekday and throughout the weekend. Doctors took turns patching up the survivors. A black woman, Rosie Hester, the town's most successful madam, kept her black and white ladies so busy that she operated from more than one location. "With its bad name," longtime grocer Guy Serio recalled, "a lot of people came to Ferriday just to tear the place up . . . They'd fight over being drunk, over women or over something personal like their wives, things like that." They even fought over dogs. Kick a man's favorite deerhound, and "you might just as well kick him."[9]

Profiting from the violent madness, Cross began to fill his pockets with protection money in the years after his first election. Following his defeat in 1948, he was determined to regain the sheriff's office during a decade in which the Louisiana State Police launched an aggressive and somewhat successful campaign to eradicate gambling and prostitution. Borrowing lines from two gospel hymns, Cross reminded voters that although "Love lifted me" in 1948, it was time in 1952 to return "to the old rugged Cross." He addressed the vice issue by pointing out he was a firm believer that every person deserved the right "to enjoy certain personal pleasures."[10]

As Sheriff Love and the churches learned, fighting gambling interests meant fighting not only Cross but also the political leadership of state, including the organization formed by the late governor Huey Long and his younger brother, Earl. Before his assassination in 1935, Huey Long had made friends with New York mobster Frank Costello, who soon took over the slot machine racket in New Orleans and eventually vice operations throughout the state. The mob helped the Longs by financing their political campaigns. In the late 1930s, Costello tapped Tunisian-born Sicilian Calogero Minacore, better known as Carlos Marcello, to run Louisiana operations. By the 1950s, Marcello controlled casinos and brothels in the Crescent City and throughout southern Louisiana. His empire included strip clubs, bookies, restaurants, bars, jukebox companies, and a coin-operated vending and pinball machine company that also provided slot machines.[11]

According to a memo from the FBI's division office to Director J. Edgar Hoover, the mob had learned by 1939 that "the sheriff of the parish is generally conceded to be the political leader and in control of the political situation," while "gambling and other vice is controlled . . . by local interests."[12] The mob used this knowledge to expand beyond New Orleans, and many Louisiana politicians welcomed Marcello with open arms. A member of the New Orleans Metropolitan Crime Commission told *Life* magazine in 1967 that "in Chicago, people were generally on one side of the fence or the other—honest or crooked. But in Louisiana, there is no fence."[13]

During the 1952 campaign, Cross learned that gambling operators were upset that they couldn't open on Sundays because of the "blue laws," common in the country, that prohibited businesses from operating on the Sabbath.

Quietly, in the dark back rooms of the bars and roadhouses, Cross confided to the local representatives of the underworld—even as the parish grand jury was taking a stance against gambling—that if they wanted to operate 24-7, they better get behind "the old rugged Cross." He also advised them to register their transient employees and customers to vote.[14]

In the runoff, Cross beat Love by 230 votes. He vowed to himself never to suffer defeat at the polls again, a pledge he never broke. For insurance, he brought in a man who would become his closest confidant and friend—Judsen Lee "Blackie" Drane—a tall, dark-haired, wiry gambler who dressed in expensive jeans and cowboy boots and, like Cross, occasionally displayed a violent temper. A lounge owner who was also a pinball and slot machine distributor well connected to the Marcello mob, Drane provided two important services for the sheriff. First, the con men and gamblers he employed were quickly registered to vote. Because so many of these transients didn't live in the parish, they almost always used absentee ballots that Cross or his deputies filled out. Secondly, when Louisiana paper ballots were phased out at the polls, Drane (through Cross's political dickering) secured the state contract to maintain the mechanized voting machines, using that power to intimidate voters, who thought he could tell whether they supported Cross.[15] Drane believed a man's personal and professional business should always remain secret. He once told his son, "A fish would never get caught if it didn't open its mouth."[16]

In 1956, Cross was reelected in the runoff by 336 votes. That same year, Earl Long, who had lost to Robert Kennon in 1952, was returned to the governor's office. Although state police raids had "practically wiped out organized gambling," according to the FBI (an overstatement), Long's reelection in 1956 benefited gamblers statewide. As that industry flourished, the white Ferriday High School football team captured the state championship four consecutive years from 1953–56, a source of pride for the region. The parish's population increased by 42 percent—the greatest jump in its history—from 14,398 in 1950 to 20,467 in 1960. The opening of the Natchez-Vidalia Mississippi River Bridge in 1940, ending two centuries of ferry service, connected the southwestern Mississippi and northeastern Louisiana regions as one. This provided a labor link for thousands of men—white and black—at three Natchez mills: the International Paper Company, Armstrong Tire, and Johns Manville. Car dealerships opened, the oil and timber industries boomed, telephone service stretched into the rural areas, and subdivisions were built from Ferriday to Vidalia.[17] Prosperity reigned—for some.

In the spring of 1958, Jerry Lee Lewis, then twenty-two and as popular as Elvis Presley, returned home to Ferriday for a performance at the white high school. He had made an appearance on American Bandstand in March but by June was getting plastered by the press for marrying his thirteen-year-old first cousin once removed.[18] In late January 1959, the parish's White Citizens' Council sent $3,053.67 to support Arkansas governor Orval Faubus's white supremacy–based states' rights campaign.[19] A week later, a council rally drew four hundred people in Vidalia to hear state senator Willie Rainach (of Claiborne Parish), who led Louisiana's well-organized resistance to desegregation. Rainach pointed out that black voter registration was 7 percent in Concordia Parish, while in the three predominantly black parishes to the north there were no registered African American voters.[20]

By the end of 1959, with his political machine well greased, Cross got more votes than his six opponents combined and won his fourth term. Immediately, he launched a "thank-you" tour to celebrate what would rank as the biggest victory of his career. Dressed in a pinstriped suit and a derby hat, he accessorized with a cane and the family's pet Pekinese on a leash. To purposely antagonize the preachers who fought him in every election, he jokingly dubbed himself "Rev. Foxworth with the Christian Youth Administration." A photograph that appeared on the front page of the *Concordia Sentinel* on December 11, 1959, captured the moment, explaining that Cross was now without question "The Kingpin of Concordia Parish."[21]

BY 1960, FERRIDAY was the largest town in the parish, with a population of 4,563.[22] The town council under Mayor L. W. "Woodie" Davis made efforts to modernize city services. He was first elected in 1948, shortly after returning from World War II with a Purple Heart. When he took office, the town had $700 in the bank and $1,100 in unpaid bills. Horses and cows freely roamed, and raw sewage ran in the ditches. White roughnecks, pulpwood haulers, sawmill workers, and transients stayed in the King Hotel. Hookers, who earned their living there, resided in its small, dingy rooms. The town's recent growth had helped spark an increase in crime, and both the white and black bars and nightclubs in town were notoriously savage; the owners maintained order with fists and clubs. Davis built a communications tower and bought two-way radios for the police department, which consisted of one rundown patrol car and two men. A building to house the volunteer fire department's aging equipment was constructed. There was a jail on the bottom floor of the firehouse, and an apartment on the top floor housed the jailer and his wife, who was responsible for cooking for the prisoners.[23]

Davis had few choices in lawmen. Robert "Bob" Warren served on the town council before being named police chief in 1954 at the age of forty.[24] His officers came and went as often as the drunks in Ferriday. They were untrained and ill-suited for true law enforcement. In the spring of 1956, Ferriday's town council hired Frank Edward DeLaughter as a fireman and jailer at a salary of $250 a month.[25] Born on the Fourth of July in Brookhaven, Mississippi, during the Great Flood of 1927, DeLaughter had quit East Lincoln High School in the ninth grade.[26] In 1949, he married Lula Mae Cowart in Natchez, where the couple initially lived and where DeLaughter worked as a firefighter beginning in 1950.[27] After he was hired in Ferriday, they moved into the jailer's apartment above the fire station. Davis, who had recommended DeLaughter for the job, would later say that hiring him was one of the biggest mistakes of his life.[28]

DeLaughter sometimes rode in the patrol car with the lone police officer on duty. On many occasions, he assisted in making arrests and occasionally did so alone. Sometimes he would be the first to respond to a call. Such was the case in March 1959 when DeLaughter killed African American John Henry Keary, who died in an alley off the town's main north-south route in the black section of town. The parish coroner said Keary made several advances on DeLaughter, despite being ordered to stop. Witnesses indicated that Keary at one point "grabbed the [patrol] car and raised the front end completely from the ground ... When called on by the officer to desist, he advanced on DeLaughter several times." Keary was hit in the groin, leg, and finally through the heart. The coroner ruled that DeLaughter's actions were "unavoidable and in the line of duty." Unaddressed in the article was whether DeLaughter had used undue force in a confrontation with an unarmed man.[29]

In 2011, Charles Johnson, a black retired school-bus driver who was fourteen in 1959, told the *Concordia Sentinel* that he had witnessed the fatal encounter but was never asked about it. Prior to DeLaughter's arrival, Johnson said, Keary had punched a white man. That blow ended the argument, and no one else had been involved. Johnson watched DeLaughter move to the back of the patrol car as Keary lifted its front end almost off the ground and then put it down, certainly an intimidating display of strength. Although Keary then walked in DeLaughter's direction, Johnson said Keary kept his hands at the side, never surged toward the officer, and took slow steps. Despite two shots in the gut, Keary continued to move toward DeLaughter, who again instructed him to halt. His third shot failed to stop Keary, but the fourth brought him down. For a lifetime, Johnson wondered why DeLaughter had shot and killed an unarmed man.[30]

During DeLaughter's early years in Ferriday, most whites were concerned about the growing civil rights movement and feared segregation would end. W. E. Person, a respected cattleman, veteran of both world wars, and Citizens' Council member, wanted to represent Concordia in the Louisiana Senate. In his campaign announcement five months after the shooting death of John Keary, Person pledged that if elected he would work to protect "segregation in our schools and to maintain our Southern way of life." He further warned, "The proven price of racial integration is the enormous skeleton of dead empires." Person was victorious.[31]

DELAUGHTER WAS promoted to the police force in 1960.[32] In the spring of 1962, an event occurred that confirmed Mayor Davis's growing apprehension about him. Three black men were arrested for breaking into a general store outside Ferriday and stealing a package of undershirts. One of the men, twenty-nine-year-old Curtis Harris, later wrote the U.S. attorney in Shreveport that five Concordia policemen had attempted to beat a confession out of him.[33] Harris had served time in federal prison for a 1960 post office burglary. After his arrest in 1962, he was placed in a cellblock at the parish jail on the top floor of the courthouse in Vidalia. Later that night, he was taken downstairs to the sheriff's office, where deputies and two Ferriday policemen forced him to lie face down on a table. Harris was beaten with a strap by five officers, identified as sheriff's deputies Roy George Barlow, Bill Ogden, and Ike Cowan Jr., and Ferriday policemen DeLaughter and William Howell Harp Jr. (called "Junior"). Harp had been named Ferriday jailer when DeLaughter was promoted to full-time policeman.[34]

Harris's thirty-six-year-old uncle, Wilber Lee Henderson, was also arrested and later gave a statement to the FBI. The officers, he said,

> made me get on a table and lay on my stomach with my clothes on. Ike, Jr.,
> Barlow and a fifth man in the room, Mr. Harp . . . carrying a revolver in his
> belt holster, held me down. Then Frank DeLaughter started whipping me
> with a leather strap about 18 inches to 24 inches long, 3 inches wide and

about 1/4 inch thick. This strap was fastened to a wooden handle about 1 1/2 inches in diameter and about 9 inches long. When DeLaughter got tired of whipping me, Ike, Jr., whipped me then Bill Ogden and then Barlow whipped me in that order. In all, they whipped me for about one-half hour. They whipped me on my seat, the backs of my legs and the back of my hands, wrists and lower arms. The whipping caused me to bleed and there was blood on my undershirt and shorts. There was swelling and I couldn't set down for two days.

Ogden and Cowan told Henderson he would get a suspended sentence if he would confess. When he refused, Harp pointed his pistol at Henderson's head and threatened to shoot him. "I was scared," Henderson said. He confessed.[35]

All three defendants were forced by intimidation to plead guilty to theft of the undershirts. Harris said the officers told him that if he reported the beating and ever returned to Ferriday, he would "leave in a pine box." Harris and Henderson each got seven years. The third man, who confessed without incident and did not have a police record, got three years. In a chilling mockery of justice, only eleven days elapsed from the day of their arrests to their arrival at the state penitentiary in Angola. Although some of the prisoners upstairs in the jail saw Harris's and Henderson's injuries, none witnessed the beatings. All five police officers denied them when interviewed by the FBI. The U.S. attorney, following a two-month preliminary investigation, concluded that Harris and Henderson's charges could not be substantiated.[36]

Having been questioned by the FBI for the first time in his career, DeLaughter never again beat prisoners outside the familiar comfort of the Ferriday jail. While the parish jail in the Vidalia courthouse was comprised of open cellblocks, the jail in Ferriday consisted of a series of small cages built side-by-side with no opening for the prisoner to see inside the adjoining cell. DeLaughter could beat a man senseless in a distant room and throw the victim into a cell where his injuries would remain unseen. Other prisoners might hear the screams of the victim but were not visual witnesses to the beating.[37]

After the mayor learned of the beatings, he fired DeLaughter. Noah Cross was more than happy to add him to his payroll as a deputy. DeLaughter would become the worst of three criminally prone deputies who were at ease operating in the violent underworld the sheriff cultivated. The others were Ike Cowan, a stocky, dark-haired man of average height, and Bill Ogden, one of the oldest line deputies, who was said to strut like a peacock when excited. They were two of the best-known gamblers in the parish. Ogden had operated a boat landing on nearby Lake St. John before becoming a cop and was DeLaughter's shadow. The three deputies had little education and no training in law enforcement, and they were suspected by the FBI in a number of police brutality and color of law civil rights cases that came to light in the early 1960s.[38]

But by far the most feared and despised deputy employed by Cross in 1964 was DeLaughter, who once told a black preacher that after "you kill your first man the rest are easy." In his late thirties at the time, he was six-foot-four and weighed 285 pounds. His stocky frame supported a beer belly and sloping shoulders; his hair was black and his face clean-shaven, with a receding chin. Men detained and beaten by this lawman recalled how he leaned over them, the stench of his cigarette breath and the salty beads of sweat rolling down his neck and dripping onto their faces. Handcuffed to a chair, they looked up into his blank brown eyes as he degraded them with obscenities and racial slurs. He often accused men of crimes they knew nothing about.[39]

To be in the custody of the deputy was unthinkable. Inside a back pocket of his military-style khaki pants, pulled high on the waist, was a blackjack. Hidden in a front pocket along with his deputy badge were metal thumb cuffs, used as a torture device. By placing his finger between the two cuffed joints and exerting pressure by twisting or pulling, DeLaughter could easily break a prisoner's thumb. In another pocket, he carried a high-caliber derringer. The back of his hand was a taste of what was to come—his favorite tools for delivering a beating included a fire hose, a leather strap, and a cattle prod. His brutal interrogations were conducted in the middle of the night in the confines of a room at the Ferriday jail, where he sought to beat confessions out of his victims. Those in his custody were rarely charged—if at all—until hours after they were detained. Once freed, they sometimes found their wallets emptied of cash.[40]

When the civil rights movement reached Ferriday, DeLaughter explained the future of race relations to a local pastor: "Preacher . . . people in this town don't want to see no niggers voting."[41] So feared was he and so firm his authority that African Americans called him "Big Frank DeLaw."[42] By 1964, DeLaughter, Ogden, and Cowan were Klansmen, partly because the sheriff wanted them to keep tabs on the anti-vice segment of the KKK population that threatened the criminal operations of the sheriff's office. The man who swore DeLaughter into the Klan was a thirty-year-old truck driver from Natchez by the name of Edward "Eddie" Lennox McDaniel.

IN OCTOBER 1962, twenty-nine-year-old James Meredith became the first African American admitted to the University of Mississippi in Oxford. His enrollment followed a long court battle, ending with the U.S. Supreme Court ruling in Meredith's favor. Mississippi's segregationist governor Ross Barnett initially blocked Meredith's admission in September. White students, segregationists, and Klansmen supported Barnett, and at protests they assailed federal troops, injuring many. Two people died during the riots, including a French journalist.

In Natchez, Eddie McDaniel felt alarmed over the growing civil rights movement and wanted to stop it. Invited to a meeting in Concordia Parish, McDaniel rode with a friend to Minorca, a mile south of Vidalia. Located behind the mainline Mississippi River levee along what is known as Old River, once the main channel of the Mississippi, the little fishing community was enshrouded in darkness. A dirt road sprinkled with pebbles followed the river to a well-lighted mobile home deep in the trees along the riverbank. A large room had been added on the back. McDaniel's stomach grew queasy as he wondered just what he was getting himself into. As he listened to the muffled voices of men talking and laughing in the back room, a fully robed man emerged and shook McDaniel's hand. He was J. A. Swenson, leader of the Louisiana Original Knights. They talked. The man wondered if McDaniel was interested in joining, whether he could keep secrets, and if he could be counted on to fight the communists who were trying to bring America to her knees and stir up trouble between the races. Every decent Christian, Swenson said, knew that white men were superior to all other races, especially the black race. Jesus demanded that he take a stand.[43]

Over the past years, McDaniel had traveled the country, moving on to something else if he didn't get his way. Married twice, he was the oldest of seven children born to poor parents in Natchez during the Great Depression. In Natchez in 1959, the Johns Manville Company fired him after he broke into a milk machine and stole the contents. His supervisor found him a capable worker but one who continuously created unrest at the plant.[44] In Los Angeles, McDaniel had abruptly resigned his job as a driver with the Los Angeles Transit Authority; after getting into a fight with a passenger, he walked off the bus, leaving his passengers stranded on the highway. He was dogged by financial problems, too, and in 1961 filed for bankruptcy, citing assets of $200 and debts of $4,522.36.[45]

As he considered Klan membership, he remembered his grandfather telling him out of the blue one day that the KKK was a good group and he should join it when the time was right.[46] In Concordia Parish, the first public appearance of the local Klan and its support of Mississippi's Barnett was made known on October 5, 1962, when the *Sentinel* ran a front-page photo of six unidentified, hooded Klansmen—five in white robes, one in a dark robe—surrounding a five-foot cross. The photo had been sent anonymously. In an open letter to the editor, the Klan commended Barnett for his "fight against integration" during the Meredith issue and apologized for the "lack of interest" shown by Louisiana politicians. In 1956, three years before he was elected governor, Barnett had led a rally for the White Citizens' Council at the Ferriday Elementary School. In a second letter, addressed to Louisiana governor Jimmie Davis, the Concordia Klan expressed "disappointment by the lack of interest that you are showing during the grave situation in Mississippi in view of the fact that your campaign promise was to go to jail to prevent integration."[47]

McDaniel told Swenson he wanted to join. Led to the back room, McDaniel saw three dozen robed Klansmen standing in silence. Their leader, known as the Exalted Cyclops, called them to order. The chaplain prayed, and the ritual began. McDaniel was asked if he was willing to follow Klan rules and submit to Klan authority. He was asked to swear to keep Klan secrets: "I will die rather than divulge the same. So help me God. Amen!" Once the ritual was complete, and McDaniel sworn in as a member, the Klansmen removed their hoods and disrobed. To his surprise, McDaniel realized he knew half the men there. Some were his friends, yet he had had no clue any were Klansmen, a sign to him that this was truly an invisible empire. Afterward, McDaniel learned that he was the first man to be sworn into the Original Knights from the state of Mississippi in the 1960s.[48]

THE ORIGINAL KNIGHTS traced its origin to the country's first Klan organization, known as the Reconstruction Klan, which emerged from the southern wasteland after the Civil War in 1865. Confederate general Nathan Bedford Forrest of Tennessee, a godlike figure in the South who after the war served briefly as the Klan's grand wizard, recognized one of the organization's great flaws: Klan leaders could not control the violent actions of its members. This Reconstruction Klan and its later spawn arose when great political and social changes were underway in the country. During three specific periods—the 1860s–1870s, the 1910s–1920s, and the late 1950s–1960s—the Klan amassed substantial strength when white supremacy was challenged.[10]

During the early twentieth century, the second Klan movement produced the largest such organization in the history of the United States. The Knights of the Ku Klux Klan claimed an estimated 4 million members, making it as big as other major national organizations. Its founder was a defrocked Methodist minister who was a powerful orator and devotee of fraternal organizations. An Alabama native, William Joseph Simmons idolized the Reconstruction Klan to which his father had belonged. Simmons based the launch of this second Klan in 1915 in part on the tenet that to be a true American was to be native born. The influx of immigrant Jews and Catholics from Europe in the years preceding World War I, the release of D. W. Griffith's pro-Klan silent movie *Birth of a Nation*, and the mob lynching of Leo Frank, a Jewish businessman in Atlanta, Georgia, wrongly accused of murdering thirteen-year-old Mary Phagan, fanned the hysteria that helped Simmons launch his organization.[50]

Through savvy marketing, Simmons's Klan peaked in the 1920s. A handful of its members and leaders garnered national attention for murdering white men who challenged the organization but little press for the black men they slaughtered. While this uncontrollable violent element had also defined the Reconstruction Klan, something new emerged in Simmons's Klan. He and his associates grew rich as millions of members paid initiation fees and dues and bought Klan robes. Jealous and ambitious men wanted their jobs.[51]

Confrontations over violence and money were also debilitating during the era of the third major Klan movement in the late 1950s and 1960s. In Louisiana and Mississippi in late 1963, the leaders of the Original Knights were challenged over money and over reluctance to unleash the violent acts desired by the most vocal element of the growing membership. Since its inception in late 1960, the Original Knights had spread like wildfire from northwestern Louisiana to Bogalusa and New Orleans in the state's southeastern toe. It was well organized in Concordia Parish in 1962 when McDaniel became the first Mississippi member of the Louisiana organization. The symbolic leader of the Original Knights was an aging Roy K. Davis, a preacher from Dallas, Texas, who based this group's organizational structure on Simmons's Knights of the Ku Klux Klan, of which Davis had been a member. When he resurrected the Knights in 1960, he adopted Simmons's constitution and organizational structure, and this new Klan was known as both the Original Knights and the Old Originals. Although Davis served as the paid imperial wizard of the Original Knights, he had little to do with day-to-day operations. J. D. Swenson and Royal Young were the true leaders.[52]

As the chief recruiter, Swenson had traveled Louisiana organizing klaverns, individual Klan units that typically required a membership of fifty to be chartered, each having its own Exalted Cyclops. A new member went through a "naturalization" ceremony before taking an oath in which he swore to keep Klan secrets. Afterward, the new Klansman purchased a robe for $10, paid $10 as an initiation fee, and paid $1 per month in dues.[53]

With more than forty klaverns in Louisiana by late 1962, Swenson directed the Original Knights' eastward momentum into Mississippi. In early 1963, E. L. McDaniel was tapped to help Swenson recruit and organize in the Magnolia State, while another Mississippi man, Douglas Byrd, was appointed grand dragon of the newly formed Mississippi Realm of the Original Knights of the Ku Klux Klan. Swenson was now intent on making the Old Originals a true national organization, just as Simmons had done decades earlier. It became Royal Young's job to organize the growth. In his fifties, Young was a locomotive engineer for the Louisiana Central Railroad in Bossier City, located across the Red River from Shreveport. He was experienced in union work with the railroad, and his organizational skills drew Swenson to make Young his right-hand man.[54] Young had to troubleshoot growing dissension from local Klan leaders who, by late 1963, questioned how Swenson and Young were spending Klan money. Young was also instructed to reorganize the Klan by assigning duties for newly created state offices and to set up a national structure.[55]

Among the state officers appointed by Swenson was forty-year-old Robert Fuller of Monroe. The owner of a sanitation service and septic tank business, Fuller was named head of the Klan Bureau of Investigation (KBI). Violent projects by secretive hit squads known as "wrecking crews" required the approval of the KBI chief. Fuller was greatly feared and admired in Klan circles. In 1960, he had shot five of his black employees, killing four and critically injuring one, in what he called a dispute over money. He told authorities that the men attacked him outside his home with knives and linoleum hooks and that in self-defense he took his double-barreled twelve-gauge from his truck and shot all five men with seven rounds, having to reload three times. Although he was charged in the shooting, a grand jury chose not to indict him in 1961.[56]

McDaniel, Byrd, and new recruit Ernest Gilbert, of Brookhaven, quickly established klaverns throughout southwest Mississippi. They then turned on

Swenson and Young, accusing them of lining their pockets with the Mississippi money collected for robes and membership. Unrest in Louisiana resulted in a number of klaverns withholding payment of their membership dues.[57]

During this crisis, the Klan was jolted on June 11, 1963, when President John F. Kennedy proposed what would become the Civil Rights Act of 1964, proclaiming that a legal issue over equal rights had now become a moral one. The Rev. Martin Luther King Jr. praised Kennedy's proposal. Nine days later, the Louisiana House of Representatives passed a resolution by a 64 to 11 vote, trashing Kennedy's plan as simply a vindictive means for the federal government to maintain authority over the states. The *Concordia Sentinel* and other southern newspapers printed U.S. senator Richard Russell's (Georgia) spin on Kennedy's stance: "The fact that every citizen has the same right to own and operate a swimming pool or dining hall constitutes equality." But, Russell maintained, "Federal power to force the owner of a dining hall or swimming pool to unwillingly accept those of a different race as guests creates a new and special right for negroes in derogation of the property rights of all our people to own and control the fruits of their labor and ingenuity."[58]

In klaverns in Louisiana and Mississippi, Klansmen advocated violence, and the dissension grew from a growl to a roar. Some called Young an incompetent leader because he would not allow revolting Klansmen to burn crosses during the Louisiana gubernatorial campaign of 1963. Concordia Parish native Shelby Jackson, a segregationist and the state superintendent of education then seeking the governor's post, drew the support of Louisiana KKK members. At the core of the discontent, however, were two things: Certain men wanted the power that Swenson and Young held, and the money that came with it. Other Klansmen, having lost all faith that local and state politicians could hold off integration, concluded that violence was the only remaining option. Young told a congressional committee in 1965 that what was happening could be summed up in two words: "Power purge."[59]

News accounts made it clear that neither the civil rights movement nor southern resistance was going away. When Byron De La Beckwith, a member of the Mississippi White Citizens' Council, was charged and jailed for the June 12, 1963, murder of Mississippi NAACP field secretary Medgar Evers, public officials and Klansmen rallied to his aid. Four months later, on September 15, a bomb exploded at the 16th Street Baptist Church in Birmingham, Alabama, killing four girls, three of whom were fourteen and the youngest only eleven. Members of the United Klans of America (UKA), led by Robert Shelton and headquartered in Alabama, would later be implicated in the murders. During the summer, the Ruston klavern of Original Knights broke away and quietly joined Shelton's UKA. Dissident Original Knights members organized emergency meetings throughout northeastern Louisiana to plot the ouster of Young and Swenson.[60] To counter the growing rebellion, Young organized a meeting with the opposition faction in the Caldwell Parish town of Columbia on the Ouachita River, not far from the home of John McKeithen, who would be elected governor in March 1964. Complaints were raised, especially over finances.[61] IRS records cited during congressional hearings in 1966 revealed that Swenson was paid $16,944 from 1962 to early 1964 by the Louisiana Rifle Association, a front organization for the Original Knights. Swenson's Klan pay was $10,690 in 1963 alone; Young pocketed $8,500.

On December 26, a few days after the Caldwell Parish meeting, Young met with Louisiana Klan officers at his home, where he expressed fear that the Original Knights units in Mississippi would be lost to Byrd and McDaniel. Young traveled to Natchez to meet with the two, but he and Byrd spent the evening arguing. At one point, Young stood and started preaching, which drew Gilbert's ire. "Sit down!" Gilbert shouted, and "go to hell!"[62]

Three days later, Young banished McDaniel, Byrd, and Gilbert from the Mississippi Realm of the Original Knights, as well as three leaders from the Louisiana Realm.[63] In a desperate final move, on January 11, 1964, Young reserved the Shamrock Motel restaurant banquet room in Vidalia to meet with two dozen Mississippi Original Knights representing six klaverns. Among the Mississippians attending were E. L. Caston, the former sheriff of Amite County, and his former chief deputy, Daniel Jones, who had recently been elected sheriff. Jones would soon become the chief suspect in the murder of African American Louis Allen, a logger gunned down in Liberty twenty days after the Shamrock meeting. Caston and Jones promised Young their support in maintaining the Original Knights in Mississippi and voiced their opposition to those revolting to form the White Knights.[64]

But the Original Knights were done in Mississippi. Neither McDaniel, Byrd, nor Gilbert was given the top post in the White Knights. Despite the fact that the Louisiana-Mississippi Original Knights relationship was severed, the connection between the Concordia Parish Sheriff's Office and the Natchez Klan remained intact, linked by E. L. McDaniel and Deputy Frank DeLaughter.

1964

3

ABDUCTIONS, WHIPPINGS, AND MURDER

IT WAS COLD and raining in Louisiana on Monday, February 3, 1964. It was dark around 8 p.m., when a battered red pickup eased onto the gravel driveway in James White's backyard, nine miles west of Ferriday in Concordia Parish. Eleven members of White's family were inside his home, including his wife, mother, father, sister, and six of his seven children.[1]

The forty-four-year-old White raised pheasants and quail on his small farm and sold men's apparel in black communities in the area. Like his best friend Frank Morris, he was among a handful of black men in the parish who owned property. In the 1940s, White had been a member of the NAACP before quitting in frustration when he learned that Sheriff Noah Cross had a spy in the organization who reported on every meeting.[2] White knew that because he owned land and a business, some local white men considered him uppity. But he didn't care. He was physically a large man, fearless but not reckless. He backed down from no man, white or black, who threatened him or his family.[3]

During the previous weeks, his property had been fired upon in the night on seventeen occasions by unknown assailants passing by on the Monterey-Stacy Road that ran along the west side of his home. White had no idea who was responsible for the drive-by shootings but was well aware the Ku Klux Klan had a local unit that represented the communities of Monterey, Lismore, Acme, and Eva. This unit was commonly called the Black River Klan because those communities bordered Black River and a horseshoe bend of the old river channel known as Black River Lake.

On the night of the third, White heard someone calling him from outside the house. A male voice he didn't recognize said he wanted to look at White's birds. It was not unusual. Potential buyers often stopped by at night to view or purchase the pheasants penned on the front corner of his property. He put on his raincoat, grabbed an umbrella, and ventured out into the cold. Outside, he saw a man standing in front of the pheasant pen situated between the house and the highway, illuminated by a lone street light. The man wore a cap, the bill pulled down so low it covered his eyes, and a military-style jacket with its collar pulled up shielding his cheeks. Puffing on a cigarette, he appeared nervous and stuttered when he told White he wanted to buy two hens and a male pheasant.[4]

Before White could answer, the man suddenly pulled a revolver with a six-inch barrel from his waist and barked, "Get in the truck!" Near the back corner of the house, by the old red pickup parked in the driveway, another man, holding a shotgun, arose from a crouched position. When the man with the pistol poked the barrel into White's stomach, White decided to make a stand rather than be forced into the truck. He shouted for help, pointing his umbrella at his attacker as if it were a gun. Startled and trembling, White's assailant took a few steps back.[5] In a flash, White's wife handed him a loaded shotgun while the man with the pistol stumbled over the fence that paralleled the highway, firing wildly in White's direction. As the red pickup pulled onto the road, White returned fire. He was certain he had hit one of the men.[6]

The following day, White reported the attack to the sheriff's office. A short time later, deputies Frank DeLaughter and Bill Ogden arrived. White had used a washtub to cover and preserve a perfect shoe print in the mud left by the man with the pistol. DeLaughter snickered and walked over the spot. Sheriff Cross came by later, told White he knew who the culprits were, and promised to bring them by later for White to identify. Cross never returned. White reported the incident and the other shootings—including one that occurred two weeks later—to the district attorney. Nothing was done.[7]

White never knew that four men in his yard that night became suspects in many of the major Klan-related crimes in Concordia Parish and in Natchez and Adams County, Mississippi, over the next three years, including the murder by arson of Frank Morris. The FBI would learn in 1967 that the "wrecking crew" that had set out to abduct and beat White was led by Raleigh Jackson Glover, who commonly went by the nickname "Red," though some called him "Jack."[8] Also present that night was Tommie Lee Jones of Natchez, the man White saw rise from the corner of the house with a shotgun. Jones had pulled both triggers of his double-barreled weapon only to hear two clicks. He had forgotten to load it. Seconds later, when the red pickup was pulling away, White shot Jones in the face. Original Knights leaders in Louisiana contacted Brookhaven Klansman Ernest Gilbert, who made arrangements for Jones to receive medical care from the Lincoln County health officer, a drug-addicted alcoholic who had lost his medical practice months earlier.[9] Other Klansmen involved were Jones's best friend, Thore L. "Tog" Torgersen, also of Natchez, and James Lee Scarborough of Ferriday. Like Jones, they were employees of International Paper Company (IP) in Natchez. Scarborough would soon rise to the top position of Exalted Cyclops of the Ferriday-Clayton Klan unit.[10]

GLOVER, A BALDING forty-three-year-old former Navy Seabee, had served in World War II and the Korean conflict. He had more recently served as Exalted Cyclops of the Vidalia Klan and had helped organize the Black River Klan, as well as the Harrisonburg and Sicily Island units in neighboring Catahoula Parish. Glover had aligned himself with Murray Martin of Winnsboro, the new leader of the Louisiana Original Knights who had helped engineer the revolt against the leadership of John Swenson and Royal Young. Like Glover, Martin was an advocate of violent resistance to civil rights and was furious over plans for Freedom Summer, designed to register blacks to vote in Mississippi. In part because it was known that White had belonged to the NAACP, the Klan had falsely labeled him a Black Muslim, one of several Black Nationalist organizations that advocated black power. Strengthening this belief was the fact that White sported a goatee, a type of facial hair that the Klan associated with radicalism.[11]

An employee of Armstrong Tire Company in Natchez, Glover had a reputation as a fanatic on the race issue.[12] Klan informants later filled the ears of FBI agents with stories concerning his hatred of blacks. The "sight of a Negro infuriates Glover," said one.[13] Another said that Glover would like nothing more than "to pump some caps on any Negro." He lived in Vidalia on the Louisiana side of the Mississippi River during the Klan's most violent years—from 1962 to 1967. In 1962, Glover told newly elected Natchez police chief J. T. Robinson that he had shot and wounded a black man, alleging that the man had attacked him with a Pepsi bottle. Robinson interviewed the victim, who agreed to come by the police station to fill out a complaint once he was released from the hospital. Instead, he disappeared.[14]

Glover had been bent on demonizing blacks and pondering ways to physically assault them since at least his teenage years.[15] An acquaintance told the FBI that during the 1930s Glover's family was "run out of Natchez" because one of his sisters was "running around" with black men. Shamed and humiliated, Glover was shunned by the white community. Hardened by the ostracism, he developed a reputation as a hothead and a "cocky braggart." At times, he frequented the strip of bars and bawdy houses owned by Blackie Drane and others on the Ferriday-Vidalia highway. One night in the 1940s, Robinson, not yet a policeman, was drinking beer with friends in one of those lounges. Across the room Glover, smoking a cigar, suddenly jumped onto a table. Switching the lit end of the cigar "so that the fire was inside his mouth," Glover "chewed up the cigar, fire and all," and dared any man in the room to a fight. No one accepted the challenge.[16]

In 1967, the FBI investigated the attack on James White. Shown photographs of the suspects, White was unable to identify any of them.[17] The case went cold. His attack had been followed by the beatings of at least seven men in Concordia Parish and across the Mississippi River in Adams County during the month of February 1964. The second Concordia attack had happened on February 13, ten days after the attempted abduction of White. African Americans Richard James and Robert Watkins were rounding a sharp curve on a gravel road near Branche's store on Workinger Bayou, six miles from White's home, when they saw a 1955 or 1956 Ford, white over blue, parked in the road with the hood up. A balding white man with red hair and a ruddy complexion was standing by the driver's side. The two men pulled abreast of the man, who said he needed help to start his vehicle. Watkins emerged from the passenger side of James's car. As he prepared to look under the hood, the white man suddenly pulled a pistol.[18]

"This is a holdup," he said. Suddenly, five or six hooded men rushed out of the bushes on the side of the road, some carrying sawed-off shotguns. As they surrounded James and Watkins, the unmasked white man warned, "If you want to live, don't yell!" James and Watkins were taken to an abandoned oil-well site, forced to strip, and beaten severely. Watkins appeared to be the main target. His supposed offense remains unclear. A few days before the beating, he had called a white woman to report that her husband's cows had wandered onto another man's property. Klansmen likely made something more provocative out of the call and decided to attack Watkins in order to emphasize that a black man should never converse with a white woman on the phone or in person.[19] A Klan sheet circulated in the area at that time alluded to a white woman in Ferriday allegedly dating a black man. That man, a schoolteacher, left town.[20]

After the beating, James stumbled into the yard of a white couple, Mr. and Mrs. Nelson Flaherty, who called Sheriff Cross to report that James and

Watkins had been abducted on the side of the road and beaten.[21] The next day, Watkins's mother was warned to get her son out of Concordia Parish. He boarded a train in Brookhaven, Mississippi, bound for Chicago. There, in 1967, he was shown photographs of the suspects. He recognized only one—a photo of the unmasked man who pretended his car was broken down. That man was Red Glover.[22]

For years afterward, Glover manifested sadistic glee in recalling the beatings. He once told another Klansman that one of the victims asked for a drink afterward to cool his body. Instead, Glover scooped up a cupful of salt water from the abandoned oil well pit and poured it over the man's bleeding wounds. Every time he told the story, Glover bowled over laughing.[23]

The FBI wasn't surprised the sheriff's office showed little interest in the case. Sheriff Cross said his investigation into the beating yielded no conclusions. Additionally, he said there were no investigative files. When asked by agents if he thought the Klan had committed the beatings, he said certainly not: "There is not now nor never has there been a Klan group in Concordia Parish."[24]

At the time of the attempted abduction of James White and the beatings of Richard James and Robert Watkins, Cross had begun his sixth term in office, having been reelected under a cloud of suspicion in December 1963. Cross was reported the winner with an eleven-vote lead over two other candidates. The second-place finisher was James Hartwell Love Jr., the son of Cross's old nemesis, Hartwell Love, who had defeated Cross in 1948. Love Jr. filed suit, alleging that Cross and his deputies, employees, and agents, along with the clerk of court, had stolen the election to avoid a runoff. Specifically, Love charged that Cross, with the clerk's consent, "opened various of the envelopes containing absentee ballots which had been legally cast and changed those ballots" to votes for Cross.[25] However, the Louisiana Third Circuit Court of Appeal upheld a district court ruling that in part found that even if four of the absentee votes allegedly marked for Love had been changed to favor Cross, the incumbent sheriff still would have won by a three-vote margin.[26]

ACROSS THE MISSISSIPPI River in Adams County, Odell Anders had become the new sheriff in January, replacing Billy Ferrell. In Mississippi, sheriffs could not serve consecutive terms, and often the new sheriff had little to no law enforcement experience, as was true of the forty-year-old Anders, who had received the Klan vote. A Democrat, Anders defeated his Republican opponent, George Gunter of Natchez, by 226 votes out of 5,284 cast. A nineteen-year Natchez resident who had been an FBI agent for twenty-one years, Gunter reminded voters that Anders had no experience. Anders labeled Gunter a crony of President Kennedy, who was despised by many whites for his pro–civil rights agenda. In his campaign ads in the *Natchez Democrat*, Anders asked voters if they wanted to elect a man like Gunter who was "trained in guerilla warfare, supervised and directed by the Federal government." On November 6, 1963, Anders was elected. Sixteen days later, Kennedy was assassinated in Dallas, Texas. Ironically, the Klansmen who delivered Anders his victory immediately became the biggest problem he would face during his four-year term.[27] After Anders took office in January, Klansmen of the newly formed White Knights began terrorizing Adams County. By mid-February, Anders had taken statements from four black men who had been abducted in three separate attacks at gunpoint, taken to remote locations, and beaten with straps and whips. A white man also had been attacked.[28]

The metamorphosis of the Original Knights in Mississippi into the White Knights was completed by February 1964. Although the Old Originals' banished leaders, E. L. McDaniel, Douglas Byrd, and Ernest Gilbert, had led the revolt, Sam Bowers hijacked the movement. The slim thirty-nine-year-old, who had never been married, was the grandson of a four-term Mississippi congressman. Bowers spent part of his youth in New Orleans. Growing up, he was considered intelligent, a competent writer who loved erector sets and "anything mechanical." He and his business partner and occasional roommate, Robert Harry Larson of Chicago, met at the University of Southern California School of Engineering in Los Angeles. By 1964, they were operating Sambo Amusement Company in Laurel, Mississippi, distributing coin-operated pinball and cigarette machines. Larson managed the company, while Bowers maintained the machines. Bowers's mother, who lived in Jackson, Mississippi, was disappointed that he didn't become a lawyer and believed her son was misunderstood because he was so fanatically opposed to communism. She longed for the days before the civil rights movement when "our niggers had all they wanted. They were happy. We took care of 'em. Now the common people and trash from the North have come down here and got our niggers all dissatisfied."[29]

When he joined the Original Knights in 1963, Bowers became famous for his tirades, his lack of humor, and his fascination with guns and explosives. His father, who had reared him, and his brother both disowned Bowers when he became a Klansman. In early February 1964, two hundred Original Knight defectors transformed themselves into White Knights at a meeting in Brookhaven. While Bowers muscled out Byrd for the top position of imperial wizard, Gilbert was voted head of the Klan Bureau of Investigation and became the officer who spearheaded wrecking-crew projects. McDaniel was named the province investigator for southwest Mississippi.[30]

Four White Knight units were established in Adams County. One was located in the Morgantown subdivision on the north end of Natchez, where a building was adapted for use as a meetinghouse by all four klaverns. A second klavern was organized in Cloverdale, five miles south of downtown Natchez near the IP plant. A third, in the southern Adams County community of Kingston, was called the Sligo unit, after an old plantation. The fourth klavern was in Fenwick along US 84 in north-central Adams County. Each klavern elected an Exalted Cyclops and subordinate officers. Violent men who had lashed out at Original Knights leaders Young and Swenson for not giving the green light to wrecking-crew projects now felt empowered to pounce like their brothers in Concordia Parish.[31]

On Friday, February 7, four days after the failed kidnapping attempt of James White, Alfred Whitley was stopped at a roadblock after midnight. He had just gotten off work at Armstrong Tire, where he had worked as a janitor for eighteen years. Armed, hooded men yanked Whitley from his car, then blindfolded and bound him. They took him to the Homochitto National Forest, stripped him, beat him with bullwhips, and forced him to drink three ounces of castor oil, a laxative that causes excessive diarrhea.[32] The men cursed Whitley, accused him of being the "leading nigger in the NAACP," and repeatedly ordered him to identify the "white leader" of the organization. Whitley didn't know what they were talking about. In addition to the humiliation and physical pain they inflicted on Whitley, the Klansmen stole his wallet, which held forty-five dollars in cash and a sixty-three-dollar payroll check. They also took his pocketknife and car keys.[33] Sheriff Anders, who had been in office only a month when the beating occurred, said his office questioned the main suspect, Catfish Smith, and twenty-five to forty employees at the tire plant but developed no relevant information. However, Anders made a suspect decision in the days ahead: he destroyed the records on the case to ensure that "innocent people" would not be incriminated.[34]

On February 8, a white man, Roy J. Beason, was abducted and beaten by Klansmen in southern Adams County for allegedly having an affair with a black woman. Two days earlier, two officers with the Mississippi Highway Safety Patrol (MHSP) had charged Beason, who cleaned septic tanks for a living, with drunk driving. Sitting in the front seat with Beason when he was arrested was a black woman. According to white custom, the black woman should have been sitting in the backseat. A Klansman was in the car with the troopers.[35]

On February 15, James C. Winston, an African American cafeteria worker at International Paper, was walking home at 8:45 p.m. when three masked white men forced him at gunpoint into a car. They made him lie on the rear floorboard and covered his face with a hood. His assailants rifled through his wallet, stealing the two dollars inside and taking his Social Security card. He was driven to the community of Sibley near the Mississippi River. En route, he was asked if he was in the NAACP, which at that time was dormant in Natchez, and was ordered to identify some of the leading blacks in the community. When asked if he would send his children (he had none) to school with white children, he answered that he supposed he would—not the answer the Klansmen wanted to hear. Once the car stopped, the men stripped Winston, forced him to lie on the ground, and cursed him and called him derogatory names. They beat him on the back and stomach with a bullwhip and abandoned him in the woods. After midnight, he located the home of a black man who gave him sanctuary, clothed him, and arranged for him to get back to town.[36]

Days earlier, the International Paper Company had integrated its restrooms, drinking fountains, and payroll line; in the weeks to follow, however, black workers, for their own safety, continued to segregate. Everyone sensed the growing tensions. Scores of Klansmen from Louisiana and Mississippi worked at the paper mill and at Armstrong Tire Company. In fear, blacks and whites armed themselves.[37]

Within an hour of Winston's beating, at 12:45 a.m. on February 16, Archie Curtis, a black businessman who operated a funeral home in Natchez and often used his hearse to transport rural sick people to the hospital, responded to an emergency call. A man claimed his white friend's wife was in immediate need of medical care and needed a ride. At the end of Palestine Road in rural Adams County, five men wearing white hoods abducted Curtis and his employee Willie Jackson and forced them at gunpoint into a 1958 Ford Galaxy.[38]

At a nearby Humble Oil Company well site, the men forced Curtis to remove his pants and Jackson to strip entirely. The men blindfolded them, made them lie on the ground, and beat them with bullwhips and a razor strop. Curtis was the obvious target. His attackers repeatedly tried to force him to admit that he was in the NAACP, which was months away from being reactivated. A leader in the black community of Natchez since the 1950s, Curtis had been a registered voter since 1956. The circuit clerk for Adams County had described Curtis in a letter to the Mississippi Sovereignty Commission, which spied on civil rights groups, as having "a reputation in this community as being a rather smartalec [sic] negro . . . in my opinion he would be the type Negro to take part" in a "subversive" organization. By white standards in Mississippi in 1964, the NAACP was subversive.[39] Almost a half century after the beating, when the *Concordia Sentinel* approached his widow for comments on a story on the attack, Mary Curtis asked that no story be written. "I am a widow," she said, "and those people still live here." The newspaper obliged.[40]

Overwhelmed by the violence, Sheriff Anders asked for help. Although informants said Anders had joined the White Knights, others indicated Anders had attended at least one meeting simply as a law officer gathering intelligence on the Klan. Hours after the Curtis beating, the sheriff contacted the MHSP and the FBI and told them "something was up." He drove to Jackson and asked Gov. Paul Johnson for assistance. The governor sent two MHSP investigators to look into the whippings and beatings and to determine if any MHSP patrolmen were involved in the Klan. Three patrolmen were identified as Klansmen. Two were fired.[41]

No suspects were ever identified in the beatings of Roy Beason and James Winston. Only one victim, Alfred Whitley, could identify a suspect—Catfish Smith, a white coworker at Armstrong Tire. Three men were considered the prime suspects in the beatings of Curtis and Jackson. The first was Jack Seale, one of E. L. McDaniel's best friends and head of security in the White Knights. The second was Douglas Byrd, who had previously served as Grand Dragon of the Mississippi Realm of the Original Knights before becoming a White Knights leader. The third, Jasper Burchfield, a thirty-five-year-old IP worker, was an Adams County constable in Fenwick, not far from where Curtis and Jackson had been abducted and beaten.[42]

After consulting with city police and the sheriff's office, the MHSP added two names to the suspect list. One was Tiny Lewis, who operated the Barbecue Pit on the northern end of Natchez, a known Klan hangout where early discussions of the formation of the White Knights were held. Another suspect was Ernest Avants, a violent Klansman who once compared White Knights leader Sam Bowers to Jesus Christ. "In the City of Natchez," MHSP investigators reported, "there appears to be a break down in racial harmony. It is felt that this is the culmination of several things," including politics and the integration of restrooms, cafeterias, and other areas of the International Paper Company and Armstrong Rubber Company.[43]

IN 1964, ITS FOURTEENTH year of operation, IP's rayon pulp mill in Natchez was the largest industrial employer in the region. The mill had 1,800 workers, produced 1,000 tons of pulp daily, and kept log trucks rolling in more than a dozen parishes and counties on both sides of the Mississippi River.[44] While thousands of employees working at the Natchez mills rode in groups to work, few carpools were interracial. But for a number of years, Clifton Walker had ridden in a carpool with one other black man and three white men.[45] They met at Woodville, located south of Natchez in Wilkinson County, which anchors the southwestern corner of Mississippi. The county was named after an American traitor, James Wilkinson, who when a commanding general in the U.S. Army was on the payroll of Spain as a spy. Wilkinson oversaw the construction of Fort Adams, twenty miles west of Woodville; the Mississippi River fort was named after President John Adams when the Mississippi Territory was created in 1798.[46]

Woodville, the county seat, was founded in 1811. The community was the childhood home of Kentucky-born Jefferson Davis, future president of the Confederate States of America, whose family moved to the outskirts of town in 1812.[47] Clifton Walker was born in 1927, thirty-eight years after Davis's death and a few miles from his boyhood home. Although Walker was the youngest of nine, his older siblings so admired him that they called him "Man." In 1945, he married Ruby Phipps. Following his U.S. Army service in Korea, Walker secured a job in the woodyard at IP, which provided him, Ruby, and their five children a good living.[48]

There were many rumors circulating about Walker, including that he had a girlfriend. The most damning rumor, however, was that he flirted in a bold way with white women. Although the "Whites only" and "Colored only" restroom signs had been removed at IP, workers continued to segregate themselves when using the bathrooms, showers, and water fountains. Because of the growing anti-integration rhetoric at the plant and before the rash of whippings and beatings in Adams County and Concordia Parish, Walker had placed a pistol in the glove compartment of his car. For the past year, Ruby had watched her husband become increasingly agitated. In late December 1963, a Natchez doctor had prescribed medicine to calm his nerves.[49]

Twelve days after the beating of Archie Curtis and Willie Jackson, on February 28, Walker and his fellow carpool riders clocked out at IP an hour before midnight. All five men sipped whiskey from paper cups as they traveled south along US 61 from Natchez to their rendezvous point at a home near Nettles' Truck Stop, six miles north of Woodville. The road cut through the Mississippi hilltops, which rise two hundred feet above the lowland on a thirty-five-mile stretch of scenic countryside. The narrow highway was framed by towering cliffs, their tops cleared by heavy equipment during construction of the highway three decades earlier. On moonlit nights, a glance to a connecting gravel county road revealed shadows from overhanging oaks, reminiscent of a lovers' lane.[50] Heading south, US 61 crosses the Homochitto River and the swamp, which mark the boundary between Adams and Wilkinson counties. Then there's a steady climb into the Wilkinson County hills that peaks atop Doloroso Hill, offering a commanding view for miles.

Arriving at the rendezvous point at 11:45 p.m., the men said goodnight and climbed into their cars to drive their final stretches home. A mile south on US 61, Walker turned his cream-colored Impala left onto Poor House Road, the shortcut to his home a few miles away along State Highway 563. Three hundred yards down, the Impala came to an abrupt stop in the middle of the road.[51] His body was found the next day at 1 p.m., fourteen hours after Walker left his carpool. MHSP patrolman R. W. Palmertree, one of three patrolmen then under investigation for alleged Klan connections, claimed he was flagged down on US 61 near Nettles' Truck Stop by Prentiss Mathis, a local resident who said he had driven by the car earlier but didn't stop. Why Mathis waited until his second pass by the Impala before alerting authorities remains a mystery. All of the windows in the Impala, which was parked in the middle of the gravel road, were shattered, and the car's body riddled with bullet holes.[52]

Wilkinson County's newly elected sheriff, Charles T. Netterville, soon arrived at the scene. As the county's top law enforcement officer, the investigation was his to conduct. Walker's body was stretched across the front seat. Whatever he had witnessed once his car was stopped obviously had alerted him that he was in grave danger. He had pulled the key out of the ignition and unlocked the glove compartment, where his chrome-plated, four-inch barrel .38 Smith and Wesson was hidden. The Impala was in high gear, the keys hanging from the dash compartment lock, the drawer open.[53] It appeared that

Walker's path had been blocked by another vehicle. Did Klansmen quickly surround his Impala? Knowing about the previous beatings, did Walker decide to make a stand like James White four weeks earlier? Did Klansmen abandon a kidnapping plan and open fire on Walker when they realized he was reaching for a gun in his glove compartment? Why else would they risk shooting one another in a crossfire?

Part of the steering wheel had been blown away, and several gunshot holes were seen inside the car's body. Evidence indicated that a number of men with shotguns, standing two to three feet away, had opened fire on Walker from both sides of the vehicle. A full load of buckshot, fired from close range, entered just below his left ear, while another load, fired into the right side of his face from a distance of three to four feet, had blown away chunks of Walker's mouth, chin, and neck. The bone damage to his face was so severe that it required great skill by the mortician to prepare the body for viewing. Walker's son recalled looking inside the glass-topped casket and realizing that his father's face resembled that of a mummy.[54] Sheriff Netterville immediately requested assistance from the MHSP Identification Bureau, which ultimately thought that the homicide was connected to the Adams County beatings.[55]

Wadding from a shotgun shell was found inside the car, which was towed to a Woodville car dealership. Walker's body was turned over to a black-owned mortuary in Natchez. It was obvious as his clothes were cut from him that the attack had not been a robbery—his wallet had $148 inside. Williams and Williams Funeral Home had already begun embalming by the time investigators arrived shortly after 7:30 p.m. The process was halted until a pathologist could perform an autopsy. A review of the body by the MHSP indicated no powder burns, but embalmers had already partially cleaned the wounds, thereby contaminating key evidence. No fingerprints were retrieved from Walker's vehicle due to another unalterable mistake: the coroner's jury, according to Sheriff Netterville, "had gone all over the car." Among the six members of the panel was Mathis, who had discovered Walker's body. The next morning, investigators found two pieces of gunshot wadding at the crime scene, one from a twenty-gauge and another from a twelve-gauge.[56]

There were many stories as to why Walker had been murdered; most concerned alleged passes at white women, including a seventeen-year-old. A handful of suspects were identified, but there was no direct evidence tying any of them to the murder. (The sheriff's office, the MHSP, and the FBI's revived probe a half century later never mentioned the men most likely to have killed

Walker.) These suspects could be linked to a part-time waitress who had previously worked at Nettles' Truck Stop. Geraldine Vines had been an employee there during the fall of 1963 when the revolt within the Original Knights was leading to the creation of the White Knights in Mississippi. Vines claimed that during September or October 1963, a few months before the murder, Clifton Walker had made a pass at her. Vines said she immediately ordered Walker out of the cafe.[57]

MHSP investigators asked Vines if she had told anyone about the incident. She said she had told her three brothers and her two brothers-in-law, one of whom was Douglas Byrd, who in 1963 was the Grand Dragon of the Mississippi Realm of the Original Knights of the Ku Klux Klan. (After his banishment that December, he became a White Knight.)[58] Adams County sheriff Billy Ferrell, whose term ended that year, had told the FBI in September 1963 that he suspected Byrd was involved in the arson of a black church on lower Palestine Road near Natchez. The sheriff also reported that one of Byrd's closest associates was Claude W. Fuller, an IP employee who by February 1964 had left the Original Knights to become a member of the White Knights Sligo unit.[59] In 1966, Fuller would be charged in the murder of a black farmhand. Another of Byrd's closest associates was Tommie Lee Jones, who had been involved in the attempted abduction of James White. Jones lived just four miles from the IP plant and as an active Klansman would have been aware of the allegations against Walker.

Five years after the murder, an FBI informant was riding in a car with Glover in the Woodville area. The informant asked Glover about the attempted 1964 arson of an African American Masonic lodge by Glover's wrecking crew, which included Jones, Thore L. Torgersen, James L. Scarborough, and James "Red" Lee. The lodge was located in Laurel Hill, a community along US 61 in northern West Feliciana Parish, Louisiana, near the Wilkinson County, Mississippi, line. The lodge was the site of voter registration clinics led by local black activists and the Congress for Racial Equality during the fall of 1963. Glover told the informant that Jones and Torgersen were preparing to ignite gasoline inside the lodge but aborted the arson when lights were turned on nearby. Don't ever mention this, Glover told the informant, because something else had happened on the night of February 28, 1964, that he wanted to shield from the authorities. The aborted arson occurred the same night Clifton Walker was ambushed. The lodge building, which still stands, is located ten miles from the Walker crime scene.[60]

4

SUPERIOR BY BLOOD

AS KLAN VIOLENCE moved eastward from Concordia Parish, Louisiana, and the southwestern Mississippi counties of Adams and Wilkinson during the spring of 1964, rumors flamed that African American militants—figured to be Black Muslims—were stockpiling weapons in preparation for an insurrection or, as some termed it, a race war. In Franklin County, Mississippi, members of the White Knights klavern centered in Bunkley, eight miles south of the county seat of Meadville on US 84, suspected that a nineteen-year-old black lumber mill worker in Roxie was an insurrectionist.[1] Henry Hezekiah Dee stood out to Klansmen partly because he wore a head scarf. Klansmen considered the bandana, like the goatee, a revolutionary statement.[2] While there was no evidence Dee was involved in revolutionary activity, the Klan's hysteria over the growing momentum of the civil rights movement and potential federal legislation was at panic level. Dee had within the past year returned from an extended visit with his aunt in Chicago. Had he traveled north, Klansmen wondered, to plot an uprising with his militant black brothers?[3]

Bunkley was home to aging Klan leaders Archie Prather and Clyde Seale, the White Knights klavern's Exalted Cyclops. They were relatively well-off farmers whose families had been county residents since the nineteenth century. Prather turned seventy-five in 1964 and, like Clyde Seale, who was sixty-two, was considered a mean and fanatical racist. Seale was the father of four sons, two of whom were violent Klansmen.[4] The youngest, James Ford Seale, a twenty-eight-year-old truck driver, was a member of his father's Bunkley Klan and was considered as hateful as the man who raised him.[5]

In 1963, the Seales and Prather had banished the pastor of the Bunkley Baptist Church after he disagreed with Prather's Sunday school comments that there were circumstances when blacks should be killed. Once, while brandishing a sawed-off shotgun, James Ford Seale had bullied the nervous pastor, asking, "What do you think would happen if I just walked into a nigger joint and started shooting?"[6] The younger Seale was so confrontational that he had rushed onto a school bus one morning to confront a fourteen-year-old girl who had gotten into a scrap with his daughter.[7]

When discussing alleged gun smuggling by black militants in the spring of 1964, Charles Marcus Edwards, a young father of four and an IP employee, told fellow Klansmen about Dee.[8] Edwards alleged that Dee acted like a militant and that he occasionally from a distance peeked through a window at Edwards's wife. Immediately, the Bunkley klavern leadership decided to interrogate Dee. Edwards was working in his garden on May 2, a Saturday, when Klansmen came by to inform him that Dee had been spotted in Meadville. Edwards laid aside his hoe and left with the men.[9] When James Ford Seale, alone in his white Volkswagen, approached Dee, the teenager had been joined by a friend, Charles Eddie Moore, who was also nineteen. A talented football player and well liked, Moore had recently been suspended from nearby Alcorn A&M College for taking part in demonstrations seeking more social activities on campus. The boys were hitchhiking on the highway near an ice cream stand called the Tastee Freeze. Dee was heading to the Haltom Lumber Company in Roxie to pick up his paycheck of $29.43, while Moore was headed home.[10]

In addition to Seale, the Klan wrecking crew included Edwards, Clyde Seale, Archie Prather, and Curtis Dunn, who were watching from a pickup nearby. Although the teens had been looking for transportation, they declined Seale's offer of a ride before he commanded them into his car, claiming he was an IRS agent looking for illegal whiskey stills. At the nearby Homochitto National Forest, Seale covered the boys with his shotgun as the other Klansmen pulled up.[11]

The men tied the two captives to trees and beat them with beanpoles, trimmed saplings used in gardens to support the weight of growing bean vines. Limber and strong, a bean stick makes a powerful weapon, producing a "swish" sound with every swing. In powerful hands, it can strip bark from a tree or flesh from a human. The men struck the teenagers thirty to forty times over thirty minutes, all the while interrogating them: Who is "stirring up all the niggers" in Franklin County? Where are the guns?[12] Neither teen knew anything about Black Muslims or insurrectionists or gun smuggling. They pleaded for mercy. Hoping to end the torture, one of them falsely claimed that a local black pastor, the Rev. Clyde Briggs, was hiding guns in the Roxie Colored Baptist Church. A World War II veteran and teacher, Briggs had been involved in black voter registration.[13]

While James Ford Seale and Dunn stayed behind with the teens, Clyde Seale, Prather, and Edwards headed out. As they left, Edwards asked Dee an ominous question: "Are you right with the Lord?"[14] The three Klansmen stopped at Meadville, where they told Sheriff Wayne Hutto and Deputy Kirby Shell what had transpired. Hutto, like Odell Anders in Adams County and Charles T. Netterville in Wilkinson County, had only been in office since January. He had no training in law enforcement and considered his most important job to be county tax collector. Rather than arrest the Klansmen, who were in the process of committing the crimes of kidnapping and assault, Hutto traveled with them to the Roxie church while Deputy Shell and a state highway patrolman located Reverend Briggs and brought him to the site. Without a warrant, the Klansmen searched the church but were unable to find any guns.[15]

In Natchez, Jack Seale received a call from his father, who, mindful of gossipy operators, said the code word, "Kiwu," a distress signal that meant: "Klansmen, I want you." Seale and fellow KKK member Ernest Parker headed for Clyde Seale's farm, where Dee and Moore were being held.[16] Jack, a married father of three, operated a trash pickup service in Natchez, where he lived. He was stocky and strong, with an arrest record dating back to his navy days.[17] Parker, thirty-five, was the wealthiest Klansman in Mississippi and Louisiana, maybe in the South. Well respected in the white community, he owned thousands of acres of valuable land in both states, resided in Natchez, and was self-employed in the cattle, dairy, oil, and timber businesses. As a zealot Klansman, Parker used his money and time to support the Klan's offensive against integration.[18]

At Clyde Seale's farm, James Ford Seale restrained Dee and Moore with twine and covered their mouths with duct tape. His captives were bleeding so copiously that the Klansmen used a tarpaulin to line the trunk of Parker's red 1964 Ford Galaxie 500.[19] Link Cameron, an African American man who lived along Bunkley Road, was parked in a briar patch having an amorous encounter with a woman in the backseat of his car when he heard the unmistakable sound of moaning coming from a car emerging from Seale's farm.[20] Parker and the Seale brothers headed west via US 84 through Natchez, crossed the Mississippi River Bridge into Vidalia, and began the remaining forty-mile leg of their journey. They traveled through Ferriday and at Clayton turned north on US 65.

By now, Dee and Moore likely were certain of their fate. Bound and crowded in the pitch dark of the trunk, their mouths taped, they were probably unable to communicate on the ninety-minute drive. The Klansmen's destination was an island along an offshoot of the Mississippi River bordering Madison Parish, near the town of Tallulah in northeastern Louisiana. In 1964, Parker and his brother Robert Lee Parker III of Tensas Parish owned thousands of acres on the island, where they hunted, fished, and raised cattle. Some in Natchez referred to it as Parker Island, but it is most commonly known as Davis Island.[21] The Parkers had built a boat landing on the Louisiana side of Old River and used a barge to transport themselves and supplies, as well as vehicles and livestock, over to the island, where they had camps, sheds, barns, and other outbuildings.[22]

Once at the landing, the Klansmen opened the trunk and were astounded to find Dee and Moore still alive. Jack Seale asked one of the boys if he knew what was going to happen. There is no record as to whether there was a response.[23] The Klansmen tied Dee to a 1944 Willys Jeep engine block, and the Seale brothers rowed out into the water and dumped Dee overboard. Then they returned for Moore and threw him overboard in the same manner. The teenagers drowned immediately.[24]

TWO DAYS LATER, on Monday, May 4, Ernest Gilbert, head of the White Knights' Klan Bureau of Investigation, met Ernest Parker and Jack Seale in Natchez at a quiet spot on the bank of the Mississippi River. Seale and Parker told Gilbert that they had "put two niggers in the river." After learning that the two boys had been alive when dumped overboard, Gilbert complained that the treatment was inhumane. "I didn't want to shoot them," Jack Seale replied. That would "have gotten blood all over the boat."[25]

Parker feared that if the Jeep motor block were found, authorities could trace the serial numbers back to him. This worry, rather than the memory of what they had done to Dee and Moore, was keeping Parker and Jack Seale from sleeping at night. Something else also was bothering Parker: His brother Lee, when crossing Old River to the island, liked to dip his hand into the water for a drink. Lee Parker was unaware of the murders, and Ernest Parker told Gilbert he was petrified by the thought of his brother drinking water "off a dead nigger."[26]

Now a cover-up was launched. Clyde Seale considered Charles Marcus Edwards the weak link in the Bunkley Klan's wrecking crew. Although Edwards had taken part in beating the two teenagers, he had not participated in their drowning. Clyde Seale warned him to remain silent and to "make damn sure" his wife kept quiet as well. Edwards was as terrified of the Seales as were others in Franklin County.[27] He also felt bound by the so-called Christian oath of silence he took when joining the White Knights to battle Satan's communist-led conspiracy to mix the blood of the races. Edwards knew that revealing the secret acts committed by the Klan to ensure white supremacy would earn him a death sentence as well.[28] But deep in his soul, Edwards felt guilt and remorse. Had he never brought up the name of Henry Hezekiah Dee at a Klan meeting, Dee and Charles Moore would still have been alive.

Rather than lie low, however, the Bunkley klavern continued its attacks. Five weeks after the murders, they abducted and beat a white man for being too friendly with black people, and they attacked a young African American suspected of being among the local black militants. In the meantime, along a county highway, Seale ran over and killed another black man in what local and state authorities ruled an accident. But on July 12, a Louisiana man fishing on Old River at Davis Island hooked what appeared to be a human torso snagged in a log. The partial remains were determined to be those of Charles Moore. That same day in Concordia Parish, Joseph Edwards, a young porter at the Shamrock Motel in Vidalia, went missing; his car was found abandoned on the highway near Ferriday. The next day, July 13, the partial remains of a second body, that of Henry Dee, were retrieved from the river.[29]

The discovery of the bodies drew the immediate interest of the FBI. Since June 22, agents had been searching for three missing civil rights workers—James Earl Chaney, Andrew Goodman, and Michael "Mickey" Schwerner—in Neshoba County, Mississippi. The men were feared dead, but their bodies had not been found. Once Dee and Moore were identified, however, the nation's focus returned to the Neshoba case.

Despite his concerns about being linked to the murders, James Ford Seale went on the attack in a letter to the weekly *Franklin Advocate* in Meadville. He urged citizens to fight the recently enacted Civil Rights Act of 1964 that was "supposed to help the nigger get equal schools," warning that "they want to eat in the white cafe, sleep in the white hotel or motel, swim in the white pool, go to the white church, go to the white school. In short, they want to marry your white daughter, or live with her."[30]

September brought a major break in the Dee-Moore case. Gilbert began informing to FBI agent Clarence Prospere in Natchez. The bureau determined that the "best way to corroborate information in this particular case is to locate the piece of physical evidence, namely, a jeep motor block alleged to be in the Mississippi River at a point near where the bodies were found." Because Gilbert did not know where the beatings had taken place, the FBI was unaware that the crime scene was in a national forest. Had the agents known, they could have pursued federal charges. Without that knowledge, the bureau concentrated instead on assisting state authorities in developing murder charges against the Klansmen.[31]

In October, divers working under the FBI's supervision recovered an army-issue Willys Jeep motor block near the Parkers' landing on Davis Island. Attached to the block was a T-shirt containing human bones, and nearby, a skull was found. The motor block, determined to have been manufactured during the 1940s, was potentially an evidential treasure.[32] James Ford Seale and Charles Marcus Edwards were charged on November 6 with murdering Dee and Moore on warrants issued by Franklin County justice of the peace Willie Bedford. FBI agent Leonard Wolf informed Seale of what the bureau believed at that point: "We know that on Saturday afternoon May 2, 1964, you picked up in your car Henry Dee and Charles Moore, two Negro boys from Roxie. You and Charles Edwards and others took them to some remote place and beat them to death. You then transported and disposed of their bodies by dropping them in the Mississippi River. You didn't even give them a decent burial. We know you did it, you know you did it, the Lord above knows you did it."[33]

"Yes," Seale responded, "but I'm not going to admit it. You are going to have to prove it. I'm not going to say anything more." Never again did he answer any questions from authorities about the murders.[34]

Edwards, on the other hand, was nervous and afraid. Time and again, he expressed concern about his wife and children. The joint MHSP-FBI interview had gone on for nearly two hours before Edwards admitted that his wife had accused Dee of "peeping" at her from the roadway at night. Edwards admitted, too, that he had attended Klan meetings. Finally, he confessed that he was involved in the whipping of the two boys but said he knew nothing about their murders.[35]

On November 10, MHSP investigators, Louisiana state troopers, local officials, and FBI agents arrived at Parker's Landing to search the Parker property for the frame that had held the engine block found in the river. Shortly after the search began, a Jeep frame was located near the caretaker's house. Despite exhaustive efforts, however, officials were unable to find a paper trail connecting the motor and frame, nor could they directly connect them to Ernest Parker.[36]

On January 5, 1965, District Attorney Lenox Forman indicated that he was unwilling to move forward with the probe. He said that the case might "have been greatly prejudiced" because Seale and Edwards had "put out the story" that they had been "brutally mistreated" by the MHSP after their arrests. Forman told the MHSP and the FBI that if they obtained new evidence, a new grand jury slated to convene in August would investigate. In the meantime, the charges against the two Klansmen were dropped.[37]

THE DEE-MOORE killings alarmed Klan leaders. The Bunkley unit had taken action without getting the permission of White Knights leadership, particularly that of Gilbert, whose job as head of the KBI was to approve and supervise such projects. Even Sam Bowers, the imperial wizard, did not learn of the murders until after they occurred. Bowers early on had discovered that, although he had devoted Klan followers in southwest Mississippi, he couldn't control the violent men who dominated the membership there. In fact, he involved himself little in White Knight activity in southwest Mississippi, concentrating instead on Jackson and the eastern parts of the state.

By June of 1964, there was also a growing rift between Natchez Klan leaders and members of the Sligo White Knights. The Sligo klavern was responsible for the attempted murder in April of twenty-five-year-old African American Richard Joe Butler, a shooting that drew statewide publicity. Butler had worked for Haywood Benton Drane Sr. (no relation to Blackie Drane), a prominent rancher who had served in the Mississippi House of Representatives and as president of the Adams County School Board. Drane and his wife Louisa lived twenty-one miles southeast of Natchez on Deerfield Plantation in the Kingston community.[38] The southern portion of the county had been settled in the 1770s by slaveholding religious immigrants from New Jersey at a time when the British held possession of Natchez. The White Knights klavern organized there in 1964 was named after the 2,500-acre Sligo Plantation, once owned by Judge George Armstrong Sr., a wealthy Texas oilman, rancher, industrialist, and white supremacist.[39]

Armstrong's opinions had become widely publicized when he tried, in 1949, to bail out Jefferson College, five miles east of Natchez. The military school, attended briefly by Jefferson Davis, had been founded following the formation of the Mississippi Territory in 1798 and named after President Thomas Jefferson. After the World War II years drained the college's finances, the trustees asked Armstrong for help. He was eager to lend a hand in a big way. He proposed donating 26,000 acres of his Adams County land and one-half of his foundation's mineral rights from rich oil-producing fields, a financial windfall that would support the school for eternity. But there was a catch: he demanded the trustees adopt a policy excluding Jews and blacks from attending.[40]

Armstrong had long been "opposed to mixing races in our schools for it will inevitably lead to conflict, to mongrelization and the deterioration of the Anglo-Saxon race." He believed that as a white man and as one of "God's chosen people," he was "superior by blood" to every other race on the planet. After the offer became the subject of negative national headlines, the trustees declined the gift, but Armstrong's name, which still adorns the Natchez public library, was from then on revered in the Klan world.[41]

Fifteen years after the Jefferson College debacle, on Sunday, April 5, 1964, Butler walked into the Dranes' barn, preparing to feed the livestock. Four or five armed, hooded men jumped him with sawed-off and long-barreled shotguns. As he was being led away, Butler broke and ran, shouting for help from Mrs. Drane as the Klansmen opened fire. Butler was hit in the right arm and leg. Despite the danger, Mrs. Drane ran to Butler's aid as the Klansmen fled. She transported the bleeding man to Jefferson Davis Hospital, where her husband was a patient.[42]

Sheriff Anders and the MHSP investigated the shooting. Butler told investigators that a month earlier, two carloads of white men had followed him. The MHSP learned that the Sligo klavern believed Butler was having an affair with the niece of two of its most violent Klansmen, brothers Ed and Claude Fuller. Claude was known to regularly encourage attacks against African Americans,[43] and Ed was widely regarded as a hoodlum. By the end of 1964, Ed was Blackie Drane's right-hand man in Concordia Parish, where he developed a savage reputation for using brass knuckles and ax handles against the "drunk and helpless."[44]

A short time before Butler was shot, a cross had been burned in front of the home of his step-grandfather, who identified the man lighting the cross as Marvin McKinney. Marvin and his brother, J. L. "Big Mac" McKinney, were Sligo Klansmen.[45] Marvin McKinney believed black male civil rights workers intended to "plant a baby in every white girl in Mississippi."[46]

A man Butler identified as one of the attackers, twenty-six-year-old Billy Woods of the Sligo group, was arrested on April 7, 1964. Leaders in the Morgantown White Knights klavern in Natchez were furious that Sligo Klansmen had acted without authorization. Gilbert told the FBI that Natchez Klan leaders believed Marvin McKinney and Billy Woods were the shooters, but no one could prove it. A short time after his arrest, Woods was freed on $1,000 bond. Six months later, Ed Fuller and William Bryant Davidson were charged with assault and intent to kill Butler. Charges against all three were dropped after Butler, fearing for his life, fled the county.[47]

AFTER DEE AND MOORE were killed, Bowers agreed to place Marvin McKinney on trial for violating his Klan oath of secrecy by talking publicly about the Butler shooting. On June 13, the dozen Klansmen chosen as jurors were unable to reach a verdict, and a mistrial was declared. On June 22, a second trial was held at the Morgantown klavern headquarters in Natchez, with Bowers serving as judge and jury. The proceedings drew 150 White Knights from across the state. Fifteen came from Wilkinson County, led by Constable Bud Jeter, one of the suspects in the February shooting death of Clifton Walker in Woodville. Clyde Seale and his sons James Ford and Jack were also in attendance, along with three dozen Franklin County White Knights. Grand Dragon Julius Harper, the former sheriff of Mississippi's Copiah County, served as McKinney's defense counsel.[48]

Bowers acquitted McKinney. Many Klansmen in southwest Mississippi were renegades. Bowers knew they couldn't be controlled but admired their willingness to act. Yet the Sligo Klansmen were despised by their Natchez peers, and a split within the White Knights, only weeks after its formation, was already beginning. That same June, thirty-three-year-old Ernest Avants, a suspect in the February beating of black businessman Archie Curtis of Natchez, shot up the Morgantown klavern building with a pistol. Avants, a loyal follower of Bowers, was furious over the dissension within the Klan.[49] A short time later, the owner of the building kicked the Klan out. From that point on, meetings were held in homes or camps, in cafés or beer joints, along riverbanks or levee tops, in deserted parking lots, deep woods, or cow pastures. This incident so upset Klansmen that many left the KKK for good, while others turned to the United Klans of America.

FBI agent Paul Lancaster taped two interviews with Frank Morris four days before Morris's death in 1964. (*Concordia Sentinel*)

FBI agent John Pfeifer's investigations in Concordia Parish led to the federal convictions of Sheriff Noah Cross and Deputy Frank DeLaughter in connection with the Morville Lounge, operated by the Carlos Marcello mob. (*Concordia Sentinel*)

FBI agent Billy Bob Williams, who followed KKK members for eighteen months in Natchez, got into a fistfight with Silver Dollar Group Klansman Jack Seale in 1966. (*Concordia Sentinel*)

FBI AGENTS

Ferriday police chief Bob Warren in the 1970s. (*Concordia Sentinel*)

Noah Cross in Ferriday, circa 1940. His long tenure as Concordia Parish sheriff began in 1941.
(Photo courtesy Glen B. McGlothin Jr.)

Natchez police chief J. T. Robinson (*seated*) with detectives Charlie Bahin (*center*) and Frank Rickard (*left*). All three worked behind the scenes to help the FBI.
(*Concordia Sentinel*)

LAW
ENFORCEMENT

Noah Cross wept "freely," reported the *Concordia Sentinel*, when taking the oath for his eighth term in July 1972, a few months before going to federal prison. (*Concordia Sentinel*)

Vidalia police chief J. L. "Bud" Spinks. (*Concordia Sentinel*)

Noah Cross (*right*) with Frank DeLaughter a short time after their release from federal prison in the 1970s. (*Concordia Sentinel*)

Raleigh J. "Red" Glover, head
of the Silver Dollar Group
(FBI file photo)

NORMAN HEAD
COMMUNITY SERVICE STATION
VIDALIA, LOUISIANA

Kenneth Norman Head
(*Concordia Sentinel*)

Homer T. "Buck" Horton
(FBI file photo)

Elden "Junkman" Hester
(FBI surveillance photo)

**MURDER
SUSPECTS**

Tommie Lee Jones
(FBI file photo)

E. D. Morace
(FBI file photo)

Ernest B. Parker
(House Un-American Activities
Committee file photo)

Coonie Poissot
(FBI file photo)

James L. Scarborough
(FBI file photo)

Sonny Taylor
(Photo courtesy Cherris J. Nichols)

James Ford Seale
(FBI file photo)

Myron Wayne "Jack" Seale
(House Un-American Activities
Committee file photo)

5
A GREAT STORM GATHERING

PRESIDENT LYNDON JOHNSON pressured the FBI to make the Neshoba case its top priority and to stop the Klan violence, but bureau agents in the field knew how tall the order was. Black males had gained the vote during Reconstruction but had been denied it in the South through various means during the Jim Crow era. In the 1950s, after almost a century, the U.S. Supreme Court outlawed the segregation of public schools, and Congress passed two civil rights acts. The first, in 1957, created the Civil Rights Commission and the Civil Rights Division of the Justice Department. It was the duty of division lawyers to find a means to enforce the act and the one that followed, in 1960, which gave the Justice Department a potentially effective avenue to secure the ballot for blacks: the authority to inspect and photograph voter registration records. The federal mandates were supposed to prevent white public officials, such as the county registrar of voters, the sheriff, or the police chief, from discriminating against African Americans who attempted to register to vote, and to investigate anyone, private citizen or public official, who threatened, intimidated, or used coercion in any manner to do so. From 1960 to 1963, the Justice Department uncovered numerous ploys used by southern registrars that had prevented generations of blacks from voting. As the cases of discrimination came to light, police officers and their white civilian allies increased the levels of intimidation and violence, especially in Mississippi.[1]

On June 5, 1964, a month after the murder of Henry Hezekiah Dee and Charles Moore, Attorney General Robert Kennedy established a nine-lawyer unit from the Civil Rights Division to investigate the terrorist acts in southwest Mississippi. The division was also supposed to determine the numeric and arms strength of the Klan and ascertain the level of its infiltration into law enforcement.[2] In a May 3 "Imperial Executive Order," White Knights imperial wizard Sam Bowers had advised that "within a very few days, the enemy will launch his final push for victory here in Mississippi." He predicted Freedom

Summer would result in "massive street demonstrations" between blacks and whites, creating "civil chaos and anarchy." White resistance to "communist authorities" within the federal government could result in the siege of Mississippi by a declaration of martial law. He urged white Mississippians to prepare their fists and guns.[3]

His followers thought Bowers prophetic when on June 17 Joseph Alsop wrote in the *Washington Post*, "A great storm is gathering—and may break very soon indeed—in the State of Mississippi and some other regions of the South." Civil rights organizations were transporting several hundred black and white students from the North to register blacks to vote. The *Post* quoted one black student as saying that African Americans might start "killing the white people in Mississippi very soon." Harvard's student newspaper, the *Crimson*, editorialized that Freedom Summer would be a "massive, daring, probably bloody assault on the racial powers of Mississippi" and that for "the first time, active self-defense and actual retaliation (by Negroes), though not officially advocated, are being openly discussed."[4]

On June 21, James Chaney, a local black resident, and Andrew Goodman and Michael Schwerner, northern white men, went missing in Neshoba County. As part of the Freedom Summer effort, the three were investigating the burning of a black church, which had been designated by the Congress of Racial Equality as the site for a freedom school. Neshoba County deputy sheriff Cecil Price reported that he had booked the three for speeding and released them from jail before midnight.

Although numerous murders and attacks against black men in southwest Mississippi and Concordia Parish, Louisiana, had occurred since February, it was the Neshoba case that enraged the nation. Dee, Moore, and Clifton Walker had been dead for weeks. But they were ordinary black men, uninvolved with civil rights and without outside advocates, whereas the Neshoba case concerned civil rights workers, two of them white. As the case became major national news, the FBI brought in Joseph Sullivan to manage the investigation. An agent since 1941 and a bureau legend, Sullivan had served as a troubleshooter for the FBI and in 1963 had been named major case inspector. He would inspire Justice Department lawyers in 1965 when he stood in the midst of Klansmen in Bogalusa, Louisiana, and dressed down white police for failing to keep them from harassing black demonstrators. In June 1964, Sullivan informed FBI director J. Edgar Hoover that "Mississippi was badly undermanned, and that Washington was out of touch with the resident agents in Mississippi, and that the agents there were too close to local Mississippi officials."[5]

On July 2, Congress passed the Civil Rights Act. Southern leaders fumed, and Klansmen vowed revenge. U.S. senator Russell B. Long of Louisiana vilified the legislation, even as he claimed that he had "the kindest feeling toward the good colored people of this nation, and particularly the good colored people of my state . . . What I object to is this bill forces people to mingle or mix with company they do not choose." Many southern leaders likened the legislation to a second invasion by carpetbaggers.[6]

The *Meridian Star* reported in a front-page article that local congressman Arthur Winstead thought the stories about the missing civil rights workers were all hoaxes.[7] In Philadelphia, Mississippi, the *Neshoba Democrat*'s publisher speculated that the three young men had purposely dropped out of the area for publicity to raise money for their cause.[8] In the *Concordia Sentinel,* a front-page columnist opined that the missing students might be safe and sound in their communist Cuba hideout.[9]

Southern whites complained that the northern news media were purposely portraying the South in a bad light. "To white Southerners," wrote historian Adam Fairclough in a chronicle of the times, "the appearance of those 'outside agitators' acted as a red flag to a bull." White supremacy had survived since Reconstruction "because southern whites had persuaded northern whites not to interfere with the South's 'Negro problem.'"[10] Don Whitehead, in his 1970 book on the Neshoba case, reported that it was "a time of crisis for Mississippi. Emotionally, the state was on edge. The daily predictions of violence and bloodshed . . . were used by the Far Right extremists to support their claims that civil rights leaders were deliberately trying to force a federal occupation of the state."[11]

Yet Congressman Charles L. Weltner of Atlanta, an original opponent of the legislation who changed his stance and supported it, urged fellow southerners to do the same and to "move on to the unfinished task of building a new South. We must not remain forever bound to another lost cause." Florence Mars, a Philadelphia native whose family helped settle Neshoba County, believed society would "act against its own best interest to protect itself from the truth." She wrote in her 1977 book that many white women at the time realized the missing students were likely dead and that the FBI was the only entity standing between the thugs and the decent people.[12] Hoover announced on July 10 that he was increasing the bureau's strength in Mississippi to 153 agents, with the bulk assigned to the Neshoba case. A Mississippi division office was reopened in Jackson.[13]

TWO DAYS AFTER Hoover's announcement, shortly after midnight on July 12, 1964, the manager of the Dixie Lane Bowling Alley on the Ferriday-Vidalia highway closed up and went east toward Vidalia for a drink at Blackie Drane's lounge. He was heading west toward home when a white, unmarked Oldsmobile passed him, a red light flashing on its dashboard. The late-model (possibly 1964) Olds had two rear antennae on the trunk and appeared to be a police car.[14] He watched the Oldsmobile pass a two-toned, white-over-green 1958 Buick and pull it over to the shoulder across the highway from the bowling alley. As he drove by, he saw a large white man sitting in the driver's seat of the Oldsmobile. The right front door was open. One or two white men were standing next to the driver's door of the Buick. A man wearing a green shirt, possibly plaid, was the lone occupant. The witness couldn't tell whether the occupant of the Buick was white or black.[15]

Both vehicles were pointed in the direction of Ferriday, three miles to the west. A few feet from the two cars was the mainline Mississippi River levee. The witness was continuing on to Ferriday when the Olds sped by him with a number of occupants inside. When questioned later, he told the FBI he was certain that neither Concordia Parish sheriff Noah Cross nor Deputy Frank DeLaughter was among the men he saw. He didn't know Vidalia police chief J. L. "Bud" Spinks, but when shown a photo of the 1964 white Olds Spinks drove (which had a light mounted on the roof), the witness said that was not the car he had seen on the highway.[16]

For the next few days, the Buick remained parked on the highway across from the bowling alley before it mysteriously was moved onto a street beside the Dixie Lanes. Inside the Buick, a spot of blood the size of a silver dollar was found on the floor under the steering wheel.[17] Word soon spread that the Buick's owner, twenty-five-year-old Joseph Edwards, a porter at the Shamrock Motor Motel in Vidalia, was missing. Despite countless hours of searching and contacting friends and neighbors, his mother, Bernice Conner, had not been able to find her son. She had even checked the jail. In late July 1964, she reported to the FBI and the Natchez police that Edwards was missing. "The Klan got my boy," she cried to FBI agent Billy Bob Williams, who had just been transferred from San Diego.[18] Conner feared Edwards was dead.

Known by his friends as "Joe-Ed," Edwards had grown up in Sibley, eleven miles south of Natchez. From an early age, he was playful, talkative, and restless. As he grew older, he spent much of his time gambling and chasing girls. In the 1950s, he moved with his grandparents from Mississippi to Clayton in Concordia Parish and attended but never graduated from Sevier-Rosenwald, the black school in Ferriday. He was small in stature, standing five feet, six inches, and weighing 160 pounds. He wore neatly pressed clothes and a wristwatch decorated with small diamonds.[19]

In 1961, when he was twenty-one, he entered into a common-law marriage with Augree Taylor. Deaf and mute, Taylor communicated by sign language or by writing. The next year, while employed by T. E. Mercer Trucking Company in Vidalia, Edwards was using gasoline to start a fire in a steel drum when the fumes ignited and flashed in his face. (Family members and friends recall him spending two days in the hospital but believe a grease fire on the stove caused the burns.) A cousin remembers that during his hospital stay, Edwards rather flamboyantly attempted to flirt with the white nurses. A few months after the fire, he was fired by his Mercer supervisor for dishonesty concerning a request for an advance on his salary.[20]

By 1963, Edwards and Augree had two children. By early 1964, however, Edwards was rumored to be seeing other women, including white women. In mid-February, when bill collectors were hounding Edwards, and Klansmen abducted and beat black men in Concordia Parish and Adams County, a Natchez doctor diagnosed the young man with psychoneurosis, a minor mental disorder caused by emotional stress. Two months later, he was treated at the Jefferson Davis Hospital emergency room with sodium luminal to relieve nausea and tension.[21] Not long afterward, he got a job as porter at the Shamrock in Vidalia. One mile west of downtown Natchez, the Shamrock was a typical 1950s-style motel, located near the foot of the Mississippi River Bridge. The 58-room facility featured a long L-shaped wing of rooms connected to the registration office at the front. A few steps away, a separate building housed a busy coffee shop with booths, a restaurant, and a lounge. Sandwiched inside the motor court between the guest rooms and coffee shop were a swimming pool and covered sitting area.[22]

Edwards's duties included mowing, cleaning guest rooms, and a host of odd jobs. Although he could enter a room to clean it, as a black man in the segregated South of 1964, he could not spend the night in one, nor could he use the bathrooms. Aware of the debate in Congress over civil rights legislation,

Edwards expressed to his first cousin Carl Ray Thompson on more than one occasion his readiness for a new world. At the coffee shop that spring, Sonny Boyd, the son of Earcel Boyd, a preacher who worked at Armstrong Tire with Red Glover, sat alone eating a hamburger as his dad and other Klansmen met with Glover in an adjoining room. Edwards leaned his elbows on the counter and asked Sonny Boyd what had happened to his partially bandaged head, which Sonny had injured in an automobile accident. Sonny observed that Edwards also had a wound—on the side of his neck was a white scar, apparently from the burns he had received two years earlier.[23]

While the Shamrock was a popular stopping point for travelers and a meeting place for Klansmen, it also did a bustling restaurant and lounge business. Pimps and prostitutes frequented the motel. There was a legendary brothel on Rankin Street in Natchez known as Nellie's, named after Nellie Jackson, who had first opened her establishment in the 1920s, and it was rumored that she sent some of her prostitutes to entertain guests at the Shamrock. The ten-mile section of the Ferriday-Vidalia highway known as "The Strip" offered its customers gambling tables, poker games, booze, greasy barbecue sandwiches, ladies of the night, and bouncers who beat senseless many unruly customers or debtors. It was rumored that Edwards was involved in some of this activity. Some people said that while working at the Shamrock, Edwards had begun pimping black women to white men. Some also believed that he was pimping a white prostitute whose son drowned in the motel pool on June 27, but the relationship was never proven. Edwards told his cousin Carl Ray that he had been threatened after accidentally walking into a room where a white couple was having sex. He told several friends he dated white women. Friends begged Edwards to stop his interracial affairs and quit the Shamrock, as Klansmen frequented the coffee shop and restaurant. Edwards didn't see the problem.[24]

AT THE SHAMROCK MOTEL coffee shop during the late spring of 1964, Red Glover expressed frustration and anger at the leaders of all three Klan groups—the Original Knights, the White Knights, and the United Klans. The constant infighting and arguments over leadership disgusted him. The southern way of life was under attack as a second civil war neared, he believed, and all the while, Klansmen were wasting time arguing over formalities and chains of command. Meanwhile, hundreds of civil rights workers were mounting a campaign to register blacks to vote in Mississippi. Congress seemed hell-bent on passing a civil rights act that would place white and black children on the same buses and in the same schools, cafeterias, and bathrooms. To Glover, the prospect was unacceptable.[25]

Glover was prepared to bust the heads of northern agitators, white and black, and their southern co-conspirators. He didn't think he needed the permission of a Klan officer to do the work that needed doing. At the Shamrock, Glover gathered his trusted inner circle and told them that he was launching his own secret underground cell—a Klan within a Klan. There would be no robes, no formal meeting place, no officers, no oaths, no cross burnings, no ceremonies, and no dues. Everything would be done simply and in absolute secrecy. He would recruit only hardcore Klansmen, those who already had blood on their hands and who held sacred the privilege of going head-to-head against the communist agents of the federal government that intended to ram integration down white people's throats. Admission would come only at Glover's invitation. His men would work in teams. They would kill whenever he thought necessary. Racial mixing of any kind, but especially between white women and black men, would be met with deadly force.[26]

Glover's symbol of unity was the silver dollar. To each of his first recruits that spring, he handed coins minted in the year of their birth. Glover chose only men he believed would keep their mouths shut until death. The FBI would identify this Klan within a Klan as the "Silver Dollar Group" and cite as its objective "the total segregation of the races by whatever force necessary."[27]

AS THE NATION celebrated Independence Day on July 4, Edwards drove his mother, whom he called "Bean," and his nineteen-year-old sister Julia from Natchez to Clayton to the home of his grandparents, Jake and Mary King. A host of family members gathered for a holiday barbecue. Julia recalled it being a happy day. On the way home, "Bean" playfully fussed at her son for driving too fast and joked that she would never ride with him again. "Don't say that, Bean," Julia said to her mother. "You don't ever know!" It was the last time Julia saw her brother.[28]

On Monday, July 6, Edwards finalized the purchase of a 1958 white-over-green Buick four-door sedan from Purvis Pontiac in Ferriday. He made a $50 down payment on the $495 vehicle. Three days later, James Goss, a forty-three-year-old Louisiana probation officer and welfare caseworker, checked into the Shamrock. Every week, Goss visited Concordia Parish to run down clients, many of whom were delinquent in child-support payments. Goss was a big man, standing six feet, six inches, and weighing 265 pounds. His size had always garnered attention. In 1937, at age sixteen, he had attended the first Boy Scout jamboree in Washington, D.C., and a newspaper had noted that he was the biggest Scout in America, towering over his fellow Scouts and their leaders. In World War II, he served in the South Pacific before returning to the northern Louisiana town of Ruston in 1945. After a series of jobs—including telephone operator on a military base and mail carrier—he landed a position in 1961 with the Louisiana Department of Public Welfare as a caseworker for dependent children.[29]

Goss met Edwards on his first stay at the Shamrock. During a later stay, he met a twenty-two-year-old switchboard operator and registration clerk named Iona Perry. The daughter of a sawmill worker, Iona was a pretty woman who had been diagnosed with polio as a child. She had missed school for a year, and when she returned to elementary school, she was in a wheelchair. Her classmates cheerfully took turns pushing her from class to class. She never missed school after that and always made good grades. Like many of her classmates, she came from a poor family and ate biscuits dipped in sugar syrup for lunch.[30]

Goss was immediately attracted to the young motel clerk, although he was married and the father of a teenage son and a recently married daughter only a year older than Iona. He was impressed by Iona's determination to earn her own way in life despite the crippling disadvantages of polio that required her to wear braces on her legs and use crutches to walk. Initially, he didn't tell Iona he was married. Soon a romance bloomed, and Goss even considered divorcing his wife. As he checked into the Shamrock on July 9 during his routine Thursday visit, Iona began to cry. She told Goss that a short time earlier, as she walked from the switchboard to the bathroom, Edwards had grabbed her arms and kissed her on the lips against her will. Goss was furious. After taking Iona home to Natchez, he returned to the Shamrock in search of Edwards, but he already had left work for the night. Twelve hours later, on Friday, July 10, Goss drove a block east on the highway to the Concordia Parish Courthouse, where he saw Spinks, Cross, DeLaughter, deputies Bill Ogden and Ike Cowan, and jailer Ernest Clark. Goss pulled Spinks aside and related what had happened at the Shamrock the night before. He wanted Edwards charged with assault. Spinks told the deputies about the alleged incident.[31]

On Saturday, Spinks, accompanied by Natchez Police Department captain J. L. Wisner, a known Klansman, visited Iona at her boardinghouse in

Natchez. The forty-five-year-old Spinks had been elected police chief a few months earlier. Iona told them that she had no desire to press charges against Joseph Edwards and was furious that Goss had reported the incident. She wished she had never said anything to him. As the two officers departed, however, Spinks told her not to worry because Edwards "would be taken care of."[32]

The FBI would learn in 1967 from E. D. Morace, a Ferriday Klansman and FBI informant, that in early 1966 Vidalia Klansman Kenneth Norman Head, while drunk, said that Spinks had asked Glover to "take care of" Edwards. Head said that he, Glover, and Thomas "Buck" Horton had killed Edwards but didn't say how. He reportedly said that Edwards "wouldn't be popping up" in the river, meaning that Edwards's body was not thrown into it.[33]

The thirty-five-year-old Head was a mechanic who operated the DX Service Station on Carter Street. He had once served as Exalted Cyclops of the Vidalia Klan. Head was known to live "for violence" and was convinced of an impending race war. Like Head, the twenty-eight-year-old Horton had served in the Marines. According to a military psychiatrist, Horton had suffered an emotionally unstable childhood and had difficulty controlling his temper.[34]

At 10:30 p.m. on July 11, the night he went missing, Edwards stopped at Robert Taylor's bar in Ferriday. He drank two beers and told Taylor that he was "shitting in high cotton" because he was heading to the Shamrock to meet a white woman. "Stay away from those white girls," Taylor warned. Around 11 p.m., Edwards arrived at the motel.[35] Whether he actually met a white girl at the Shamrock, or was simply lured there as part of a police/Klan setup, is unclear. What is certain is that his murder wasn't the only violence of the night. Before dawn, sixteen miles south of Natchez in Kingston, home of the Sligo White Knights unit, two African American churches—Bethel Methodist Episcopal and Jerusalem Baptist, located six miles apart—were burned to the ground before dawn, mere hours before Sunday church services were to begin. At daylight, Klansmen abducted a fifty-five-year-old white man named Dewey White in the Monterey area of Concordia Parish and beat him. With his black fishing buddy sitting in his car, White had a day or two earlier walked into Buckley's Café on Horseshoe Lake and ordered two hamburgers. The owner, looking through the window at the black man, asked White if he planned to "bring that nigger" into the café. White answered no but reminded the owner that his friend Lewis had every right to enter under the new civil rights law. The proprietor furiously cursed White, who realized immediately that he had stirred up a hornet's nest. He quietly paid for his burgers and left the café.[36] A few hours later on July 12, Charles Moore's body was found off Parker's Landing. Henry Hezekiah Dee's body would be found the next day.

Three months later, a commercial fisherman at Deer Park Lake along the Mississippi River seventeen miles south of Vidalia discovered flesh-like material near the shore. In 1967, when it intensively investigated the Edwards case, the FBI learned of the discovery and wondered if the fisherman had found Edwards's remains. The bureau sent divers to search the lake on two separate occasions. FBI agent Billy Bob Williams had heard a rumor, as had others, in 1964 that Edwards had been hung up, skinned alive, and thrown in the river. More than forty years later, the *Concordia Sentinel* learned during its investigation that the origin of that rumor was a Ferriday prostitute who said she had been told that Ed Fuller, her boyfriend and Concordia gambling kingpin Blackie Drane's chief enforcer, had committed the act, but it was never proven. She also indicated that Fuller was involved in the murder of Clifton Walker and the attempted murder of Richard Joe Butler.[37]

While only one informant pointed to Glover, Head, and Horton as Edwards's murderers, several pointed to Concordia Parish sheriff's deputies. The Rev. Robert Lee Jr. told the *Concordia Sentinel* in 2007 that not long after Edwards went missing, civil deputy Raymond Keathley told him, "the [line] deputies got Jo-Ed." Keathley also told the bureau that in 1964, when he asked the deputies whose abandoned car was parked by the bowling alley, DeLaughter replied that it belonged "to the nigger who smarted off to the girls at the Shamrock. We won't be bothered with that black SOB any more." A female witness heard Deputy Bill Ogden say of Edwards, "That serves him right and they ought to bundle up all the niggers and get rid of them."[38]

Probation officer James Goss, whose complaint put Edwards in the crosshairs of the Klan and the sheriff's office, found himself in a vulnerable position when the flesh-like material was found in Deer Park Lake. He had asked Ogden earlier whether the sheriff's office was going to arrest Edwards for the alleged indiscretion with Iona. When he asked Ogden at a later date about Edwards, he said Ogden told him to sink his victims away from the reach of fishermen. Goss asked what he meant. Ogden replied, "You ought to know! You put him there!" Until his death in 2009, Goss would recall many times to his daughter how Ogden and DeLaughter had tried to frame him in a Concordia Parish murder.[39]

According to Ferriday preacher Julian Massey's interview by the FBI in 1967, Ogden told him that he and DeLaughter had pursued Edwards after receiving a complaint that he was causing a disturbance in a Ferriday nightclub. In Massey's account, Ogden said they overtook Edwards at the bowling alley and pulled him over. Edwards jumped from his car and ran onto the levee. With DeLaughter chasing on foot, Ogden followed in his patrol car to the top of the levee, but he claimed Edwards got away. Picking up where Ogden's story left off, a Klan informant told the bureau that he had heard from Louisiana Klansmen that Edwards was taken to the levee, "possibly to whip him, and they over did it." The perpetrators had "rolled him [Edwards] down the levee, thinking he was dead or had buried him on the levee."[40]

The FBI was given two different accounts, then. In one, an unmarked white Oldsmobile with a flashing police light chased Edwards from Vidalia. In the other, Ogden, in his patrol car with DeLaughter, chased Edwards from Ferriday. It seems significant that in both accounts, the chase ended at the bowling alley. After 250 interviews, the FBI closed the Edwards case in 1968 but would reopen it more than four decades later.

A FEW DAYS AFTER Edwards went missing, Agent Williams visited the new FBI offices on an upper floor of the downtown bank building in Jackson. The offices were still under construction. There was one teletype machine, a bank of telephones yet to be installed, wires sticking up in the floor, and a lone clerk sitting at the only desk.[41] Williams was there to talk to Roy K. Moore, who had been named by Hoover as special agent in charge of that field office. There was not an agent in the country who hadn't heard of the storied Moore. He had served seventeen years in the Marines before joining the bureau in 1940, where he trained new agents in the use of firearms. Moore had led the probe in the 1963 Birmingham church bombing that claimed the lives of four girls.[42] Fifty years old, Moore had some of his best work still ahead of him.

Moore welcomed the twenty-nine-year-old Williams, also a Marine, with a handshake. Williams was the second agent to report at headquarters. The son of sharecroppers in New Mexico, Williams had started his bureau career in San Diego and after eighteen months there had gotten orders to go to Mississippi.[43] He had never been there before. Moore gave Williams a brief overview of what had transpired over the past weeks. Outspoken and confident, Williams thought he would have some input on where he was assigned, but Moore began talking "about this sleepy little town called Natchez with Spanish moss hanging on the trees and beautiful antebellum homes." Remembering the meeting later, Williams said, "It became apparent that's where he wanted me to go."[44] Moore, Joseph Sullivan, and other top FBI officials knew the war against the Klan in the area would be brutal. Assistant attorney general for civil rights John Doar found southwest Mississippi's "law enforcement problems were the worst," while "Natchez and its environs had been an intimidation trouble spot for years."[45]

Moore told Williams about the three different Klan groups, and while he didn't sugarcoat the job, he didn't give Williams many details. Williams was to become a part of the community and help local authorities by passing on FBI intelligence when appropriate. After a two-hour conversation, Moore looked at his watch and told Williams he should be in Natchez by 6 p.m. He told Williams to report to Natchez resident agent Clarence Prospere, "an old-timer who had grown up in Natchez."[46] Prospere's one-man operation was headquartered in his kitchen. One of the most experienced bureau agents in Mississippi, Prospere had days earlier refused to share information with the Justice Department task force sent by Kennedy to investigate the Klan. John Doar thought Prospere "very uncooperative . . . He stated that in many matters the FBI considered the Justice Department attorneys 'outsiders.'"[47]

A North Carolina native, Prospere's father had served as the superintendent of Jefferson College early in the twentieth century. The young Prospere and his brother had been cadets there from 1926 to 1933.[48] Before World War II, Prospere became an FBI agent. He served in New York City, Long Island, Niagara Falls, Tennessee, and New Orleans before returning home to Natchez to complete his bureau career just as the civil unrest erupted. Williams recalled Prospere as a big, gregarious man with a graying flattop. He had a deep southern drawl, didn't curse, and was set in his ways.[49] Agents called him "Pross," while some locals knew him as "Toots." One former Adams County sheriff recalled Prospere as "an old [J. Edgar] Hoover guy, old school."[50] Prospere was constantly fidgeting with his pipe, often relighting the tobacco while talking. In 2008, he responded politely to a call from the *Concordia Sentinel* seeking comments about the FBI and the cold cases that had been reopened. "No, sir," the ninety-four-year-old former agent said. "I don't get into the FBI's business."

Prospere's initial refusal to cooperate with Kennedy's task force in the summer of 1964 was symbolic of the uneasiness between the FBI and the Justice Department. What Doar didn't know was that Prospere had already developed crucial information on the White Knights. Prospere learned that three

Natchez police officers, including a captain, a Natchez fireman, and a deputy sheriff, had been among the first to join the White Knights in February.[51]

Before joining Prospere in Natchez, Williams stood at the door of the FBI office in Jackson as Roy Moore wished him good luck and gave him final instructions. A half century later, Williams remembered them clearly: "You go down there and do whatever you think is right and I'll back you 100 percent. You use your judgment on what it looks like needs to be done. But I don't ever want to hear of you backing down to the Klan. And if you ever draw your gun, use it."[52]

AS THE WHITE KNIGHTS violence accelerated in Mississippi, Robert Shelton's Alabama-based UKA continued to move west. Shelton's recruiters had first entered Louisiana in late 1963 but didn't make much headway until Original Knights dissension boiled over, resulting in the creation of the White Knights in Mississippi. While Sam Bowers operated the White Knights like a military dictatorship, Shelton's UKA was taking a different approach following the breakout of violence in Louisiana and Mississippi during the early months of 1964. UKA's strategy in the Magnolia State was to paint itself as a nonviolent political organization and hope that its involvement in past atrocities, such as the Birmingham bombing, would be forgotten. Although the nonviolent image never stuck, the UKA moved through the 1960s as the predominant Klan group in the United States. On May 16, Shelton spoke at a membership rally at the fairgrounds in McComb, where he attacked the "communist-led" federal government's attack on the "southern way of life."[53] In the days ahead, McComb, soon to become a UKA stronghold, was labeled the bombing capital of the South. Following a series of bombings and arsons, a number of white men were arrested and convicted. Civil rights leaders howled when the men received probation, and Judge W. H. Watkins, showing sympathy for the defendants, blamed the activists for inciting the violence.

FBI and MHSP intelligence from McComb also revealed surprising news: E. L. McDaniel of Natchez, who had been banished by the Original Knights in late December 1963 only to help form the White Knights, had become Shelton's top UKA leader in Mississippi. By way of money and deception, McDaniel had managed to obtain the White Knights position of province investigator for southwest Mississippi, which included the responsibility of delivering justice involving internal Klan matters.[54] During the spring of 1964, while handling his investigative duties, however, McDaniel began looking at the UKA as a new vehicle for his ambition. Meanwhile, he dug deeply into the White Knights coffers, causing great dissension among the members until Bowers set a limit on McDaniel's spending. All the while, McDaniel was secretly recruiting for Shelton in Mississippi and had surreptitiously administered UKA oaths to several of the men arrested in the McComb bombings.[55]

In early August, twenty-five Adams County Klansmen, including McDaniel, met at a Natchez bowling alley, where they voted to defect from the White Knights and organize into a UKA klavern under the cover of the Adams County Civic and Betterment Association. Later that month, Shelton announced his appointment of McDaniel as the first grand dragon of the Mississippi Realm of the United Klans of America. With Shelton's blessings, McDaniel opened a UKA office in downtown Natchez on the corner of Canal and Main. On the night of August 29, Shelton led a UKA rally in the city's Liberty Park. A twenty-foot-tall cross was raised and burned in the center of the baseball field before approximately one thousand spectators.[56]

Now a state Klan leader, McDaniel stretched his influence across the Mississippi into Concordia Parish, where he had first become a Klansman in 1962. One of his recruits, Frank DeLaughter, soon put his family to work for the UKA. DeLaughter's sister, Mildred DeLaughter Garner, owner of a beer joint known as Cario's Drive-In on the Ferriday-Vidalia highway and a UKA member herself, took out an ad during the summer in the *Concordia Sentinel*. The ad proclaimed: "All KKK are welcome and invited to this establishment as our special guest [*sic*]. You are always welcome whether recognized or not." UKA applications were kept in the bar. When Delbert Matthews, a local white teen, drove one of Garner's female black employees to work, Garner put the barrel of a .38 caliber pistol between his eyes and commanded, "Don't ever do that again." When Matthews explained that the woman needed a ride to work, Garner warned, "Let her walk!"[57]

6

A DECLARATION OF WAR

CIVIL RIGHTS WORKERS opened more than three dozen freedom schools in Mississippi in 1964 with the purpose of teaching young blacks how to become socially, economically, and politically involved in their communities, particularly through activism. Klansmen monitored every move made by those involved. Keeping the peace in towns polarized by racial disharmony was an impossible job. In Natchez, Mayor John Nosser and Police Chief J. T. Robinson were caught in the middle of the growing tensions. The Klan and the civil rights groups both despised the two men, and each thought the town officials favored the other cause. To make matters worse, Nosser and Robinson didn't like each other.

The sixty-five-year-old Nosser had months earlier been narrowly reelected for a second term as mayor. Of Lebanese descent, he had settled in Natchez in 1939 and over a quarter century had become one of the town's most successful businessmen. He owned two Jitney Jungle grocery stores and a 15-tenant shopping center (known as Nosser City) that had been built in 1956 for $500,000.[1] Because he spoke broken English instead of with a local accent, the garden club was never comfortable when he stood at the podium at antebellum pageants and at balls held during the tourist season. Known to be temperamental, he once kicked Robinson out of his office when the police chief told the mayor that Nosser's two sons had joined the Klan.[2]

At thirty-seven, Robinson, unlike most police officers in the region, had experience and training in law enforcement. Elected chief in 1962, he had served more than a decade on the Natchez police force and had worked as chief criminal deputy for the previous sheriff. Robinson's father and four of his brothers were experienced lawmen as well.[3] An ex-Marine, the chief stood six feet, two inches tall; he was thin but tough. As a young man, he had been considered a good boxer and fought many competitive bouts at the city auditorium. When in uniform, Robinson wore a white shirt with his badge pinned to the pocket and carried in his holster a Smith and Wesson Centennial, a small five-shot hammerless revolver.[4] Many who knew the chief considered him a fair man who used comedic flair to break up tense moments. He was known for his one-liners.[5]

Several things divided the mayor and the chief. Because the chief was elected rather than appointed, Robinson answered to the voters, not the mayor. In fact, the mayor and the city council had little control over the 40-member police department, which was under civil service protection. This situation was also a problem for Robinson because he had no authority to hire or fire. Although the mayor had made it known that he wanted to remove the police department from civil service, Robinson didn't want the mayor meddling in his business. There were reasons for that, too.

Early in 1964, Robinson realized he had moles in his department who were leaking police business to the Klan, particularly to the Sligo White Knights unit at Kingston. He soon found the primary source, Captain J. G. Wisner, who was also informing the mayor on internal affairs within the police department. Robinson knew Wisner was a close friend of two of Nosser's sons, George and Joe, and Ed Fuller, the Exalted Cyclops of the Sligo unit, of which the Nosser brothers were members.[6] Fuller's brother, Claude, was also a member. At International Paper Company where he worked, Claude Fuller was known as one of the most venomous racists in the county. In two years, Claude Fuller would lead a Klan wrecking crew of three in the brutal murder of a sixty-five-year-old black man by the name of Ben Chester White.

Ed Fuller had been identified by the MHSP as a suspect in the February murder of Clifton Walker in Woodville and the attempted murder of Richard Joe Butler in Kingston in April. When the Nosser brothers joined the renegade Sligo unit, no one was more enraged than UKA grand dragon E. L. McDaniel, who wanted the klavern dissolved because its leaders refused to follow Klan leadership. For this and other reasons, McDaniel was a political enemy of Nosser's.[7]

Nosser and Robinson at first had been reluctant to publicly attack the Klan. Nosser claimed that, although illegal, the Klan was a "patriotic" organization, and he had delivered a speech at a KKK rally.[8] Robinson acknowledged at a Civil Rights Commission hearing in 1965 that he had been the principal speaker at a meeting of the Americans for the Preservation of the White Race (APWR). He also had attended the UKA rally in Liberty Park in Natchez when its local office was opened. The event "impressed me," Robinson said.

"I couldn't see anything that might would make you think they were anything but upstanding people." Robinson testified that being a member in the APWR would not keep someone from being a part of his police force, while being a Klansman probably would. But membership in the NAACP, he said, which he considered a subversive organization, would definitely bar employment.[9]

THE CIVIL STRIFE between the Klan and the civil rights community, as well as the contention between the mayor and the police chief, was revealed in an electrifying article published in early September in the *Chicago Sun-Times*. Written by the colorful reporter Nicholas von Hoffman, the story was head-lined, "Anti-Antebellum Natchez: How Things Do Change." Widely circu-lated throughout town, the lede read, "Somebody has taken all the charm out of once-genteel Natchez." In the story, von Hoffman pointed out that while the Klan was allowed to meet at Liberty Park on August 29 to preach about "segregation, communism and the need for more Christianity," blacks were not allowed to use the same public park for a civil rights rally. Among those turned away was Robert Moses, head of the Mississippi Summer Project, who had been at work in the state for years and had been beaten in Amite County in 1961 when attempting to register blacks to vote. Von Hoffman, who had been followed by Natchez police during his visit, received an apology from the mayor, who was quoted: "I have no control over the chief of police." A chamber of commerce receptionist told von Hoffman, "I don't know what to say to you. We like for people to take pictures of the lovely homes, but we've had too much tension here." And a police officer warned him, "Be careful. This isn't like any other town in Mississippi."[10]

The mayor said blacks and whites were afraid because of the ongoing violence, and he blamed the town's problems on "white radicals" and a "well-armed underground." Orrick Metcalfe, a banker and car dealer, indicated Nat-chez was nearing a state of chaos. Metcalfe expressed sympathy for Nosser, whose "primary administrative headache" was "a police chief responsible to voters." Metcalfe said the mayor's "hands are tied," while the police depart-ment was "terrible, just terrible." Von Hoffman also discovered that the po-lice department and city hall were not well thought of in "the slum-ridden Negro quarters down by the big river." He quoted twenty-year-old activist Jesse Barnard, who noted the failed effort made to hold the civil rights rally: "They smother everything here."[11]

Across the river in Vidalia, at 11:40 p.m. on Sunday, September 13, there was an explosion on Cedar Street at the home of Bob and Tammy Doyle and their five children. Northern born and Catholic, Doyle was a schoolteacher who had served in previous years as night editor for the *Natchez Democrat.* He was outspoken against the Klan. In 1963, he had made friends with Father August Thompson, a black Catholic priest who had arrived there a year earlier. Thompson pastored St. Charles Catholic Church in Ferriday, which served Concordia Parish's black population. He was in the process of building a community center for African American youth. During the months preceding the bombing, the priest had been a guest for supper many times in the Doyles' home, and the two men had become close friends. The Vidalia Police Department building was visible from the Doyle home, and officers often drove by when Thompson was a guest. Also conspicuous from time to time were Klansmen, who parked on the street and glared at Doyle. Soon, the community ostracized the family. Doyle was dropped as a parish teacher at the public school before the Catholic school in Natchez gave him a job. As racial tensions mounted on both sides of the river, Doyle often expressed his belief that "every man has a right to a voice in his own destiny."[12]

The bomb exploded twenty feet from the Doyle home near the bedroom of one of his sons. No one was hurt, and damage was minimal. Despite his reporting background, Doyle couldn't get the *Concordia Sentinel* or the *Natchez Democrat* to publish a story.[13] But the bombing did get coverage in the *Miss-Lou Observer,* a new weekly published by lawyer Forrest A. Johnson and his partner Wilhelm Winkler, a retired Army officer. The paper took a hardline stance against the Klan, challenged McDaniel, and reported Klan violence. For this, Johnson's name was smeared in Klan publications and his life threatened. His and Winkler's efforts were heralded in the months ahead by national journalist Drew Pearson, whose weekly column, "The Washington Merry-Go-Round," was published in more than six hundred newspapers, including the *Natchez Democrat,* despite Klan protests that the column be dropped. Shortly before the *Observer* folded, Winkler published an open letter to House Un-American Activities Committee chairman Edwin E. Willis of Louisiana. Winkler reported that by late 1965, the Klan's campaign against the *Observer* was so effective that the publication had dropped from twenty-four pages weekly to four, and revenue had spiraled from $1,200 weekly to less than $15. "I'm a redneck, born in Mississippi," Johnson told Pearson. "But people whom I have known for twenty years don't speak to me on the street anymore."[14]

Bob Doyle immediately notified local police and the FBI about the bombing of his home. Although he refused to investigate, Vidalia police chief Bud Spinks was furious that Doyle had contacted the bureau. "If you don't like the people around here," he said, "why don't you leave?"[15] Nine months later, Doyle's story appeared in the June 1965 issue of *Good Housekeeping* in an article entitled "My Problem? How Much Should a Family Buckle Under?" Written after Doyle and his family had relocated to Colorado, the story was modified to protect their identity.[16] A short time after the story's publication, a lawyer with the HUAC investigating the Klan contacted Doyle, who said that he had found himself unemployable in Vidalia and that his children had been suffering too much to continue living there. Prior to the move, however, he had served as co-chair in the fifth congressional district for Lyndon Johnson's presidential campaign. Doyle believed that he had been the only white man in a ninety-mile radius of Vidalia with an LBJ sticker on his car.[17]

AFTER MIDNIGHT on September 14, less than two hours after the Doyle bombing, stink bombs were hurled into Mayor Nosser's grocery stores. The missiles broke windows and delivered a sulphuric payload that damaged the floors. That same night, a brick was thrown through a window at Orreck Metcalfe's Chevrolet-Cadillac dealership, clearing the way for a jar of acid, which landed on a new Cadillac. While investigating the matter, Chief Robinson was greeted on the scene by three Klansmen—the Nosser brothers and Ed Fuller. Robinson asked Joe Nosser who was responsible. Without hesitation Nosser answered, "Jack Seale." But he had no proof.[18] By now, the Sligo unit was blaming every instance of Klan violence on the newly formed UKA unit, and the UKA was blaming the Sligo bunch.

Everyone in the city of 24,000, populated almost evenly by blacks and whites, knew things were getting out of hand. Ten days after Nosser and Metcalfe's businesses were targeted, the mayor met with McDaniel, whose UKA office was so scenically positioned between the Mississippi River and the heart of downtown that no tourist could miss it. Nosser wondered what could be done to calm the tensions.[19] The next evening at 9:18 p.m., however, an explosion rattled windows in Natchez and Vidalia and shook the Mississippi River Bridge. This time the target was Nosser's home at 207 Linten Avenue. In an upscale neighborhood accented by live oaks and beautiful Victorian homes, the street was anchored on the north end by the Ritz Theatre. Five minutes prior to the blast, Nosser and his wife had been outside watering flowers. His daughter and her friend had crossed the lawn just before her parents went inside. The blast blew out all of the windows on the front of the house, cracked the brick foundation, and split the plaster in the living room. Next door, windows were blown out of the home of Rawdon and Kathie Blankenstein. Their three sleeping children, ages two, three, and five, were covered with glass.[20]

Robinson, who was patrolling at the time, raced to the scene, where he found a crowd of neighbors on the front lawn and a visibly upset mayor. After his two detectives arrived at 9:35 p.m., two more blasts were heard across town. On Pine Street, the homes of two black men were damaged, although less severely than Nosser's. One of the victims was Willie Washington, a contractor who had been targeted by the Klan during the summer when a Molotov cocktail was thrown on his lawn. But Robinson soon realized these bombs were not gasoline based. Soil samples taken from the scenes failed to reveal any residue that would identify the type of explosives employed, but other evidence showed that the bomb thrown in Nosser's yard was a plastic explosive, likely set off by a timing device. Investigators believed that the bombers had waited until authorities arrived at Nosser's home before delivering the second bomb at the other location. The obvious motives for the bombings were Nosser's criticism of "white radicals" in the von Hoffman article and his hiring of Washington to perform construction work.[21] That night, the chief placed ten shotgun-toting, uniformed patrolmen at locations throughout the city.[22]

Nosser met with McDaniel again to plead for an end to the violence. On September 27, in an article in the *Natchez Democrat*, Nosser claimed that he had been misquoted in the *Chicago Sun-Times* and clarified that the racial troubles in Natchez were caused not just by white radicals but also by some of the "colored," noting that a fraction of each was at fault. He urged citizens of the town "to stand up for law and order at a time when it appears that radical elements are threatening not only the properties but the lives of the people who live here." He warned, "If this situation continues, we may be confronted by the intervention of federal forces," and Natchez "will become a ghost town."[23] The next day, in a letter printed on the front page of the *Democrat*, McDaniel claimed the UKA had nothing to do with the bombings and other violence and didn't condone any of it. He tried to persuade a skeptical public that his group demanded law and order as much as the average citizen.[24]

* * *

AFTER MEETING longtime resident agent Clarence Prospere, FBI agent Billy Bob Williams had visited the Natchez Police Station to meet Robinson. On the wall of the chief's desk were four Marine Corps Division patches. As Robinson stood to shake his hand, Williams said, "Semper Fi." They hit it off instantly.[25]

Williams soon learned that Robinson's two most trusted employees were the department's detectives, lieutenants Charlie Bahin and Frank Rickard. Bahin had served as police chief years earlier, had worked as chief deputy for the sheriff's office, and had been an officer for the MHSP. Easygoing, Bahin roamed the night, stopping in black and white lounges for a beer to find out what was going on. Oftentimes, his mere presence kept the troublemakers at bay. Equally important, he reported daily to the chief what he learned on his nightly rounds.[26]

Born to a German mother in Coblenz and an American father who had served as part of the U.S. occupational force following World War I, Rickard possessed a loyalty to Robinson that knew no bounds. While Bahin frequented the bars in order to monitor the pulse of the city, Rickard personally enjoyed the nightlife. During the day, he helped Robinson administer the police department. The two became so close that when Robinson went through a divorce in later years, he slept on Rickard's couch.[27] Rickard was renowned in Natchez for his physical strength and was the subject of gossip because of his alleged contacts with the New Orleans underworld. Williams once watched him drive roofing nails with the edge of his bare fist. On the streets, Rickard was said to have enough karate skills to kill somebody.[28] He delighted at intimidating the most hardcore Klansmen. Even Jack Seale, a muscular and powerful man feared by his KKK brothers, was afraid of Rickard.

Often, in the late afternoon, Williams joined the detectives and the chief for a visit to one of the bars where Klansmen were known to hang out. On one occasion, as the lawmen entered a lounge, they encountered a group, led by Jack Seale, heading out. Rickard and Seale stood face to face. Like his Klan associates, Seale was wearing a white shirt and a red tie with the initials "KKK" running vertically down the length of the material. Rickard took the tie in his hand and examined it closely while talking loud enough for everyone to hear. "Look at this!" he proclaimed. "You know you have to be a big man, a tough son-of-a-bitch, to wear something like this and back it up." Then Rickard raised the tie to his face and blew his nose on it. Seale trembled with anger, stepped aside, and left the bar.[29]

Such encounters were not rare. Although Rickard intimidated Seale in the Natchez bar, there was no doubt that Seale and his comrades were in control of the night. With the violence escalating, Williams realized that there was no mechanism in place that could realistically stop it. With civil rights workers, local businesses, private citizens, and even the mayor under attack, he feared that Natchez and southwest Mississippi would soon be soaked in blood. He had been called out to bombing scenes in McComb and had visited the sites of Klan attacks in Wilkinson and Franklin Counties. He was familiar with the savage violence committed by Klansmen and hoodlums across the river in the lawless land of Concordia Parish. So intense was the situation that, with Prospere's help, Williams had strung chicken wire beneath his rented home, which was on blocks, so the Klan couldn't throw a bomb beneath it. He often thought of Roy Moore's instructions to never back down to the Klan. One morning while driving to work, he decided it was time to do something. He detoured to Mississippi FBI headquarters in Jackson. There, he quickly made his way to Moore's office. "We're losing the battle down there," he said. "That's all there is to it. We've got to get a handle on it."[30]

Williams watched as Moore quietly studied the situation in his mind. Soon, he snapped to and began writing names on a list. He called in his secretary. "Find these people and send them teletype transfers to get down here as fast as they can and to come prepared to stay awhile." Williams hadn't realized that Moore had such power. Moore picked up the phone, called headquarters in Washington, and reported that he had sent out orders to have twenty-five agents transferred to work in southwest Mississippi. He contacted the MHSP and made arrangements to pair each agent with a patrolman. Because the FBI didn't have jurisdiction in many of the cases of violence, it was going to beef up its assistance to the MHSP. Moore looked at Williams and said, "We're fixing to declare war on the Klan down there."[31]

Within days, the FBI opened its first office in Natchez in a bank building downtown. The office was soundproofed. In addition to fourteen special agents, eleven uniformed and fourteen plainclothes Mississippi state troopers were working out of the office.[32] In the meantime, to help nudge witnesses forward, the mayor and aldermen offered a $5,000 reward to anyone who could help solve the crimes, a move similar to the action taken by the business community in McComb. Government leaders called for the public to report crimes to the authorities and make a stand. Failure to do so would be nearly as bad as committing the criminal acts. The town couldn't survive without tourism and industry, but no one would visit Natchez under the current dangerous conditions because "we do not know when, or where or whom the terrorists will strike next."[33]

SOON THE COORDINATED effort paid off. Within days, nine Klansmen were charged in three separate cases—those involving the beating and attempted murder of two civil rights workers in 1963, the attempted murder of Richard Joe Butler in April 1964, and the murders of Henry Hezekiah Dee and Charles Moore in May 1964. The first arrests came on October 22, when the MHSP booked five Klansmen for two separate attacks on civil rights workers Bruce Payne, a twenty-one-year-old white Yale political science major, and George Green, thirty, a black Tougaloo College student in Jackson who was working on the staff of the Student Nonviolent Coordinating Committee (SNCC). The two had visited Natchez in October 1963 as part of the Freedom Ballot campaign orchestrated to prove that black Mississippians could and would vote if given the opportunity.[34]

Then-governor Ross Barnett and other political leaders had long insisted that black citizens were so satisfied with state government that they had no desire to vote and that blacks were intellectually incapable of understanding the election process. Several carloads of white students from Yale and Stanford came to the South to take part in a mock election with black candidates held in conjunction with the regular statewide election for governor and lieutenant governor in Mississippi. Civil rights groups knew some of the activists would likely be arrested and beaten by police and Klansmen, but they also knew such events would give the movement publicity and make the nation aware of conditions in Mississippi. Public outrage might push Congress to act, while at the same time blacks might be encouraged to risk the dangers and register to vote. But in Mississippi and Louisiana, the statewide elections only served to ferment more white support for segregation. In Louisiana, Governor-elect John McKeithen, a North Louisiana lawyer who subsequently would become a moderate on racial issues, defeated former New Orleans mayor deLesseps Story "Chep" Morrison. Morrison was politically connected to President John Kennedy, who would be assassinated a few days later. About his victory, McKeithen said, the "people have illustrated for the entire nation that the people of a sovereign state are not going to allow the NAACP to come in and elect a governor."[35]

In late October 1963, Payne, Green, and Nick Bosanquet arrived in Natchez, where they met with black male and female leaders, white Catholic women, and Father William Morrissey, a white activist who was pastor of Holy Family Catholic Church, which served a black congregation. Morrissey was the first white person to hold office in the Mississippi NAACP. The next morning, Natchez police arrested Green on trumped-up traffic charges. Robinson later acknowledged at a Civil Rights Commission hearing in Jackson that he had Green arrested in order to "see who he was." Like most law enforcement personnel, Robinson resented the presence of activists because it complicated his work.[36] FBI agent Williams believed that many civil rights workers didn't realize, or care, how gravely they endangered the lives of local blacks who would remain in a community after the activists left.[37]

Payne and Green stayed at the rooming house of future Natchez NAACP president George Metcalfe, an employee at the Armstrong Tire Plant. (He would be seriously injured in a Klan bombing in 1965.) When driving by Metcalfe's house, Klansmen and other whites shouted obscenities at the activists. On the afternoon of October 31, 1963, as Payne, along with Green and veteran black activist Ella Baker, departed Natchez for Jackson, he observed two cars following him. When Payne stopped for gas at a station in Port Gibson, the Klansmen attacked. Three of the four attackers slugged and kicked Payne several times, but because he adhered to Dr. Martin Luther King's pledge of nonviolence, he didn't fight back. All the while, a dozen local black and white witnesses said and did nothing. After this incident, Payne was interviewed about the attack, and the story made national news. One goal set by the activists had been reached.[38]

Among the four men arrested a year later was thirty-two-year-old Ernest Avants. After leading the attack, Avants had told Payne and Green, "Don't come back to Adams County and show your tail any more."[39] Neither Payne nor Green was intimidated. They were back in Natchez two days later. When leaving town, they soon realized they were once again being pursued, this time by just one car, at speeds in excess of one hundred miles per hour. Green, who was driving a rental, was forced to pull over near Fayette, twenty-four miles north of Natchez. Hemmed in, the two men watched as Avants, now clearly identifiable to both, trotted to the driver's side of the vehicle and aimed his revolver at Green's head. Before Avants could open the door, Green hit the gas. As they sped away, their car was riddled with bullets, but they eluded their attackers.[40]

Of the three men booked in this attack, Avants and Jack Seale were charged for assault and battery with intent to shoot and murder. Those involved in the first attack were booked with assault and battery with intent to kill. On October 23, 1964, the day after the arrests, Sheriff Odell Anders, with MHSP and FBI officers present, seized from Seale's home on 172 Booker Road in the Morgantown subdivision in Natchez a shotgun, two high-powered rifles, a bayonet, a set of handcuffs, a hunting knife, and twelve boxes of shotgun, rifle, and pistol ammunition.[41]

On October 26, a phone company survey team working along the riverbank at Natchez discovered twenty-four pounds of dynamite. Authorities suspected an unknown quantity had been thrown into the river.[42] An MHSP informant had reported that Natchez Klansman Ernest Parker had been using his personal plane to fly in explosives to his landing strip on Davis Island, where he and brothers Jack and James Ford Seale had murdered Dee and Moore the previous May.[43] Also on October 26, the FBI and MHSP announced the arrests of Ed Fuller and fellow Sligo Klansman William Bryant Davidson, twenty-seven, in connection with the April shooting of Richard Joe Butler. Billy Woods, another Sligo Klansman, had been arrested in April. Fuller's release from jail was secured on a $2,000 property bond signed by Mayor Nosser's sons, Joe and John.[44]

On October 29, Sheriff Anders and Police Chief Robinson jointly announced that the sale of whiskey and all gambling activities would be prohibited, effective at midnight. The two men told the *Natchez Democrat* that they were acting on orders of Gov. Paul Johnson, who indicated that if the two lawmen didn't want to do it, the Mississippi National Guard would. Though illegal, gambling in the backrooms of bars had long been tolerated, as had the sale of whiskey. In Natchez, a bar owner could pay a black market tax to the city to obtain a license to sell hard liquor. The paper reported that the FBI and the MHSP believed the ban on gambling and alcohol would reduce the violence and help solve the bombings and other crimes. Immediately, MHSP patrolmen fanned out across the county and informed individual bar owners of the ban.[45] Many citizens claimed they were illegally pulled over by patrolmen. In the weeks ahead, there was an outcry by public officials.

Sen. Bill Jones of Brookhaven berated an MHSP investigator for "mistreatment of the public" and alleged that Klan suspects and one black man had been roughed up.[46] Former Adams County sheriff Billy Ferrell sent a telegram to Governor Johnson: "Have we been placed under Marshall [*sic*] Law?

Twenty patrol cars make it appear that way. Agree that something needs to be done about bombings, etc., but illegal search and harassment of decent citizens upon hwys. at night by over eager officers not the answer."[47] Mayor Nosser complained that twenty-five to thirty families were "hurting" because of the ban on whiskey sales. Sheriff Anders alleged that since the shutdown as many as eight package liquor stores had opened across the river in Vidalia. Dozens of men identified by law enforcement as hoodlums, such as Ed Fuller, had moved across the river, where Concordia's prostitution and gambling business was not only thriving but growing.[48]

On November 1, the *Natchez Democrat* ran a front-page article on the Adams County Civic and Betterment Association's resolution attacking the MHSP. The article didn't mention that the newly formed group was a front for the UKA. John Dawson, an ordained Baptist minister and IP employee, said by informants to be the man behind the UKA and McDaniel, claimed that the MSHP had created a "police state" by conducting unlawful arrests and searches. He asked for donations to help those defendants recently arrested in Natchez. Foster blamed the turmoil on the "communist-front" civil rights groups.[49]

Five days later, James Ford Seale and Charles Marcus Edwards were charged in the May 2 murders of Dee and Moore. In the days after his arrest, Seale had been praised in Klan circles. Bob Doyle, the schoolteacher whose family had survived a bombing in Vidalia in early September, had once thought Seale "a swell fellow until the Klan made a kook out of him . . . I saw him on the street all duded up like a cowboy, he assured me he didn't do it, and then at a Klan meeting that night he was treated as a hero."[50]

ON NOVEMBER 3, the nation elected Lyndon Johnson, the former vice president who had ascended to the presidency following the assassination of Kennedy a year earlier. Johnson, the Democrat, garnered 61 percent of the vote. The man who had pushed the Civil Rights Act of 1964 through Congress and was preparing to push through a voting rights act, Johnson was soundly rejected in southwest Mississippi and Concordia Parish. There were a number of issues discussed during the campaign, but civil rights was without question the number-one issue locally. Five southern states supported Arizona senator Barry Goldwater, the Republican candidate, who condemned racism during the campaign. While he got 56 percent of the Louisiana vote, Mississippi cast

87 percent for Goldwater in a solid stance against civil rights.[51] One reason the Council of Federated Organizations had targeted Mississippi for Freedom Summer was that only 6.2 percent of the state's eligible black voters were registered, the lowest percentage in the nation.

In Wilkinson County, where Clifton Walker had been murdered in an ambush, 93 percent of the voters favored the Republican. In Franklin County, where Dee and Moore were kidnapped before their murders, Goldwater got 96 percent of the vote. In Natchez and Adams County, where a dozen men had been beaten during the winter of 1964, Richard Joe Butler shot, and the mayor and others targeted by Klansmen, 84 percent of the 6,993 registered voters went for Goldwater. Across the river in Concordia Parish, where Klan wrecking crews roamed the nights and Joseph Edwards had vanished, Goldwater received 83 percent of 4,831 votes cast.[52]

7

"THE COLORED PEOPLE OF CONCORDIA PARISH"

AT THE END OF 1964, the FBI's attention shifted from southwest Mississippi to Ferriday. Although Concordia is in Louisiana, the parish's association with Natchez predates 1716, when the French built a fort and trading post atop the bluff. Before then, the Natchez Indians and their Native American forebears had harvested wildlife and cypress from Concordia's vast forests for generations. The English and, in turn, the Spanish, based in Natchez from 1763 to 1798, grazed their livestock on the rich grassland of Concordia and fished its lakes and rivers. By the time of the Civil War, Natchez planters, who had amassed great wealth thanks to cotton, buttered their biscuits and built their mansions with the income derived from the rich Concordia bottomland worked by some thirteen thousand enslaved Africans, who also built the levees, nursed the masters' children, and emptied the chamber pots. Most white families were under the thumb of the Natchez planters, too, serving as plantation overseers and managers. For decades, Natchez considered Concordia its hired hand. While the communities are as one in many ways, they do have separate identities. Concordia has secrets that will never be revealed. Natchez lives in eternal fear of its secrets being exposed.

On the morning of December 23, 1964, *New York Times* reporter John Herbers sipped coffee at the Eola Hotel in downtown Natchez before driving to Ferriday. He had learned a few days earlier about the fiery death of a black shoe-shop owner. It had come at a time when Klan violence in southwest Mississippi and much of the state had become eerily quiet.[1] The beefed-up presence of the FBI and the MHSP statewide had made a difference. The White Knights of the Ku Klux Klan had placed a moratorium on violence in late fall of 1964 and urged their members to lie low. The UKA in Mississippi, through its grand dragon E. L. McDaniel, headquartered in downtown Natchez, issued letter after letter to newspapers condemning the violence and attacking the communist-backed civil rights "agitators" for dividing the white and black populations, which, McDaniel claimed, had for generations lived in perfect harmony. The biggest Klan-related news had come early in December, when twenty-one White Knights were arrested for the June 1964 murders of the three civil rights workers in Neshoba County.

Herbers spent years writing about racial issues for the United Press in its Jackson, Mississippi, bureau before joining the *Times*. He had covered racial murders for a decade—from the 1955 Emmett Till trial to the 1963 16th Street Baptist Church bombing to the Neshoba case. Klan leaders knew him. Herbers considered Sam Bowers, head of the White Knights, a menacing and paranoid man, while he thought that UKA leader Robert Shelton, whose Klansmen had bombed the Birmingham church, was in some ways a savvy public relations man who was at ease with the press. Whereas Bowers avoided attention, Shelton loved it. Only McDaniel, Shelton's top man in Mississippi, drew more headlines. Herbers knew Ferriday and Natchez as "the scariest places" in the South.[2] FBI agent Billy Bob Williams recalled that Concordia was so infamous as a killing ground that the bureau called it "a maggot-infested mess."[3]

In Ferriday, Herbers found the community tense and shocked by the murder of a respected town citizen, whose shop looked like a scene from *Gone with the Wind*. Herbers wrote, "Frank Morris's (leather) sewing machines are exposed to the sky and remain upright in the blackened ruins of the building, a stark reminder of the man who repaired the shoes of everyone in town, white and Negro." Morris "was a man of varied interests and it is possible he could have acquired enemies in the course of his business. However, the crime has aroused suspicions because it occurred in an area of racial tensions and because it fit the pattern of terror that has been carried out only a few miles away in southern Mississippi." The journalist reported that Ferriday, a town of 4,500, was the "business center for Concordia Parish, which lies flat and black below the river levee. It has cotton and cattle land, bayous, dense forests and a large but silent Negro population . . . Natchez, a city of 24,000, has hills, antebellum homes and factories. Many who work in Natchez live in Concordia Parish, mostly in the parish seat of Vidalia."[4]

WHEN WHITES IN Ferriday told FBI investigators they thought race relations were harmonious prior to Morris's murder, they were either ignorant, lying, or naïve. A year earlier, the writer John Howard Griffin had spent a few days in Ferriday with Father August Thompson, the black priest at St. Charles Catholic Church. In 1962, Griffin had published a book called *Black like Me*, an account of his six-week journey by bus through the Deep South. Although he was a white man, he had artificially darkened his skin, successfully passed himself off as black, and suffered a daily dose of racism and hatred.

He visited Ferriday in September 1963 (as a white man) to do a piece on Thompson. He also kept a diary, a narrative on the political and social climate of Ferriday and the necessity of having to conceal from the Klan and the police that he was a guest of a black priest. Griffin's stories were published in the Christmas 1963 issue of *Ramparts* magazine, a publication the *New York Times* described as "the most freewheeling thing on most American newsstands." Griffin's visit coincided with the September 15 Birmingham bombing, as white people in Ferriday were growing more and more concerned over the civil rights movement, especially school integration, voting rights, and growing rumors of a black revolution.[5]

Visiting downtown for a haircut, Griffin listened to the conversation of middle-aged and elderly men who condemned blacks "for seeking their rights." A young man said, "We're going to see the niggers don't get the vote." At a gas station, a white man told Griffin he "was trying to get Negroes fired from jobs held around town—to teach them a lesson. He ranted against Kennedy, said he wouldn't be surprised if someone assassinated the President if he ever dared come into that area." (Kennedy was assassinated two months later in Dallas, Texas.) A service station attendant told Griffin blacks were getting uppity and hoarding guns and ammunition. He predicted violence. "When it comes March, it gets windy around here. Well, if the niggers haven't cut out all this ungodly crap about their rights by then, there's about fifty of us going to meet here some night, each of us take five-gallon cans of gasoline. And we'll put on masks and go right down through niggertown and burn the whole place out."[6]

Griffin described the black section of Ferriday, which was divided by the main drag—Highway 65—on which Morris's shop was located. The business strip was a mixture of black-owned and white-owned businesses, while the interior of the neighborhood was "a clutter of grey-weathered houses and dust-powdered chinaberry and cottonwood trees. The humid air carried the fragrance of fields into town." All of Ferriday, Griffin wrote, was a "place of blindness, ignorance, anguish."[7]

When Griffin told Father Thompson about the threatening comments, the priest smiled: "Well, of course, we just might have something to say about that.

Do they think Negroes here are just going to set there and let themselves be massacred?"[8] In fact, Thompson knew that in the churches and homes of African Americans in Ferriday there was ongoing talk of the changes in the wind. Blacks were ready to claim their rights as Americans and as human beings. They had been governed by two partnering entities throughout their existence in the South: the master and overseer prior to the Civil War, and the Ku Klux Klan and police afterward. If blacks were going to be massacred in Concordia Parish as a result of gaining the right to vote, it wouldn't be the first time.

WHEN RECONSTRUCTION ended, so did federal government oversight of southern elections. During the congressional referendum of 1878, the purge of black power in Louisiana initiated by the Knights of the White Camellia a decade earlier and carried on by the White League was taken up by a group of men known as the "Bulldozers," yet another name for the Klan. They intended to "bulldoze" black men from office and strip them of their vote and power. Concordia and neighboring Tensas Parishes were targeted.[9]

Men who had been rich planters and slaveholders prior to the war only to fall afterward into poverty and be governed by their former slaves found the situation incomprehensible. In Natchez, John Roy Lynch, born into slavery in Vidalia, served as justice of the peace during Reconstruction. Educated and bright, he would later serve in Congress after becoming the first African American elected as speaker of the house in the Mississippi legislature. When an elderly black man filed a complaint against a white man who had cursed and threatened him, Lynch issued a warrant for the white man's arrest. In court, Lynch asked the accused how he pled to the charges. The man appeared shocked: "Why, do you mean to tell me that it is a crime for a white man to curse a nigger?" The man obviously sided with the infamous opinion of Supreme Court judge Robert B. Taney, who in the 1857 Dred Scott case opined that a black man "had no rights which the white man was bound to respect." In Natchez court, Lynch showed the white man the statute. "Well, I be damned!" the man answered.[10] As historian Eric Foner has written, "The reaction against Reconstruction was so extreme because the extent of political and social change was so unprecedented."[11]

Other whites shared the disbelief of the white defendant in Lynch's court. They thought that men like Lynch were nothing less than "uppity niggers." In Natchez in the 1930s, Charlie Davenport, a former slave, recalled a moment during Reconstruction when a small group of black men integrated a performance held at Memorial Hall, a public building in Natchez. Once the black men seated themselves in front of the auditorium, the whites left in silence. That night the Klan came calling, and every black man seen in the theater disappeared, just as Joseph Edwards would in 1964. Davenport told his interviewer that Klansmen were "devils a-walkin' de earth a-seekin' what dey could devour."[12]

For several days in 1878 in Concordia and Tensas Parishes, well-organized companies of white planters, businessmen, and former Confederate officers, acting with military precision, hunted down black politicians as well as those who supported them. The *New York Times* reported that on October 12, "a party of armed white men" attempting to capture a black preacher and political leader named Alfred Fairfax rushed into his home "late at night, and at once began to shoot at the five colored men found there. Fairfax and his brother escaped. The three other men were severely wounded. The women fled in terror. One of the wounded men died after a few days of suffering. He was shot down by Capt. Peck, who emptied his revolver into his prostrate body." Although Peck was killed in a crossfire of bullets from his own men, it was Fairfax who was accused of killing him.[13]

Newspapers in Louisiana and the *Natchez Democrat* in Mississippi published accounts of the shooting, labeling the bloodshed the result of "a Negro insurrection" to which leading white citizens had heroically responded. The white community seems to have believed these lies. A U.S. Senate committee investigating the violence and allegations of election fraud learned during hearings in New Orleans in January 1879 that at least twenty-five black men were massacred, although some claimed as many as one hundred were slaughtered. Some were killed in front of their wives and children, some hung, at least one decapitated. Blacks hid in the swamps and the woods for days. Vidalia quickly filled with black refugees from the countryside arriving, one black man recalled, "in droves, women and children."[14]

Yet, in the years to follow, local whites remembered the massacre as little more than an unpleasant necessity for a return of good government. Robert Dabney Calhoun, a noted lawyer in Vidalia, expressed the sentiments of many whites in his 1932 history of the parish when he explained that the election of 1878 had been a time when "substantial citizens were forced to engage in election manipulations and to make political dickers and alliances from force of necessity, and not from choice, which would be reprehensible today. They fought fire with fire, as best they could, while they prayed for the dawning of the new day of white supremacy." He suggested, too, that black politicians were little more than "illiterate dishonest and sweating black men," who "perfumed our Legislative Halls with an overpowering odor."[15]

In 1879, the *New York Times* reported that no "attempt has been made to indict the men who tried to murder Fairfax, or to punish any of the members of the armed companies who maltreated and assassinated the blacks." While black leaders were economically ruined and displaced like hundreds of other blacks, the Klansmen who destroyed their lives lived on, unpunished and unrepentant, their evil deeds buried with them in their coffins. Some of their children and grandchildren were running things when Frank Morris opened his shoe shop in Ferriday in the late 1930s.[16]

HERBERS REPORTED in 1964 in the *Times* that whites in Ferriday genuinely feared a black uprising. Several editions of the Klan's propaganda sheet, "The Fiery Cross," had been distributed at the time of the arson, most accusing and identifying white women of having affairs with named black men. Herbers interviewed a number of people, black and white, but no one would acknowledge knowing anything about Morris's murder. Herbers recounted the story told by everyone in town: During the early morning hours of December 10, 1964, Morris was awakened in the backroom of his shop by a noise and "found two white men pouring gasoline about. When he tried to flee . . . one of the men forced him back inside with a shotgun. The fire followed."[17]

While Herbers reported that the FBI showed "considerable interest in the case," local and state authorities refused to acknowledge the fire was anything more than an accident.[18]

"Don't call it arson," said Mayor Woodie Davis, who made a genuine effort to keep a lid on the violence. "That has not been determined."[19]

Louisiana governor John McKeithen said he would "be shocked if it is foul play. While I disagree with the civil rights law, we don't resort to murder and mayhem in any attempt to circumvent."[20]

"How can he say no foul play?" an unidentified white man asked Herbers about the governor's remark. "Everyone around here knows better than that."[21]

Other newspapers carried wire service stories about the Morris arson. The Associated Press reported that the police and fire departments in Ferriday refused to comment on orders of the mayor, while a "man at the Concordia Parish sheriff's office in nearby Vidalia . . . said Sheriff Noah W. Cross was 'out in the woods hunting' and not available." Herbers reported that, like Morris's killing, a number of crimes in southwest Mississippi had been committed against blacks "who apparently had no enemies and were not involved in the civil rights movement." Herbers was the first to report that Joseph Edwards had vanished in July. He asked Concordia assistant district attorney Roy Halcomb about Morris. Halcomb expressed remorse in a very mixed way: "My ten-year-old daughter prayed for that nigger every night."[22]

FRANK MORRIS was born in 1914. His parents were not married, and a year later, his mother, Charlotte, died. That same year, his father, Sullivan, who operated a shoe shop in Natchez, married Ethel Bacon, the owner and operator of Ethel's Café. Reared by his grandmother, Morris grew up working in his father's shoe shop, where he learned the trade, and he attended Broomfield, the local black school. He learned about business from his father and stepmother, both entrepreneurs.[23]

By the late 1930s, Morris was in business for himself in Ferriday. He quickly became known for quality work and good service, and he learned how to successfully cater to both blacks and whites. To achieve longevity as a black businessman with an interracial customer base had never been done in Concordia Parish or in most areas of the South. In the context of the parish's savage racial history, Morris's longtime success was nothing short of amazing. By the 1950s, his shop was thriving. "Open Every Day and Half the Night" was a slogan he used in his weekly ad in the *Concordia Sentinel.* On one side of the shop, he repaired shoes, boots, saddles, and bridles, while on the other side he sold hats, dyed purses, tap shoes, inexpensive jewelry, and clothing. He considered himself a "shoe builder" and occasionally purchased new equipment. Many local black boys got their first paying jobs working in Morris's shop, where he taught them to treat all people well. Others recalled that Morris was charitable and patriotic, often buying war bonds during World War II. "I'm buying some hats for the boys," he was often heard to say.[24]

In Ferriday, Morris was known as a jolly man. Honk your car horn and wave when you passed his shop, and Morris would sprint to the front door, wave, and shout a greeting. He always laughed and joked. A white girl whose parents operated a grocery store across the street from the shoe shop in the

1950s spent hours watching Morris cut leather and hammer soles onto shoes. He often greeted her with a bag of plank cookies.[25] When Morris's granddaughter, Rosa, was baptized at the age of ten, Morris, her Aunt Polly, who was blind, and others surrounded her. Just as the pastor prepared to immerse Rosa, Morris yelled out, "Everybody stand back so Polly can see!" Laughter filled the sanctuary.[26]

Rosa and her brother Nathaniel, who was called Poncho, were Morris's only grandchildren. Their mother was Clementine, his only child, born during a relationship he had in the 1930s with Rosie Hewing. He was married for a few years to Edna Brown, a seamstress. The couple had no children and divorced in the late 1940s. By the early 1960s, Clementine moved to Las Vegas. Rosa lived with Aunt Polly and Poncho with Morris.[27]

An usher in the Mercy Seat Baptist Church, Morris also hosted a gospel program on the Ferriday radio station from 6 to 7:30 a.m. on Sundays. He dedicated gospel songs to black and white listeners, male and female, and occasionally had a pastor as a guest. It cost him seventy-five dollars a month to air the show. White and black businessmen occasionally sent him donations for mentioning their establishments on air. On many occasions, Morris traveled to attend gospel music events.[28]

At his death, Morris had $1,800 in three bank accounts, assets of $33,933, and debt of $10,000. He owned the lot where the shop had stood.[29] Many in the white business community remember him as an honest man who paid his bills on time. When a Jewish businessman in town died in 1963, Morris wrote a letter to the editor of the *Concordia Sentinel* praising the man, noting that even though in segregated Ferriday blacks were "unable to attend the funeral, we lined Fourth Street in an effort to show him honor and pay him tribute." Morris wrote the letter on "behalf of the Colored Citizens of Concordia."[30] Those same citizens would turn to the federal government for justice in the Morris murder, the same government that had abandoned them during Reconstruction.

Morris's banker considered him a good credit risk, and his attorney (since 1948) told the FBI that Morris was ethical and respected. Morris's ex-wife had sued him once over back payment of a divorce settlement, but the suit was filed during the only period when Morris was known to have experienced financial troubles, a time in which the region was in an economic slump. In 1962, Morris settled with a Houston hotel over an injury he had suffered while a guest. Morris's daughter Clementine was expected to receive almost $21,000 ($158,000 today) as the sole heir, while grandson Poncho was to collect on the small insurance policies.[31]

The day after the arson, a three-paragraph story appeared on the front page of the *Concordia Sentinel* with a top-of-the-page one-column headline: "Fire Destroys Frank's Shoe Shop in Ferriday Thurs." By that time, the FBI had interviewed Morris three times in Room 101 at the Concordia Parish Hospital in Ferriday. He consistently told authorities he didn't know his attackers.

AT THE OUTSET, the FBI wanted to know if Morris's killers had violated any federal civil rights laws. A preliminary investigation revealed that Morris had been secretary of the local NAACP, but the chapter had not been active for at least five years, nor had Morris been involved in voter registration drives or in civil rights activities. Father Thompson and Father John Gayer, the white priest at St. Patrick's Catholic Church, said whites continuously threatened blacks, harassed them on the telephone, and occasionally threw rocks at them, but both were shocked at Morris's killing. Gayer said he had no faith in local police but had asked the mayor to enforce the law.[32] Mayor Woodie Davis arrived at the scene of the fire before it was extinguished. Almost fifty years later, he told the *Concordia Sentinel* that he saw an FBI agent at the scene and turned the case over to him, advising the agent that Ferriday would provide the bureau any assistance it could.[33] But the FBI at that moment had established no federal jurisdiction to take over the investigation.

In January 1965, U.S. senators Clifford Case and William Harrison of New Jersey expressed concern over the murder. Each notified FBI director J. Edgar Hoover that they had been contacted by Willie R. James, president of the Burlington County, New Jersey, branch of the NAACP. James, a cousin of Morris, had been called by another relative who told him that "white persons were responsible for the bombing and that he [Morris] was afraid to identify them."[34] There was no evidence of a bombing, however. Morris's relatives, including his father and stepmother, and the many friends who visited him in the hospital told the bureau that Morris repeatedly said he didn't know his attackers. He said the same thing to FBI agents twelve times in recorded interviews, but because of the onslaught of Klan violence in 1964, the FBI considered the arson a Klan attack. However, by mid-January, the bureau notified the Justice Department's Civil Rights Division that Father Thompson had talked to a woman, Della Mae Smith, who claimed that Deputy Frank DeLaughter had ordered the arson and that local police had set the blaze. With this news of a possible civil rights violation involving police officers, the bureau was authorized to launch a full federal investigation.[35]

A mother of seven, Smith had been friends with Morris since 1951. She said that Ferriday officers George Sewell and Timmy Loftin, who had transported Morris to the hospital, were the arsonists. Smith, who worked as a maid at the hospital, told the bureau that while changing the linen in Morris's room she asked him who had set the fire and he named the police officers. According to Smith, Morris revealed that, while one man held the shotgun, the other threw gas on him and said, "I want you to see yourself die." Morris confided that months earlier Lula DeLaughter, the deputy's wife, had tickled the palm of his hand, a signal that meant she wanted to have sex with him. Morris told Lula he would call her later. When he didn't, Lula, feeling scorned, told her husband that Morris had made a pass at her.[36] DeLaughter confronted Morris at the shop with Lula's allegations and also contended that Morris had made obscene phone calls to her. Morris denied the allegations, saying they were lies. The two men argued. DeLaughter warned Morris to leave Lula alone.[37]

Agents interviewed Sewell and Loftin separately on January 25. They related how they had picked up Morris from the burning shop after midnight and delivered him to the hospital. Both said they arrived at the scene in Ferriday's lone police car from the other side of town. Two weeks later on February 4, however, both admitted they had lied about their location prior to the arson. Another witness had seen Sewell and Loftin, with a third man in the backseat, on the Ferriday-Vidalia highway and had followed the patrol car into town. The young officers acknowledged that they left town, with their friend as a passenger, to follow two pretty waitresses who were headed toward Vidalia. They had lied because they were afraid they would lose their jobs if Mayor Davis and Police Chief Bob Warren found out they had left their city jurisdiction on a non-emergency call in the patrol car and because of the liability involved in having a passenger in the cruiser.[38]

Eight FBI agents worked the case, including two from the bureau's Alexandria, Louisiana, office, which considered Concordia Parish its territory. A Navy veteran, Paul Lancaster, had been named resident agent in Alexandria in 1964. He had recorded the Morris hospital interviews with an IBM dictaphone. Don McGorty, a former captain in the Marine Corps, had begun work in the Alexandria office that same year. He served as case agent in the investigation.[39]

Agents interviewed more than sixty people in the area around Morris's shop and talked to his former employees, friends, and relatives. FBI forensic tests on soil and debris turned up nothing useful, while a determined search to find who left a five-gallon fuel can at the shop proved fruitless.[40] A piece of a finger belonging to a black man was found in the shop rubble but was never matched to anyone, although Morris's best friend, James White, said he looked at Morris's hands during a hospital visit and observed that he was missing part of a finger.[41] There was also some speculation that a black man may have been the third man seen by Morris at the arson and that he was either a participant or observer. In 2007, the son of Junious "Tee-Wee" Kelly told the *Concordia Sentinel* that his father had witnessed the arson from a distance. A short time after the fire, someone fired into the Kelly home with a shotgun, an incident the family believed was a message for Kelly to keep quiet. Afterward, DeLaughter and Bill Ogden came by, honked the horn, and called Kelly outside. They told him to leave town. Before leaving, Kelly saw Rosa Williams, Morris's twelve-year-old granddaughter, on the street. "I know what happened to your grandfather," he told her, but he didn't name names. On his deathbed in 2000 in Monroe, Louisiana, Kelly was asked by his son who killed Morris. "Son," Kelly answered, "you don't have to look no further than the police department."[42]

AS THE PROBE INTENSIFIED, agents found that most people, white and black, thought highly of Morris. Blacks could think of only two possible means by which Morris might have upset white people. One was by dedicating songs on his radio show to white women. Others said that since white women didn't go inside his shop, Morris would pick up their shoes for repair or deliver repaired shoes to their cars. Sometimes Morris would lean in to the driver's window to discuss the work to be done, or sometimes he would open the passenger door and sit on the seat. Someone might have found this offensive. During this period, Klansmen in Concordia and Natchez had been warning business owners to fire black employees and to keep their workplaces segregated.[43]

A black schoolteacher said after the arson that there was a rumor Morris may have been setting up interracial liaisons. There also were stories in the black community that in 1947 Morris had been romantically involved with the wife of the white man who owned the Billups Service Station. Morris's ex-wife said he allegedly insulted the woman in an unspecified manner. Several witnesses also claimed Morris had a close friendship with the service station owner. Whatever the story, the couple left town not long after Morris was arrested by Ferriday police on August 10, 1947, and charged with fighting and disturbing the peace. He paid a ninety-dollar fine and served fifteen days in the parish jail in Vidalia.[44] His ex-wife said he was released on the condition that he not return to town until Ferriday police granted permission.[45]

Only two groups had bad things to say about Morris—his former girlfriends and ex-wife, and the police and firemen. Morris had a reputation in Ferriday's black community for being a ladies' man. The women in his life claimed he cheated on them. One woman said her five-year common-law marriage to Morris ended in the summer of 1964 when she caught him with his mistress in bed in the back room of the shop. She also claimed that Morris occasionally beat her up and that he liked "abnormal" sex, which wasn't specifically described in FBI documents.[46] A businessman from across the street said young black girls were afraid to go into Morris's shop because he would hit on them.[47]

By the fall of 1964, after his relationships with his girlfriend and mistress had ended, Morris began dating a woman from Clayton, five miles north of Ferriday. She alleged no abuse from him. For a few weeks, Morris and his grandson Poncho spent their nights in Clayton with the new girlfriend. On November 2, 1964, the girlfriend went to Chicago to visit her daughter. For the next five weeks until the fire, Morris spent the night in the back room of the shoe shop, while Poncho slept behind the shop in the small shack where Johnny "Snoot" Griffing, Morris's employee since 1959, lived.[48]

Once Della Mae Smith named DeLaughter, Sewell, and Loftin as the men responsible for the arson, the New Orleans FBI division sent to headquarters in Washington, D.C., a teletype identifying cases involving Concordia Parish police officers who had been the subject of preliminary FBI investigations.[49] The oldest case involved the 1962 beating of two black males in the sheriff's office, and another involved a complaint filed against DeLaughter and Sewell by Mildred Garner eight months prior to the arson. Garner, forty-two, at her office in Cario's bar along the Ferriday-Vidalia highway, complained to agents that DeLaughter had threatened her with a blackjack while both officers had called her a "nigger lover" and indicated they might have her occupational license revoked.[50] The dispute concerned a black male employed by Mildred's husband, but the specifics of the conflict are unclear. The bureau didn't know Mildred was DeLaughter's sister until Sheriff Noah Cross told them that the siblings had been feuding for years, most recently because the deputy was running around on Lula. Ferriday police chief Bob Warren reported that Lula had initiated divorce proceedings against DeLaughter and was seeking $200-a-month alimony. Because of DeLaughter's growing reputation as a brute, Mayor Davis had forbidden Ferriday police officers from associating with him, a rule the chief said Officer Sewell followed.[51]

ONE FERRIDAY POLICE officer seemed to know as much about Morris as the shopkeeper's former girlfriends. William Howell Harp Jr., known as Junior Harp, had taken the job of jailer, fireman, and policeman when DeLaughter went to work for the sheriff's office in 1962 after the mayor fired him. That same year, Harp had also been involved with DeLaughter, Ogden, and another deputy in the beating of two black prisoners in the parish courthouse. One prisoner confessed when Harp pointed a pistol at his head. Harp had nothing good to say about Morris.[52]

Interestingly, he alleged what Morris's girlfriends and ex-wife alleged— that he liked "unnatural" sex with them. He also claimed Morris was a bootlegger and sold narcotics, although he acknowledged to agents that the police could never prove it. Harp, police officer Timmy Loftin, and fire chief Noland Moeulle, who thought Morris had accidentally started the fire because he was drunk, told the bureau a suitcase filled with bourbon was found in the back room of Morris's shop after the fire. The suitcase was slightly scorched, but inside were fourteen half-pints of bourbon individually wrapped in newspaper, all unblemished.[53] How did this suitcase survive the fire? Was it planted to throw the FBI off the scent and make agents believe bootlegging enemies started the fire? FBI agent John Pfeifer told the *Concordia Sentinel* in 2011 that when he arrived in Ferriday in 1966, the bootlegging story was still being told. But he soon determined that this rumor and others, all of which cast Morris in a bad light, came from a single source: Frank DeLaughter.[54]

Harp also described Morris as a drunk and admitted to having had two confrontations with him over the previous two years. Harp claimed that in 1962 Morris's girlfriend had been arrested for theft. When Morris appeared at the jail after hours demanding to see her, Harp told Morris to go home. Instead, Morris began to force his way through, and Harp threatened him with a blackjack. At that point, Harp said, Morris left.[55] Not long after, they had a second confrontation. This one had been the source of rumors in the black community, but when Morris's friends asked him about it, he usually brushed it off as a simple disagreement. Mayor Davis explained to agents that in 1962 Morris came to his office and complained that Harp had come to the shoe shop and pulled a gun on him during an argument. The mayor said he talked to both Harp and his wife about the matter and learned that Morris had called the police department to talk with an officer. Harp's wife said she had answered the phone, and when she told Morris that Harp wasn't there, Morris "was a little abusive" in his language. Mrs. Harp "in turn got mad and said something she should not have said." The mayor felt that both were at fault. The incident escalated when Mrs. Harp complained to her husband, "who got mad and went to Morris' shop armed with his revolver." Davis said all apologized, and he assumed that afterward they were all on good terms.[56]

THE MORE AGENTS DUG, the more doubt was cast on Della Mae Smith's story about DeLaughter threatening Morris for coming on to his wife and Smith's implication of Sewell and Loftin. It was Harp and Morris who had argued in 1962, not DeLaughter and Morris. And in a short time, Smith's credibility was shattered. Everyone in the black community, even Father Thompson and Father Gayer, described her as an alcoholic who was prone to lie. And why would Morris identify the killers to her rather than his doctor, his father, his stepmother, close friends, and clergy? When confronted with inconsistencies in her stories, Smith said she personally didn't think Sewell and Loftin were involved.[57] More troubling, why would an argument between Morris and a policeman trigger an arson two years later?

After the fire was extinguished, Harp, Police Chief Mouelle, and Assistant District Attorney Roy Halcomb visited Morris in the hospital. It was at this point, Harp told agents, that Halcomb called the FBI.[58] DeLaughter told the bureau that Sheriff Cross ordered him to go to the fire scene at 2:45 a.m. DeLaughter then claimed that, at 3 a.m., he went to the hospital to talk to Morris, who told him the same story everyone in town knew.[59] After Morris was transferred from the emergency room to private room 101, his first visitors were police officers and firemen. Was he warned to keep his mouth shut?

On the night of the fire, the lone attendant at the Billups Service Station, James Simolke, heard a blast that sounded similar to a pistol shot near Morris's shop. Almost immediately, a black sedan sped out of an alley next to the shop and turned left in the direction of Vidalia. Simolke didn't know if the car then turned on a side street to exit town in another direction. A short time later, he saw Morris running through a vacant lot between the shoe shop and the gas station. At the same time, the town's Pontiac police cruiser pulled up. Morris left tracks of blood behind him, and the officers appeared "genuinely stunned" at his condition. One officer opened the back door, and Morris got in "of his own power," displaying no fear of the officers. After they left, Simolke saw a bright light emitting from inside the shop and soon heard an explosion; some of the flammable liquid inside had apparently ignited.[60]

Before the policemen drove off, one gave Simolke the fire department number and told him to call. He did, but oddly, there was no answer. He then phoned the operator and asked her to make the call. Ten to fifteen minutes passed before the firetruck was in sight. Harp told the bureau his entry book revealed that a call came in about the fire at 1:15 a.m. and that he arrived at 1:25. His wife contacted the fire chief and the volunteers.[61] Eighteen-year-old Johnny Blunschi, a future Louisiana state trooper, was a volunteer fireman and among the first to arrive at the scene. By then, the fire was blazing. Everyone kept waiting for the fire truck. When Harp finally arrived in the town's 1953 Howe fire engine, he had to open the driver's door, push in the clutch, and hold it down while reaching behind a side panel to shift it into park. Harp was so drunk that Blunschi thought he was going to fall out of the truck.[62]

It didn't take long for the bureau's investigation to hit a dead end. In Ferriday, Mayor Davis knew his police department couldn't solve the crime, as did Assistant District Attorney Halcomb. The sheriff's office didn't express the slightest interest in the case. Agents interviewed DeLaughter at the sheriff's office in Vidalia. He said Morris had never caused him any trouble, had never said one off-color word to his wife, and that he had no idea who committed the arson. He said his wife's only contact with Morris had been getting "the family shoes repaired." They had done business with Morris since 1957. During his visit to the hospital, DeLaughter claimed he didn't press Morris to identify the arsonists because he "was in great pain." The sheriff's office, he said, wasn't investigating because the crime happened in Ferriday's jurisdiction.[63]

Distraught and frightened over the arson, Morris's father, Sullivan, and stepmother, Ethel, sought haven with family members in California for an extended period.[64] Local blacks were harassed with telephone calls from white men who warned, "You're next." At least two black men—one a teacher, the other a funeral home employee—left town. In February 1965, Adams County sheriff Odell Anders, testifying before the Civil Rights Commission hearings in Jackson, Mississippi, wondered what evil possessed the men who committed Morris to flames: "I don't know what kind of a man it takes to do that. I don't know what beats in him."[65] In April, the FBI received a letter from Ferriday. The writer wondered if Morris's killers were going to get away with murder even though "the police were part of the gang that permitted this terrible thing to happen. Your office is our only hope so don't fail us." The letter was signed: "The Colored people of Concordia Parish."[66]

1965

8

"WHY DO THEY HATE US SO?"

OVER A PERIOD OF MONTHS, Red Glover tracked Natchez NAACP president George Metcalfe, a forklift driver in the shipping department at the Armstrong Tire and Rubber Company plant where both men worked. As a tire builder, Glover earned $2.70 an hour at the sprawling facility near downtown Natchez. To the west of the plant entrance, at the top of the hill on Gayoso Street, was the site of Concord, a fabled Spanish mansion that had been destroyed by fire six decades earlier. In the late 1790s, it had been the home of Manuel Gayoso, the last Spanish governor in Natchez. Gayoso had puffed on Havana cigars and sipped wine while entertaining guests at Concord. On the grounds, he had negotiated a treaty with the Choctaw and Chickasaw Indians. He was remembered as a diplomat among the Europeans and the Native Americans, but not even he could have negotiated a peace between Glover and his fellow Klansmen at Armstrong and the civil rights movement George Metcalfe was directing in Natchez.[1]

Since beginning the Silver Dollar Group (SDG) at the Vidalia motel coffee shop, Glover had recruited others into his underground Klan within a Klan. Only he knew every member. Only he knew the crimes the various members had committed for the cause of segregation. FBI agents early on tagged Glover a psychopath. He was moody, temperamental, paranoid, a loner. John Pfeifer, an agent who interviewed Glover several times, believed he "got a tremendous shot of paranoid schizophrenia" early in life. "I mean he would not trust anybody."[2]

At 170 pounds and under six feet, Glover was not a big man. He was balding with red hair, freckles, and a ruddy complexion. Some men called him "Red," while many called him "Jack," derived from his middle name, Jackson. Born in the east Texas county of St. Augustine in 1922, he grew up on a struggling farmstead during the Great Depression, quitting school after the seventh grade. St. Augustine was an old frontier crossroads, the home of revolutionists like Sam Houston (the president of the Republic of Texas) and the hideout of frontier gamblers, criminals, and misfits. When Glover was ten, his mother, Maggie, moved the children (three girls and two boys) to Mississippi, where she had family ties.[3] Glover's relationship with his father, Warren, is unclear. Glover claimed that his dad had committed suicide during his childhood, but Armstrong Tire personnel records indicate that his father was living in Summit, Mississippi, in the 1940s and in Texas in the 1950s.[4]

In the late 1930s, Glover went to work for the New Deal's Civilian Conservation Corps. He told his stepson he helped construct the Clear Springs Recreation Area in Franklin County, Mississippi, but records at the tire plant indicate that he worked in Louisiana as well, building roads and bridges. Later, he was employed as an ironworker and steelworker throughout the South. He was divorced by the time he was twenty-two. In 1943, he was drafted into the Navy and recruited into the Seabees, a construction and demolition force that built roads, airstrips, and bases, sometimes under enemy fire. While in New Guinea in the South Pacific, Glover shot himself in the left knee after accidentally striking the cap of a .45 caliber shell while making an ornament chain to hang around his neck. The Navy said the injury was Glover's fault but agreed to pay him a monthly disability stipend of $15.75 for the rest of his life.[5]

In December 1945, a few days after returning home to Natchez and about a year after his divorce, Glover married Polly Burts Watts, the widow of his best friend, who had been killed in combat in Germany. Glover reared the couple's child as his own. In 1948, Glover began work at the Armstrong tire plant, but in 1950 he reentered the Navy and served in Korea. He served as a shipfitter and pipefitter, while qualifying as a marksman on the rifle range. Glover's experience in the military, like his childhood, was a mystery to his family. He never talked about it, other than telling his stepson that he read encyclopedias and the Bible to educate himself and that, although he had sailed the seas, he couldn't swim.[6] An FBI informant said Glover occasionally looked at old photos of himself taken in the Pacific Islands during World War II. The images showed Glover in his Navy uniform as he cut off the head and genitals of a dead Japanese soldier. He was arrested once while in the military for indecent exposure.[7]

After Korea, Glover returned to Armstrong and briefly tried dairy farming. He attended church for a while, but that didn't last long either. In March 1963, he secured a Veterans' Administration loan totaling $11,855.66 and bought a house in Vidalia at 113 Lee Avenue. Stories circulated that Glover was mentally unstable. Many of his new neighbors in Vidalia had heard his tirades about "the niggers" bringing down America and about the growing civil rights movement, which he believed was fueled by communists.[8]

One of Glover's SDG recruits was Earcel "Preacher" Boyd Sr., an Armstrong employee and part-time preacher who would don a white Klan robe for a meeting on Saturday night and then preach in a black church occasionally on Sunday morning. One day while visiting the Boyd home in a subdivision along the Ferriday-Vidalia highway, Glover led Boyd and sons Sonny and Leland to his car. In the trunk were rifles, automatic weapons, and machine guns. Glover picked up one of the rifles and dry fired it. The Boyd brothers were not frightened of Klansmen or their weaponry. They had grown up with both. Often military fighter jets rocketed over the Boyd home, traveling faster than the speed of sound. The sonic booms that followed rattled the windows in the Boyd home, causing Earcel's wife, Marjorie, to scream in terror. She feared that Boyd's explosives—cast iron–shelled bombs the size of baseballs filled with black powder—would detonate in the attic where they were stored.

Glover often clowned with the teens, wrestling with them and teasing them. The brothers and their mother did, however, fear him at times. Once while Glover was visiting, the phone rang. It was for Glover. As he talked on the phone, the Boyd family watched his demeanor suddenly change from clownish to demonlike. He often experienced such transformations. None who saw them ever forgot the rage in his eyes.[9]

By the end of 1964, Glover was restless and impatient. He had led Klan wrecking crews in northeastern Louisiana and southwestern Mississippi on projects ranging from beatings to arson, and he was linked to Joseph Edwards's disappearance. But Glover could clearly see that the established Klans were achieving nothing in the war to preserve segregation. Civil rights groups and the FBI would not go away. Glover believed that it was time to go after the locals most responsible for pushing civil rights, and George Metcalfe was number one on the list. As FBI internal documents reveal, Glover was convinced Metcalfe "was a hard core active communist," and he was "consumed with the passion to kill Metcalfe."[10]

THE ARMSTRONG TIRE plant where Glover and Metcalfe worked had been built in 1939. The complex included seven buildings, all constructed with reinforced concrete, including the 198,000-square-foot main factory. Raw rubber pellets were rolled from conveyors to vats, where they were mixed with chemicals, heated, blended with fabric and steel-encased beading, and shaped in engraved molds. The process was synchronized through several stations and required vast amounts of machinery. For the employees, it was hot, noisy work.

In 1950, the company brought in Iowa native Pete Mitchell as factory manager. Mitchell had traveled the world for Armstrong, helping launch a new plant in Spain in 1933. He had trekked through Africa in the 1940s in search of wild crude rubber. In Natchez, Mitchell inherited a plant beleaguered by poor leadership and low morale. His first priority was to improve labor relations, and he also issued warnings to troublemakers: Disrupt production and face termination. He met often with the Rubber Workers' Union, listened to grievances, and had on call the dean of the Tulane Law School to act as an arbitrator if needed. During meetings, union officials attempted to intimidate him by whittling with their long-bladed pocketknives. Mitchell made fun of their bullying by reaching for his small penknife and cutting paper.[11]

By 1963, Mitchell had doubled the plant's production, with 1,100 workers producing twelve thousand tires and tubes daily for Sears. The annual payroll was $7 million. Blacks were assigned to the lower-paying janitorial and shipping jobs, but they, too, were union members. Armstrong policy was to establish a climate conducive to good race relations, which the company knew was required by new civil rights legislation. However, the growing nest of Klansmen at Armstrong made the job difficult at best. They wanted blacks perpetually barred from holding traditional "white" jobs, and they opposed the integration of bathrooms, break rooms, and the cafeteria. Mitchell found the plant, like Natchez, rife with rumors and gossip; he once noted that he had "never worked in such a small city nor been any place where people would repeat what they heard with no effort to verify it." Rumors about Metcalfe abounded. Glover often remarked that he had seen white girls sitting in Metcalfe's lap at the Council of Federated Organizations (COFO) house in Natchez. Metcalfe was often harassed at the plant and received threatening phone calls at home, and in early 1965, someone fired into his house.[12]

METCALFE WAS BORN in 1912 in Franklin, Louisiana, located between Lafayette and Morgan City near the Gulf. A slim, quiet man, serious in mind and nature, Metcalfe could also be jovial. By 1940, he and his wife, Adell, then twenty-seven, were living in Natchez, where he drove a truck for a sawmill and she worked as a waitress.[13] In 1954, Metcalfe was selling burial insurance when he met Wharlest Jackson, a Florida native, Korean War veteran, and father of five who had just moved to Natchez from Chicago. That same year, the two men got jobs at the Armstrong plant. They became best friends.[14]

Metcalfe had worked with COFO during Freedom Summer and by early 1965 was ready to relaunch the local NAACP chapter, which had been dormant for years. On March 3, the first meeting was held, with Charles Evers on hand to help reorganize the chapter. The brother of slain Mississippi NAACP field secretary Medgar Evers, Charles had left Chicago after his brother's murder in 1963 and had taken over his job. Charles Evers was often at odds with the NAACP national leadership. At the Natchez meeting, the fifty-three-year-old Metcalfe was elected president, and Jackson, thirty-five, was voted in as secretary. Jackson's wife, Exerlena, was named head of the political action committee.[15]

Four days later, on March 7, the now-famous march for voting rights from Selma to Montgomery was intercepted by Alabama state troopers, who savagely beat participants. Photographers and television cameras captured images of the brutality, and it was vividly described by journalists. The event, which came to be known as Bloody Sunday, shocked Americans. On March 15, President Lyndon Johnson lobbied Congress to pass comprehensive voting rights legislation that would ban literacy tests, give the federal government a more definitive means to oversee elections, and allow blacks a legal avenue for challenging the local election process. Despite strong opposition, Johnson pushed the legislation through. He signed the Voting Rights Act on August 6, 1965. Following a series of meetings the previous spring, the Natchez NAACP chapter had put together a list of demands to be placed before the city administration, and before the end of August, Metcalfe filed a desegregation lawsuit against the city of Natchez. His personal life, however, was in disarray, and his wife left him.[16]

AT SDG MEETINGS along the Homochitto River in Meadville, Mississippi, and at the Clear Springs Recreation Park nearby, Glover mentioned that something needed to be done about Metcalfe. Once, he said Metcalfe's home should be torched. After Glover decided on a plan to silence Metcalfe, he alone considered the best way to carry out the hit. He initially planned to lure him outside the plant, where two Klansmen would kidnap him at gunpoint, transport him to a remote location, and kill him. But the plot fizzled when Glover was unable to get Metcalfe outside.[17]

The second plan involved two participants, James Horace "Sonny" Taylor, a logger from Harrisonburg in Catahoula Parish, and James "Red" Lee, an Armstrong Tire employee who lived in the Concordia Parish community of Lismore. Glover, Taylor, and Lee spent days watching Metcalfe's every move, observing where he parked his car and spying on his approach to the plant gate. Glover's idea was for Taylor and Lee to assassinate Metcalfe under cover of darkness with Lee's Winchester twelve-gauge pump shotgun as Metcalfe walked toward the plant. A third man, described by an informant as fifty years old and heavy, was enlisted to pick up Lee's shotgun after the shooting; Lee and Taylor didn't want to chance being stopped on the highway afterward with the murder weapon inside their car. At ten o'clock on the night of the planned assassination, the third man backed out. Lee and Taylor, however, moved forward. As Metcalfe began his walk to the plant gate, Taylor covered Metcalfe with Lee's shotgun, loaded with buckshot. At the last second, however, because of the uncertainty about disposing of the murder weapon, Taylor didn't fire.[18]

After the two plans failed, Glover chose a much more grandiose mission, one that would be carried out in the light of day for all of Natchez to see. He assigned Lee and Taylor to perfect a bombing device that could be planted in Metcalfe's car. Glover gave Taylor a tightly sealed grease can that contained two red cans of blasting (black) powder and eighteen white cans filled with powerful C-4 explosives (likely primer cord), which could be safely molded, like clay, into a brick shape. Taylor, who lived in the hills outside Harrisonburg, hid the material there, possibly in a cave not far from his home.[19]

In early summer, Glover instructed Lee to host a fish fry for SDG members. Always careful to limit meetings to only a few, Glover's decision to intermix all of his hardcore members—those who had dirty hands—was outwardly a means to gather socially and at the same time to experiment with explosives. Glover also was making a master move by purposely implicating everyone there in his ultimate plan to kill Metcalfe.

With his wife and three children, Lee lived in a rented two-story house along the Black River in Lismore. The area had a dark history. A century earlier, Lismore had been the site of a plantation owned by a prominent physician and slaveholder. One of the doctor's slaves was Mary Reynolds, who, as a teenager, was freed by Federal troops following the fall of Vicksburg in 1863. Mary had watched slaves whipped by an overseer named Solomon and had suffered a savage beating by a white man that left her unable to bear children and physically scarred for life. Even as a child, she knew that her master was raping his female property. When a woman called Aunt Cheney was caught running away, Solomon unleashed the hounds, who caught her and gnawed away her breasts. After getting her freedom, Mary worked hard at farming, housekeeping, and tending white people's children, living in poverty until her death in the late 1930s (about the time Frank Morris opened his shoe shop twenty miles east of Lismore in Ferriday).[20]

Born in Orange, Texas (between Beaumont and Lake Charles, Louisiana), Lee was ten years Glover's junior and also had red hair. While his father preached at the Evangeline Baptist Church a few miles from Lismore, his mother was a high school music teacher in a neighboring parish. Lee despised blacks as much as Glover did. Once, as a patient at Jefferson Davis Hospital in Natchez after it was integrated in 1964, Lee awoke in his hospital bed and was so shocked to see a black patient in the bed beside him that he thought he was dreaming. Once reality set in, Lee called his wife. When she arrived to pick him up, he was standing at the hospital's entrance in his boxer shorts.[21]

Late on the morning of June 26, 1965, the first guests arrived at the Lee residence, including three of the SDG members' wives, who helped prepare the food. The remaining Klansmen came at intervals throughout the day, most arriving in early afternoon, when lunch was served. Several left early, but most stayed until dark.[22] Coming from Mississippi were brothers Jack and James Ford Seale, Ernest Finley, L. C. Murray, Thore L. Torgersen, and Ernest Parker. Parker brought the fish, a mess of big bass, caught in the same water where the Seales and Parker had drowned Henry Hezekiah Dee and Charles Moore the previous summer. Murray, a suspect in the bombing of Mayor John Nosser's home, served as field secretary to UKA grand dragon E. L. McDaniel, also a suspect in that case.[23] Finley had been an early recruit of Glover's and had actively helped organize the SDG in Mississippi. When he died three months after the fish fry, mourners at his funeral noticed a silver dollar on a chain in the center of a wreath.[24] Torgersen had been involved in Glover's wrecking crew projects in Concordia during the previous year. (Unbeknownst to Glover, Torgersen had given his silver dollar to a waitress at the Shamrock coffee shop.)[25]

Also on the guest list were Kenneth Norman Head and Buck Horton, both of Vidalia. They were linked, along with Glover and local law officers, with the disappearance of Joseph Edwards. Three months before the fish fry, two FBI agents asked to see Head's driver's license. As Head pulled the license from his wallet, a silver coin fell to the ground. One of the agents inspected the piece, an 1878 Liberty Head silver dollar. "Is this a lucky piece?" he asked. No, Head answered, it was just an old silver dollar he hoped to sell to a collector one day.[26]

From Ferriday came E. D. Morace, James L. Scarborough, and Woodrow "Blue" Holloway, all present or former officers in the Ferriday-Clayton Klan. Scarborough served as Exalted Cyclops in 1965 and was involved in wrecking crew projects. Sonny Taylor came from his home in Harrisonburg in neighboring Catahoula Parish. While two informants said Ernest Avants of Mississippi attended the fish fry, others didn't recall seeing him there.

After eating, Lee and Taylor left the gathering, returning a while later with two dummy grenades, a two-foot-long stick of dynamite, one roll of dynamite fuse, and one roll of pink primer cord the diameter of a cigarette. Jack Seale put a match to a section of the dynamite fuse, but it burned out. When he moved to touch the match to the pink fuse, Taylor warned him he would blow everyone up if he did that. Then the Klansmen attempted to make black powder by mixing pieces of dynamite, charcoal, sulphur, and borax. They placed the black powder mixture into a dummy grenade with the dynamite fuse stuck in the end. They lit the fuse, but it didn't explode.[27]

Although there was no success that day, Glover keenly observed the experiments with Metcalfe in mind. FBI agents would later interview known attendees of the fish fry, but none would remember discussing Metcalfe, not even those later recruited by the FBI as informants. Yet Glover had succeeded in one thing: If he successfully bombed Metcalfe, every man who had been at the fish fry would be considered part of a conspiracy and therefore be less prone to snitch.

One SDG member never made the meeting. Tommie Lee Jones was a suspect in several crimes, including the beatings of black men in Concordia Parish and Adams County and the arson of Jake's Place in Natchez. En route to the fish fry from his home in Natchez, he was arrested by Ferriday police for pistol-whipping a black man with a .25 caliber revolver. Jones claimed that the man had cut him off on the highway. At the scene of the accident, the officers observed blood pouring from a cut to the victim's head, the imprint of the pistol butt clearly visible. Inside Jones's car was a massive German shepherd. The officers instantly tagged Jones a "smart mouth" and took him to the Ferriday jail, where he was booked for assault with a gun and disturbing the peace. Once the officers realized that Jones was a notorious Klansman, fearing trouble due to the tense racial climate, they informed Mayor Woodie Davis that they had Jones in custody. The mayor, who was at a softball game, instructed the police to set bond at $500 and lock up Jones until the bond was made. Jones called his wife, who called Scarborough.[28]

Before midnight, a number of Klansmen were at the Ferriday police station. Scarborough paid the $500 bond in $20 bills. The charges against Jones were reduced because the arresting officer feared the Klan might retaliate against the black man if Jones was convicted of a felony. Jones was found guilty of disturbing the peace and received a suspended sentence of sixty days in jail or a $150 fine. He paid $50 total on July 3. The remaining balance was waived.[29]

IN LATE AUGUST, Lee summoned Morace to his house and said that he and Taylor had "a nigger they wanted to get," without identifying the target. Lee indicated that he and Taylor had failed in an attempt to set off an explosive charge placed on an oak stump and wired to the spark plugs of Lee's 1952 Chevrolet. However, when they touched the wires to the ignition coil, the charge "blew the stump to bits." Lee wondered if the coil, an electrical transformer that ignited the spark plugs, held a constant electric charge. Morace, who was a mechanic, said that it did, but if the car switch was off, there was no charge. Lee wondered if the coil on a six-cylinder Chevrolet could be reached from underneath the car. Morace said he didn't know.[30]

Later, Lee and Taylor hooked an electrical dynamite cap to the ignition coil, turned the switch, and the cap detonated. Next, they used the same method with C-4 explosives to blow up a tree stump. They alerted Glover that they had succeeded with their assignment. Glover then ordered Taylor to place the charge in Metcalfe's car; meanwhile, Glover and Lee, both Armstrong employees, would be on the job to create an alibi. Taylor chose a Ferriday Klansman, unidentified in FBI documents, to assist him in the mission. At 2 a.m. on Friday, August 27, Taylor and the other Klansman slid under Metcalfe's 1955 Chevrolet Delray. They first connected the electrical blasting cap to the ignition coil and then inserted a blasting cap in a red booster can. Next they strengthened the mixture by screwing in three or four white cans of C-4 explosives behind the red can. The charge was placed under the hood near the firewall. The two men crawled from beneath the car and slipped away.[31]

METCALFE HAD CLOCKED IN at midnight. Originally scheduled to work a regular eight-hour shift, he was asked and agreed to put in four hours over-time. He alerted an NAACP coworker that he would arrive at headquarters late. For months, the NAACP had been pressing the city administration to make major changes. Among the demands were that the city denounce white supremacy groups; that police brutality and Klan intimidation end; that schools, swimming pools, parks, auditoriums, and other public facilities be desegregated; that blacks be hired for city jobs on an equal basis; that blacks be appointed to the school board; that public works be provided in black neighborhoods; that housing codes be enacted; and that blacks be addressed by city workers with the same courtesy as whites and not be referred to as "Boy," "Uncle," or "Aunty."[32]

Although he rarely expressed personal feelings to anyone, Metcalfe opened up more than once to Marge Baroni, a white activist. Baroni held a deep personal commitment to human rights, partly because of her conversion to Catholicism in 1947 and her nurturing friendship with journalist and social activist Dorothy Day. The daughter of an alcoholic Adams County sharecropper and a no-nonsense Baptist mother, Baroni grew up amid deep-seated racism in communities throughout southwest Mississippi. Metcalfe asked her often why whites so vehemently opposed "giving the Negro a better education and the right to vote." More than once he wondered, "Why do they hate us so?" Baroni always answered, "I simply do not know."[33]

At noon on Friday, August 27, 1965, Metcalfe ended his overtime shift and clocked out. He walked by the guardhouse and along the fence and got into his car parked just outside the plant. When he placed the key in the ignition and turned the switch, the front of the car exploded. The blast was so loud, it was heard blocks away. A worker inside the company's business office watched the hood sail into the air, whirling like a saucer, before landing near the guard shack.[34] Metcalfe was blown from the car, minus his shoes, which were found intact beneath the driver's seat. The steering wheel landed in the passenger seat. All of the windows were blown out, and shattered glass was spotted twenty feet away. The left fender, front grill, and front bumper separated from the car. Two vehicles parked nearby were damaged.[35]

Minutes later, as sirens wailed in the background, a caller notified the NAACP office that Metcalfe had been killed by a car bomb. Charles Evers, who was in Jackson, Mississippi, quickly dispatched NAACP representatives to the Jefferson Davis Hospital, where Metcalfe was taken. Mary Lee Toles, who worked in the X-ray department and later became an Adams County judge, was among the first to see Metcalfe, who was alive. His face was bloody and burned. "I didn't think he was going to make it," she recalled. Although Metcalfe was gravely injured, doctors reported after surgery that he would recover. He had suffered burns, and his right leg was shattered in three places, his arm broken. Shards of glass and metal had penetrated his face, permanently damaging his right eye.[36] Pieces of skin were stripped from his body. Police guarded his hospital room and denied access to reporters. FBI agents who questioned Metcalfe had no comment for reporters.[37]

The FBI lab found that "a high order type explosion occurred and an explosive charge had been placed between the steering column and lower left rear of the motor block forward of the firewall." All broken wires discovered were due to tension breaks, not cuts. Because of the extensive damage, the bureau was unsure "what electrical circuitry was utilized to detonate the explosive charge; however, pieces of wire were removed from the coil."[38]

Throughout the afternoon, the NAACP office fielded angry calls from blacks and threats from Klansmen. Evers arrived in town at 4 p.m. The office printed fliers and posted them about town, announcing a mass meeting at No. 9 St. Catherine Street, where Metcalfe lived. Hundreds of shocked and angry supporters attended; a handful cursed police driving by in patrol cars. Evers urged everyone to stay calm and afterward asked the crowd to go home. He warned whites not to travel in black neighborhoods and told the press that if the Justice Department didn't protect the black community, "the Negroes are going to provide protection for themselves."[39] In Washington, Michigan congressman Charles C. Diggs Jr. addressed the Metcalfe bombing, saying that blacks would "no longer suffer murder and atrocities upon their homes and person without defensive action."[40]

Police Chief J. T. Robinson and Sheriff Odell Anders publicly expressed confidence that arrests would be made, and the *Natchez Democrat* condemned the bombing. Privately, however, Anders was at a loss as to what to do. Robinson, consulting daily with federal authorities, worked to keep the peace. Roy K. Moore led ten agents to Natchez and personally directed the Metcalfe probe.[41] Meanwhile, Mayor Nosser called the bombing a "dastardly crime." He quickly agreed to meet with the NAACP to form a biracial committee to seek racial harmony and address some of the black community demands, and he offered a $2,000 reward for information leading to the arrest and conviction of the bomber. He claimed to have received three anonymous phone calls warning, "We got Metcalfe today and you're next."[42]

As tension continued to build, local and state law enforcement agencies, including the FBI, feared a riot. Two nights after the bombing, young blacks threw rocks at passing cars, breaking windows. Evers feared he couldn't control them. Heavily armed Klansmen amassed in town. Also rushing to the scene were members of the newly formed Deacons for Defense and Justice, chartered in Jonesboro, Louisiana, in 1964 with a mission to provide armed protection to black communities. When city aldermen rejected a demand to speed up the desegregation process, threats of violence escalated. The city enacted a nightly curfew, primarily in black areas. On September 2, Mississippi governor Paul Johnson announced that he was sending in 650 National Guardsmen from six companies in the 31st Dixie Division, marking the first time the National Guard had been called out for a race-related matter since the September 1962 riot at Ole Miss. Guardsmen pitched tents at the Natchez armory and launched what was labeled "Operation Wet Blanket." They patrolled in jeeps, five to a car, each man armed with a rifle, sheathed bayonet, and a gas mask.[43]

IN MID-SEPTEMBER, *Jet* magazine reported that the most radical thing Metcalfe had done in the days before the bombing was to eat in a restaurant technically desegregated under the 1964 Civil Rights Act. The magazine also reported that UKA leader McDaniel complained that "police state" tactics were used against a white bombing suspect. The suspect, Odis Lavell Goode, a wiry Armstrong employee known as a Klansman and a skilled rifle shot, told friends that he had been taken to Jackson and interrogated by the FBI and the MHSP for thirty-six hours. For decades, Natchez residents believed he was the bomber.[44]

But by 1967, the FBI's main suspects became Glover, Taylor, and Lee. On August 23, 1965, four days before the bombing, Morace, one of the FBI's best informants in Concordia Parish, had reported that Lee and Taylor were experimenting with explosives. Eleven days after the bombing, Roy K. Moore and Special Agent Elmer B. Litchfield, the future sheriff of East Baton Rouge Parish, went to Concordia to talk with Morace. Morace said he had talked to Glover on September 1 about the Metcalfe bombing and that Glover had denied knowing anything about it but threw suspicion on Lee. Glover also told Morace that Lee had requested some electric dynamite caps but that Glover had none to give him. The next day, under the FBI's direction, Morace had coffee with Lee. "I see you got your nigger," Morace asserted. Lee, like Glover, pretended not to know what he was talking about. And, like Glover, Lee cast suspicion on others, including Taylor and James Ford Seale.[45]

In early August, after Morace told the FBI about the fish fry at Lee's home, two agents had gone to Lismore. Lee denied being in the Klan but volunteered that he had been trained to kill while in the army. Morace had also implicated Lee and Glover in the bombing of Hopewell Baptist Church in Catahoula Parish a year earlier. When asked about that bombing, Lee said he knew nothing about it. On September 3, a week after the attack on Metcalfe, the bureau interviewed Lee again. He repeated his denials but alleged that Metcalfe was so unpopular, there were "5,000 people who would want to bomb him." A week later, Moore, accompanied by three other FBI agents, interviewed Lee yet again. Lee continued his denials, adding that once he decided not to talk about something, he would "die first" before talking.[46] Glover was interviewed as well and denied any involvement in the bombing or the Klan.

The FBI investigation would never result in an arrest, although there were many state and federal charges—from attempted murder to the transport of explosives across state lines—that would have applied. There were no eyewitnesses. Morace, who could have testified that Lee had questioned him about placing a bomb in a car, was a protected informant. He feared Glover and knew Glover would kill him in a heartbeat if he learned of his loose tongue.

THE NAACP STAGED several marches, but its demands continued to go unheeded. Evers decided to up the ante, calling for a full-scale economic boycott of white-owned businesses that opposed the demands. His pleas for Dr. Martin Luther King to come to Natchez failed. By early October, a court order sought by the city prohibited marching and picketing by civil rights groups and the Klan. Evers vowed to defy the order and did so. As a result, marchers, including children, were arrested. At one point a group of black teenagers, jeered and heckled by whites under McDaniel's command, moved toward the Klansmen. Police quickly separated the groups. Evers urged all to go home. "Those people out there [whites] don't know any better," he said. "They are ignorant." Hundreds of marchers were arrested.[47]

When the jail filled, approximately 150 African American protestors were transported by bus to the infamous Mississippi State Penitentiary at Parchman. Forced to strip, some were made to drink laxatives, denied toilet paper, and told to drink out of the toilets. Guards threatened black males. Among the inmates was Wharlest Jackson's wife, Exerlena. Despite temperatures in the forties, prisoners were made to stand on wet floors with fans sucking in the frigid air through opened windows. One fourteen-year-old female inmate was sent home early by bus, arriving just in time to be rushed to the hospital, where she delivered a stillborn child.[48]

Evers invited Pope Paul VI to Mississippi to observe the brutality endured by blacks. By early November, some Natchez businessmen threatened to fire their black employees unless the boycott ended. Whites threatened to fire domestic servants as well. But Evers held firm. NAACP members patrolled the streets, and leaders harassed black people who crossed the picket lines to shop in white stores. Congressman Gerald Ford of Michigan, who would ascend to the presidency in 1974, canceled a scheduled speech before an all-white Republican group in Natchez because blacks would be barred from the gathering. *Jet* reported that few shoppers were seen in downtown Natchez, where business was down by 25 to 50 percent. One merchant cut advertising by 40 percent and laid off a third of his employees as the holiday season kicked off. A photograph in *Jet* showed Metcalfe sitting up in his hospital bed, his right leg in a cast and his right eye swollen shut. Another photo showed him being visited by Evers and other civil rights activists.[49]

By early December, the city caved. It agreed to desegregate public facilities, develop a housing code, hire public employees based on merit (not race), submit a $2.5 million bond proposal for sewer and street construction in black neighborhoods, and revamp the anti-poverty program under a biracial board. The *Wall Street Journal* reported that the Natchez boycott was run with military precision and ended as one of the most effective boycotts in the history of civil rights. Nosser hoped it signaled "a new era of understanding."[50]

In the days to follow, Glover lay low, furious that Metcalfe had survived, and stunned at the courage and steadfastness of the black community and its ultimate victory. His hatred for Metcalfe intensified. He brooded over his failure and bided his time.

Joseph Edwards disappeared in 1964. A half century later, a new search
was begun to locate his body.
(*Concordia Sentinel*)

VICTIMS

Earl Hodges in front of his shop, circa 1950s. Silver Dollar Group Klansmen beat Hodges to death in 1965, fearing he would implicate the KKK in the murder of two black teens. (*Concordia Sentinel*)

Frank Morris (*center, wearing visor and apron*) and workers in front of his shoe shop, circa 1950s. (Photo by William Brown/*Concordia Sentinel*)

Morris's bedroom in the back of his Ferriday shoe shop after the 1964 arson.
(FBI file photo)

Rubble of Morris's shoe shop.
(Photo by August Thompson/*Concordia Sentinel*)

George Metcalfe's car following the bombing in 1965.
(FBI file photo)

Wharlest Jackson, a Korean War veteran and treasurer of the Natchez
NAACP, was the Silver Dollar Group's final target. Jackson was killed
when a bomb planted beneath the frame of his pickup exploded in 1967.
(Photo courtesy Denise Ford)

Jackson's pickup following the bombing in 1967.
(FBI photo)

Blasting cap leg wire used in the bombing of Jackson's car.
(FBI photo)

Henry Hezekiah Dee was one of two teens killed by Klansmen from
Franklin County, Mississippi, in 1964. This photo was uncovered by
Canadian filmmaker David Ridgen in May 2007, just before the trial
and conviction of one of Dee's killers, James Ford Seale.
(Photo courtesy David Ridgen, © Ridgen Film Corporation)

Charles Moore was with Henry Hezekiah Dee in May 1964 when the two were kidnapped, beaten, and killed by Klansmen from Franklin County, Mississippi.
(Photo courtesy David Ridgen, © Ridgen Film Corporation)

From left, Thelma Collins, sister of Henry Dee; Canadian filmmaker David Ridgen; and Thomas Moore, brother of Charles Moore. The three are shown together in Meadville, Mississippi, in May 2014.

(Photo by Andy Dymond, © 2014 Ridgen Film Corporation)

Curt Hewitt was manager of the mob-run Morville Lounge. (*Concordia Sentinel*)

E. L. McDaniel, photographed here for his application to be a cab driver in Natchez in 1958, became the grand dragon of the United Klans of America in Mississippi in 1964. By 1966, he was an FBI informant. (FBI file photo)

Silver dollar given to Klansman Earcel Boyd by Silver Dollar Group leader Red Glover. (Photo by Pete Nicks, Cold Case Truth & Justice Project, Center for Investigative Reporting)

OTHER

Earcel Boyd preached in black churches while a member of the Ku Klux Klan and the Silver Dollar Group. (Photo by Leland Boyd/*Concordia Sentinel*)

Ernest Avants in 1964, following his arrest in the beating of two civil rights workers. In 1967 he was one of three men booked and exonerated in the murder of Ben Chester White in Adams County, Mississippi. He was convicted of the murder in federal court in 2003.
(House Un-American Activities Committee file photo)

Father August Thompson prayed with Frank Morris before Morris died four days after the shoe-shop arson. He also photographed Morris on his deathbed. (*Concordia Sentinel*)

Louisiana probation officer James Goss's complaint that Joseph Edwards allegedly had forced a kiss on a female Shamrock Motel employee led to Edwards's disappearance. (*Concordia Sentinel*)

L. C. Murray was one of three Silver Dollar Group Klansmen still living in 2015. (FBI file photo)

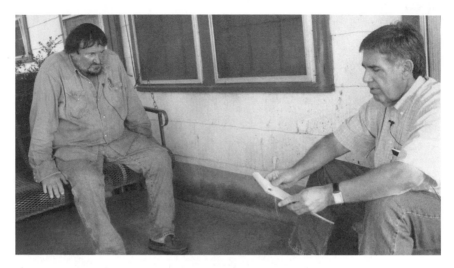

Concordia Sentinel editor Stanley Nelson interviews Klansman Arthur Leonard Spencer in 2010. Spencer, who was implicated in the Frank Morris arson, died in 2013. (Photo by David Paperny, Cold Case Truth & Justice Project, Center for Investigative Reporting)

9

"CRIPPLED JOHNNY" AND THE ALCOHOLIC MECHANIC

IN THE EVER-CHANGING world of Klan allegiances, the UKA was growing nationally and in 1965 added Louisiana Original Knight and Mississippi White Knight klaverns to its membership list. In May, the UKA in Mississippi convened at the Eola Hotel in Natchez. Imperial Wizard Robert Shelton expressed concern that some members were reluctant to attend the state convention—known in Klanspeak as a Klonvocation—because they didn't want anyone to know they were Klansmen. Shelton also instructed members to refrain from drinking in public. At the convention, he narrated the film *Birth of a Nation,* calling it the "Eighth Wonder of the World."[1]

E. L. McDaniel, who had been appointed by Shelton as Mississippi UKA grand dragon in August 1964, was elected by the membership to the position at the convention. Other Natchez men also were elected to state positions, including Paul Foster, the Exalted Cyclops of the Natchez UKA klavern, and Charles Davidson, John Dawson, and Jack Seale.[2] Davidson had been booked in the shooting of Richard Joe Butler in southern Adams County in the spring of 1964, and Seale had been arrested for assaulting civil rights workers and implicated in the murders of Dee and Moore. Charges against both Klansmen were dropped.

McDaniel announced at the meeting that he was forming a women's auxiliary group. As he recruited in Mississippi in 1964 and 1965, the UKA, which unlike other Klans loved the spotlight, capitalized on the notoriety of the White Knights, a Mississippi-only organization, as the UKA pushed a political and nonviolent agenda. At its peak there were 6,000 White Knights in eighty-two counties. By 1967, membership was down to 400. In Louisiana, the Original Knights counted forty-two klaverns at its height and at least 1,000 members, the bulk in northern Louisiana and the southeastern toe of the state. But membership dwindled to 250 by 1967.[3] UKA membership, however, rose to almost 17,000 by 1967, with seventy klaverns and 750 members in Mississippi (many former White Knights) and thirty klaverns and 700 members in Louisiana. North Carolina was the biggest UKA state in America with 192 klaverns and 7,500 members.[4]

These figures, compiled by the U.S. House of Representatives House Un-American Activities Committee (HUAC), may or may not be accurate, as Klan leaders always inflated their numbers. Although UKA rallies drew hundreds, sometimes thousands, the majority in attendance were spectators. Wherever he traveled, McDaniel was always available to the press, and he fired off letters to the editor and press releases to newspapers throughout Mississippi. While blacks boycotted Natchez stores in the wake of the Metcalfe bombing, McDaniel attacked public officials and anyone who was anti-Klan.

On October 30, during the NAACP-led economic boycott of white businesses, one hundred robed UKA members from Mississippi and Louisiana, accompanied by three UKA Klansmen waving Rebel flags and mounted on horses, assembled at the end of Main Street in Natchez and marched ten blocks to the courthouse. McDaniel used the assembly to warn Mayor John Nosser not to give in to the demands of blacks. That night, Shelton was the keynote speaker at a rally in Liberty Park attended by 150 to 160 robed Klansmen and an estimated 4,000 spectators. HUAC investigators at the rally handed out subpoenas to several Klansmen to testify at hearings scheduled for 1966.[5]

Among those subpoenaed was McDaniel. In December 1965, he took advantage of a state law that allowed anyone to sign an affidavit and have a person arrested. His affidavit called for the apprehension of Natchez police chief J. T. Robinson, who had ignored McDaniel's demand that he arrest civil rights leaders for violating a state anti-boycott law. Wire services sent the story out nationally. Sheriff Odell Anders made the arrest, but the matter went no further. In the meantime, the SDG began to attack other Klansmen. Although SDG men may have kept their membership in the UKA, White Knights, or Original Knights—mostly to keep up with what was going on within those groups—the majority remained convinced that words and political campaigns would not stop integration. For them, a secretive underground war was the only answer.

ON SUNDAY, August 15, 1965, the Beatles were on their way to becoming—as John Lennon would later comment—more popular than Jesus Christ. In New York City, the band opened its U.S. tour before a sold-out crowd (almost

57,000) at Shea Stadium. The event made headlines across the world. What happened that same day 1,134 miles away in Fayette, Mississippi, however, barely made a ripple anywhere. Located twenty-four miles north of Natchez, Fayette was founded in 1825 and named after French general Marquis de Lafayette, who fought under the command of George Washington during the Revolutionary War. In 1905, the town had built a Confederate war memorial across Main Street from the courthouse.[6]

At 1 p.m. that Sunday, gunshots pierced the heavy summer heat at the Fayette Ice House, located a block north of the courthouse on US 61, the town's main street. A crowd soon gathered near the body of the local shoeshine man, sixty-five-year-old Johnny Queen, whose blood, mixed with melting ice water, flowed down the street. His stiffening hand held a .32 caliber silver-plated pistol, known as an "owl head" because the head of an owl was engraved on the handle. Queen's killer, off-duty Adams County constable Jasper Burchfield, stood at the edge of the ice house deck (called the porch by town citizens) where Queen's body lay. With him were his sister, mother, and father, and a family friend. A short time later, Jefferson County Sheriff's Office chief deputy Robert Pritchard arrived on the scene and collected Queen's and Burchfield's revolvers. Pritchard was considered a decent man in both the black and white communities. His wife, Cecilia, was sheriff, having been elected in 1963 because her husband, who had been the sheriff, couldn't succeed himself under Mississippi law.[7]

Ninety minutes later, the parish coroner, under the sheriff's direction, convened an inquest. Five white men were randomly chosen. No witnesses testified. Pritchard presented the evidence. The panel was shown Queen's pistol and soon reported that Queen died from four gunshot wounds fired from Burchfield's .38 Smith and Wesson revolver. It reported that Burchfield had killed Queen in self-defense.[8]

The next day the justice of the peace held a hearing. Two black ice house employees and Burchfield's father, mother, and sister testified. Pritchard reported that after Burchfield arrived, Queen used "vulgar language" in the presence of the constable's mother and sister, who were seated in his car. Burchfield asked Queen to quit cursing. Queen said he could say what he wanted. Gunshots followed. The justice of the peace ruled the killing justifiable homicide.[9]

After receiving a call from Sheriff Cecilia Pritchard, FBI agent Billy Bob Williams drove to Fayette from Natchez to investigate. He found no evidence that this was a Klan killing and was certain the bureau had no federal jurisdiction. Additionally, he found no evidence that Burchfield as a constable had violated the "color of the law" federal statute—Section 242 of Title 18—because he was not performing an official duty when the shooting occurred. Williams also thought the Pritchards to be honest and reliable law enforcement people.[10]

However, the FBI had identified Burchfield as a White Knight in 1964. Two agents visited him in the Fenwick community of Adams County in February 1965, six months prior to the Queen killing. They found Burchfield, an employee of the International Paper Company who had been elected constable in 1963, critical of what he called the "Nigger situation." He alleged that the "Jews" were controlling the American dollar, felt that Governor Paul Johnson was "through in Mississippi," and complained that Natchez mayor John Nosser was "trying to burn the candle at both ends and be nice to everybody." (Klansmen hated Nosser because they felt he was taking the side of blacks on the civil rights issue.) Burchfield denied any knowledge of who had bombed Nosser's home. He also alluded to charges being dropped against several Klansmen arrested during the fall of 1964 for the attempted murder of Richard Joe Butler, the attack on civil rights workers in Fayette and Port Gibson, and the murders of Dee and Moore. If he had been in the position of those Klansmen, Burchfield said, he would have sued the FBI and Mississippi officials.[11]

As early as February 1964, an FBI mole had infiltrated the White Knights during its formation in Natchez. The informant (who provided typed reports) said Burchfield was the leader of the White Knights group in Fenwick. He also reported that Burchfield was a close friend of Sheriff Anders.[12] An Adams County deputy had named Burchfield as a suspect in the whipping of Natchez funeral home director Archie Curtis in February 1964. That same year, the FBI notified Governor Johnson that Burchfield was one of scores of law enforcement officials in the Klan, and later informants reported that Burchfield had quit the Klan shortly after his election as constable. When interviewed in 2012 by the *Concordia Sentinel* and National Public Radio (NPR), Burchfield denied he had ever been in the Klan, denied having attended Klan meetings, and denied having ever known anyone who was in the Klan.[13]

A native of Itta Bena, Mississippi, Burchfield moved to Natchez after marriage. In 1950–51, he served in the Korean War as a machine gunner, an experience he considered the worst in his life. On the day he shot and killed Johnny Queen, Burchfield and his passengers were traveling to Itta Bena. As he neared

Fayette, his car's radiator overheated. He stopped at the Fayette Ice House to buy a sack of ice to place in front of the radiator to keep it cool until it could be repaired. He parked parallel to the ice house, and the passenger doors were inches away from the ice house porch, which was four feet above ground level. On the porch, Burchfield observed a handicapped black man.[14]

Johnny Queen was a town fixture. Everybody knew him. He loved to play checkers behind Ball's Drug Store a short distance from the ice house. He had lost the use of both legs in a fall from the roof of a house during his childhood, and his legs were dead weight. Using his upper body strength, Queen stretched his arms and then dragged his legs forward. Many called him "Crippled Johnny." At some point as a young man, when shining shoes became his career, he built two small wooden boxes to store brushes, shoe polish, and supplies. Placing his hands atop each box enabled him to haul his supplies as he pulled himself about town. Young boys thought of him as a musician; as he shined shoes, he made his polishing rag go "pop, pop, pop, pop, pop" to a beat. But because his deformity made his appearance so odd, many children were afraid of him.[15]

Queen was an unpleasant, confrontational man. He drank too much, cursed in front of children, and often carried a knife or a pistol in one of his boxes, but he never physically harmed anyone. Say something he perceived as threatening, and he would immediately tell you where to go. He wanted everyone to know that neither his blackness nor his disability made him less of a man. Queen was a lot like Burchfield—opinionated, some said aggressive at times—and under no circumstances would he ever back down from a fight.[16]

After parking that Sunday, Burchfield got out of the Buick, leaving his pistol behind in the middle of the front seat. He placed his order with two black ice house employees who were on the porch along with Queen. Black teens often sat there during the hot summer months to catch a rush of cool air emerging from inside the building where ice was manufactured in blocks or crushed and packaged. Two teens on the scene that day heard Burchfield tell Queen to stop cursing in front of his wife and sister. One heard Queen reply, "I can say shit whenever I get ready."[17]

According to Burchfield's account, his mother, sitting in the backseat of the Buick, shouted, "That nigger's got a gun." Standing at the driver's door, Burchfield shifted his weight as Queen, seven feet away on the ice house porch, fired. Afterward, witnesses saw a bullet hole, allegedly fired from Queen's gun, in the house next door. Burchfield said he instinctively reached inside his car for his pistol, which the coroner identified as a ".38 state police special." Burchfield told the FBI in 2009 it was a .357 magnum. In 2012, when interviewed by the *Concordia Sentinel* and NPR, Burchfield said he still had the pistol used in the shooting but declined to produce it.[18]

The MHSP reported in 1965 that Queen attempted to fire again, but the gun clicked. At that moment, Burchfield shot Queen, who rolled over and aimed at Burchfield, who fired three more times. In 2009, Burchfield told the FBI that he initially fired two shots into Queen's waist. Afterward, Queen "slumped over," and as he attempted to sit up and shoot again, Burchfield fired twice, delivering the fatal shots. During the 2012 interview, Burchfield pointed at his forehead and said his final shot hit Queen there: "That was the end of the show … that blood shot up out of him, over down on the concrete. I mean a pile of it … and he just kind of shrunk and I knew that was it … seen too many die over in that [Korean] war."[19]

No witnesses were forthcoming in 1965 to refute Burchfield's account of the shooting. Four witnesses who reportedly testified at the justice of the peace hearing that year—Burchfield's mother, sister, and the two ice house employees—are now all dead. Only Burchfield and his sister, who was fourteen in 1965, were still alive in 2012. The sister refused to talk with the *Sentinel* and NPR, and referred the FBI to her lawyer when the bureau asked her to take a polygraph.[20]

The *Sentinel* and NPR found four men—three white and one black—who had come upon the scene immediately after the shooting. All saw the pistol in Queen's hand. All reported that Burchfield was calm. "I got good nerve," Burchfield recalled forty-seven years later, when he was in his eighties. However, he was initially hostile when NPR producer Amy Walters, accompanied by NPR investigative reporter Joe Shapiro and the editor of the *Sentinel*, showed up on his doorstep seeking an interview. When Burchfield came to the front door, I asked him about the day he shot Queen. He went ballistic and spewed profanity, just as he claimed Queen had done a half century earlier.[21]

"You ain't gonna talk to me about no shit like that," Burchfield fumed. He said it was no one's concern but his own. "I mind my own goddam business." When Walters said that they simply wanted his side of the story, Burchfield cooled down and talked for an hour. He told the same story he said he had told two FBI agents—"a man and girl"—in 2009, and he claimed to have also told the agents it "wasn't none of their damn business."[22]

There was no evidence to refute Burchfield's claim of self-defense in 1965 or in recent times. The FBI closed the case in 2013, after spending little time investigating. But questions linger. What would have happened to Johnny Queen had he been the survivor of the shooting? As word spread that a black man had killed a white man, would Queen have survived the oncoming night?

A WEEK AFTER the Queen shooting, in the neighboring Franklin County community of Eddiceton, forty-seven-year-old Earl Hodges's body was found in the backyard between his father's shotgun house and the railroad track. According to a HUAC investigator, Hodges's "body showed welts from the bottom of his feet to the top of his head. There was a hole in the top of his head. There was a split from the left side of his nose to his left eye which was deep enough so you could see the roof of his month." One weapon believed used against Hodges was a three- to four-inch strap and a belt lined with tacks that "tore the flesh every time he was struck with it."[23] The coroner found the cause of death was a heart attack brought on by the beating. An alcoholic who suffered from liver disease, Hodges's death was ruled a homicide, his injuries "inflicted by person or persons unknown."[24]

Born and reared in Lincoln County, Hodges had served as commander of the American Legion post in Meadville in 1951 following military service in occupied Europe during World War II. Fun-loving and a great dancer, he caught the eyes of the girls and spent a lot of time on the dance floor at the Eola Hotel in Natchez.[25] As a young man, he worked in automobile garages in Brookhaven and was sought out as a skilled mechanic. In 1946, he and his wife of ten years, Neva Short, built a garage and service station on US 84 in Eddiceton. Neva helped pump gas and kept the books; she also gave birth to two sons. The business thrived.[26]

During the 1950s, Hodges injured his back several times while working in the garage, resulting in numerous trips to doctors and hospitals. He had begun to drink heavily, and by 1957, he was running around with women, often married women. At times his erratic behavior frightened Neva and, although he never hit her, he threatened to do so on several occasions. Soon the marriage—and the business—fell apart. In 1961, Neva divorced Hodges and moved back to Lincoln County. Hodges moved in with his father Zeb in a three-room shotgun house along the railroad tracks, just two hundred yards from the garage.[27]

Three years later, Hodges joined the White Knights klavern in Bunkley, led by Exalted Cyclops Clyde Seale. There was another White Knights unit in

Franklin County, led by Clyde Wentworth, but everyone knew that Seale ran the Klan in that county. Along with Ernest Parker, Seale and his sons James Ford and Jack had taken part in the killing of Henry Dee and Charles Moore. (All four were SDG members.) Although the MHSP had arrested James Ford Seale and klavern member Charles Marcus Edwards for the murders during the fall of 1964, District Attorney Lennox Forman quickly dropped the charges. Seale's right-hand man in the Bunkley Klan, Archie Prather, had a son, Marcus Shelton Prather, who also was a member.

No one questioned Clyde Seale's leadership until he targeted Meadville Ford dealer Bill Scarborough. Seale believed Scarborough had given $1,000 to Klansman Charles Marshall for a list of the names of Klan members. Seale wanted Scarborough whipped, and there was talk of killing Marshall. In due time, a Klan smut sheet, prepared on Seale's orders, accused Scarborough of having an affair with the black maid he had hired to care for his children following the death of his wife years earlier. Hodges knew there was not a bit of truth to either allegation against Scarborough, and he opposed the project.[28] Others were against it, too, and soon there was a split. Seale was furious that Hodges challenged his authority and feared he might drink too much and talk. Maybe Hodges would tell his brother-in-law, Dan Vernon, a highway patrolman who had worked on the MHSP task force investigating the Klan. Hodges had expressed a desire to mend his ways.[29] Did that mean he planned to confess his personal sins as well as those of the Bunkley klavern, which in addition to committing the Dee-Moore murders had perpetrated at least nine beatings in two years, some administered at an abandoned farmhouse equipped with a homemade stockade? Mostly, Hodges wanted to be a better man. Those who knew him best later painted him as deeply troubled, maybe even fearful for his life during his final days.

IN LATE JULY, Hodges stayed briefly at the veterans' hospital in Vicksburg, trying to dry out, but soon was home and drinking again. On August 5, timber contractor Rax Marshall saw Hodges at the old Bude sawmill. Hodges sobbed, lamenting that he had been unable to see his sons.[30] On August 8, Hodges's married girlfriend, Johnnie Lee Cothren, told him that Clyde Seale had been staking out Marion King's dry cleaners in Meadville. King had been warned that unless she fired her black employees, her business would be burned. "Stay away from that no-good son of a bitch," Hodges barked.[31]

On August 12, Cothren drove into town to buy Hodges a half pint of whiskey from Doll Green, a black bootlegger in Meadville. Two white men in a white car followed her into town and back. She noticed the passenger wearing a straw hat like the one Clyde Seale was known to wear.[32] The next day, Hodges appeared at the doorstep of preacher W. H. Davis. He apologized for being drunk and told Davis he would do anything "to break the drinking habit." Davis felt Hodges was deeply troubled.[33] That night, at Hodges's request, Cothren called his brother Bill and asked him to send money so Hodges could return to the hospital to dry out. At 8:30 p.m., Johnnie Lee brought Hodges some supper while his father was away. From inside, she observed the white car pass by the house three times.[34]

Mid-morning on Saturday, August 14, Hodges arrived in his pickup at his friend J. C. Emfinger's house. He was broke and in need of a drink. They drove to Doll Green's, bought a half pint, and returned to J. C.'s, where J. C.'s wife, Lanette, fed Hodges some chicken noodle soup and crackers. Lanette found Hodges "shaky and sick." He slept for a few hours.[35]

That same morning, Hodges's ex-wife visited Rosia Roland Davis and his wife Frances, her best friends in Eddiceton, who lived diagonally across the road from Hodges. (Davis had once ordered Hodges out of his home when he arrived intoxicated.) While there, Neva called her attorney. She was considering legal action to force the sale of the garage.[36] Later on, Clyde Seale arrived at Davis's farm nearby along the Homochitto River to help Davis work on his camp. The two were close friends. Davis would later tell the FBI that shortly after noon he spotted Seale's imported gray English Ford parked in the cornfield just west of Middle Fork Creek. Beside Seale's car was a solid white, late-model car that Davis told agents he didn't recognize. The FBI would never identify the owner of that car.[37]

That afternoon, Hodges and Emfinger drove to the Adams County line to a bar. At dusk, Link Cameron, an African American man, watched four or five cars proceeding north on Bunkley Road heading for US 84 west of Meadville. He recognized some of the vehicles and immediately assumed it was the Seale-Prather Bunkley Klan group going to a meeting. Cameron told the FBI that he recognized James Ford Seale's pickup and Charles Edwards's Chevrolet.[38]

At 8:30 p.m., Emfinger and Hodges returned to Emfinger's home. Hodges got into his pickup and fell asleep. A few minutes later, Emfinger's wife heard a commotion outside and observed that Hodges had backed his truck into a ditch.[39] Seventy-five yards away, Emfinger's brother Ed sat down to supper with guest Warren Newman, who operated a furniture store in Bude, and Lucius C. DeLaughter, Newman's employee. While the men were eating steak, peas, and okra, Hodges knocked on the door and asked for help with his truck. They fixed Hodges a plate of food and decided to pull the pickup out of the ditch the next day.[40]

At some point after 9:30 p.m., Newman, DeLaughter, and Ed Emfinger squeezed into Newman's pickup to take Hodges home. DeLaughter told the bureau they arrived at Hodges's house around ten. Newman gave Hodges a half pint of whiskey and left with DeLaughter and Ed Emfinger. Newman told the FBI he was home in bed by 10:30 p.m.[41] Thirty minutes later, Cameron observed some of the cars he had seen earlier in the evening returning home on the Bunkley Road. He recognized Clyde Seale's gray car and the pickup of Mark Shelton Prather traveling at high speed.[42] At 11:50 p.m., eighteen-year-old Thomas Scott, driving home from a night out, crossed the railroad track behind the Hodgeses' house and saw what appeared to be a white-faced calf lying in the distance.[43]

Six hours later, at daybreak on August 15, Bill Campbell, a black man who had often helped an inebriated Hodges get inside his home, drove by and thought he saw Hodges lying in the backyard. He walked over and found Hodges lying face up with his right forearm in the air. There was blood on his face. Campbell raced to one of the neighbors, William Watson, for help.[44] Watson placed a bedspread over Hodges's body.[45] He then called Sheriff Wayne Hutto, a suspected Klansman who had helped Clyde Seale cover up the Dee-Moore murders. By 8 a.m., more than fifty people had arrived. Some walked through the house and others throughout the yard, contaminating the crime scene. Hodges's father had been away that night sitting up with an ill man and was still gone.[46]

Hutto found blood in the road and on the grass. Hodges's khaki trousers, soaked in blood, were discovered fifty yards from the house at the edge of the blacktop. They appeared to have been cut from his body. Blood was found throughout the three-room house, which featured a hallway on the left side running from the front door to the back with rooms to the right. The living room, which was the front room, was where Hodges slept. His father's room was in the middle, and the kitchen at the back. An electric fan was running beside Hodges's bed. At some point, he had walked down the hall to the kitchen, leaving bloody handprints along the walls and on the refrigerator. There was no bathroom in the house, no running water. The outhouse was out back. Hodges's blood was on the rope and bucket used to retrieve water from the well, which was also bloodstained. His body rested between the well and the house, his feet in the garden patch. His nose was broken, one of his eyes was almost protruding from the socket, his mouth was bloody, and his body was bruised and cut all over. Although Hutto told the FBI he had no suspects, he believed that Rosia Davis, the neighbor who had spent part of Saturday with Clyde Seale, had knowledge of the crime.[47]

The coroner found that Hodges's injuries had been inflicted around 10:30 p.m. on August 14 and that Hodges had died around midnight.[48] MHSP investigator Donald Butler reported to the FBI that Hodges was one of two or three men who caused the split in the Bunkley Klan and that Clyde Seale feared Hodges would inform on the group.[49] There was no indication that he had. There were rumors—most of them put out by the Klan—that a jealous husband killed Hodges. There was also a Klan rumor that Hodges had a black girlfriend. But Zeb Hodges said Earl's refusal to go on a Klan project against an innocent person had drawn the wrath of Clyde Seale. More than once Zeb had heard his son say he was "fed up with that old bastard giving orders."[50]

For weeks, Franklin County was abuzz with news of Earl Hodges's demise. A grand jury looked into the matter eight days after the homicide but took no action. There was an outrage against the Klan that hadn't been expressed a year earlier when black teens Dee and Moore were killed. In 1966, the HUAC questioned Clyde Seale, James Ford Seale, Jack Seale, and Charles Edwards about the Dee-Moore killings and the Seales about Hodges's murder. They all cited the Fifth Amendment and refused to talk.[51]

IN 1971, MEADVILLE ATTORNEY Max Graves asked for a meeting with District Attorney Ed Benoist to discuss a topic that had the potential to blow the lid off of both murder cases. Graves represented Warren Newman, who had driven Hodges home on the night of the murder. Newman faced charges of timber theft and was looking for a deal. He offered to tell what he had learned about Hodges's death. Benoist, Graves, and Sheriff Kirby Shell, who had been Hutto's deputy in 1965, sat down with Newman.

Newman related that he and the Emfinger brothers, all three Hodges's closest friends, had set up a meeting with Clyde Seale to resolve his differences with Hodges. The meeting took place in the vicinity of Hodges's home, maybe out in the yard, maybe in a nearby abandoned house, maybe at Rosia Davis's camp construction site. The Emfingers and Eugene Robert "Bob" Storey stood with Hodges that night. Newman was not present. At least seven men were with Clyde Seale, including Ernest Avants. Hodges's friends wanted to make peace, while Seales's men wanted to teach him a lesson by whipping him. The meeting quickly turned into a brawl.

At the courthouse in Meadville in 1971, Newman related that Ernest Avants had indicated that the intent was to beat Hodges but not kill him. The main participants in the brawl were Clyde Seale and Avants against Hodges and Bob Storey. Clyde Seale used a two-by-four board embedded with nails to deliver the final blow.[52] In 1968, Pulitzer Prize–winning journalist Jack Nelson reported that he had learned from an unidentified source that Hodges was "tied to a saw-horse and beaten . . . with a leather strap with tacks in it."[53]

In 2007, when James Ford Seale was tried in federal court for the murders of Dee and Moore, Graves presented a sheet of paper with the scribbled notes, several notations unreadable, of the late Ed Benoist. James Ford Seale's name does not appear on the list of participants in the Hodges beating, but Graves remembered Newman mentioning his presence at the fight. Because Newman was not at the brawl and had heard the details from the other participants, Benoist in 1971 considered his information hearsay, although the known participants were still alive. There was another problem: All involved, including those defending Hodges, directly or indirectly contributed to his death. Who would want to prosecute the men who had defended Hodges? Graves said in 2013 that the purpose of the meeting was for Hodges to assure the Seale-Prather group that he was not going to sell them out. But Hodges apparently made no assurances and was ready for a showdown.[54]

Until his death in 1987, Bob Storey, who had been twenty-eight at the time of the incident, was haunted by the melee and Hodges's murder. In 1967, the FBI found him in the Mississippi State Hospital at Whitfield. He had slit both of his wrists while on a drinking bender. Storey said rumors that he was partly responsible for Hodges's death were untrue because on the night of the beating, he was at his mother's home in Bude "sleeping off a drunk." A comment he had made at the crime scene the morning after—that it looked as if someone had hit Hodges in the face "with the blade of a hatchet"—had been misconstrued, Storey said. He said he had been recruited into the White Knights five to six months prior to Hodges's death and that he had quickly grown tired of the group because all Klansmen wanted to do was find a black man to whip.[55]

Only one man whose car was seen in the caravan leaving Bunkley shortly before Hodges was killed was alive in 2014. Charles Edwards, still living in Franklin County, was granted immunity in 2007 when he testified against James Ford Seale in federal court in Jackson. The FBI visited Hodges's sister, Helen Vernon, in 2007 but never reinvestigated the homicide.[56] Hodges's nephew, Keith, recalled in 2013 that the murder had devastated his father— Earl's brother Luther—who gathered his family and his shotgun for the drive from Texas to Eddiceton for the funeral in 1965. Luther talked to Earl's neighbors and friends, but everyone was silent, most too afraid to say a word. Keith was shocked when his father sought the help of a fortuneteller in solving the homicide. "We were a close family," Keith said of his uncle's murder. "This gutted us."[57]

10
OUTLAW COUNTRY

NEWS OF EARL HODGES'S beating by Klansmen in August may not have traveled much farther than Franklin County, Mississippi, but it struck the Klan community like lightning, scaring the daylights out of the average member while prompting paranoid KKK leaders to plug potential leaks. Although Red Glover spent much of 1965 planning to kill George Metcalfe, he was also directing other Klan violence. During January and February, the SDG torched two nightclubs in the Monterey-Lismore area of rural Concordia Parish for allegedly selling alcohol to minors and for gambling and prostitution. These arsons came despite the FBI's presence in Ferriday, where the bureau was intensively investigating the Frank Morris case. Glover didn't have a particular interest in the lounge arsons, but the Black River Klan often looked to him to carry out such projects, just as it had in 1964 with the beatings of three men and the attempted kidnapping of James White, Morris's best friend.[1]

While the lawlessness intensified, the sheriff's office seemed to be the head of or, at least, the coconspirator in much of it. In Ferriday, white Methodist minister Jerry Means could no longer remain silent. He was offended by the Klan smut sheets that accused white women and black men of having interracial affairs, naming them and intimidating some to leave the area. Means was the pastor of the Sevier Memorial United Methodist Church, whose members included Sheriff Noah Cross and a handful of Klansmen. The preacher spent a lot of time trying to "love the hate" out of Klansmen, knowing perfectly well what some were capable of doing. Although he didn't believe his fiscally responsible Klan churchgoers would burn the parsonage, he was compelled to move his son's crib away from the bedroom window.[2]

On February 4, 1965, the *Concordia Sentinel* ran a front-page letter to the editor in which Means, who also headed the Concordia Ministerial Alliance, repudiated the Klan and asked the general public to take a stand with him. "The only type of society which the KKK desires to preserve is a society of hatred and of the devil himself," he wrote.[3] Two weeks later, the newspaper ran a front-page story: "Law and Order Urged by Parish Civic Clubs." In a joint resolution, the chambers of commerce in Ferriday and Vidalia, along with the Vidalia Lions Club and Ferriday Rotary Club, urged local and state law enforcement to apprehend and punish the arsonists. But the groups also made it clear they remained in total support of segregation.[4]

BY LATE SPRING, Father August Thompson was busy preparing for the opening of the St. Charles Catholic Church recreational center for black youth, while the Congress for Racial Equality (CORE) was lining up volunteers from the North to move to Ferriday during the summer. When Thompson was ordained in 1956, he was one of only fifty black Catholic priests in America. He was not shocked that he faced racism in his church, but he was deeply hurt when his request that the congregation seating be integrated for his first mass was denied.[5]

Thompson was born in 1926 in Baldwin, Louisiana. The second of nine children, he was educated in a segregated black school, where every morning the students altered the final words of the Pledge of Allegiance to "with liberty and justice for *some*."[6] By 1965, Thompson was in his third year of service at St. Charles. He had been a steadfast presence in the region's underground civil rights movement, with black and white friends, many prominent in the movement, often visiting him in Ferriday. When CORE arrived in early July, FBI agent Don McGorty made twice-weekly visits after the Ferriday police, sheriff's deputies, and the sheriff himself were spotted driving by the center several times a day.[7] Despite the pleas of his friends, Thompson refused to carry a gun. If he died, whether as a result of his civil rights work or for some other reason, he wanted his mother to always remember that he "died loving."[8]

For the summer of 1965, CORE had two major goals in the area: the integration of public places in Natchez and the organization of an active civil rights movement in Ferriday, a town known statewide for police brutality. CORE leaders called Ferriday the "cutting edge in the battle for civil rights in the South."[9] In Natchez, CORE workers publicized their first attempt to integrate Duncan Park, whose golf course, swimming pool, tennis courts, and baseball and softball fields were all off limits to blacks. The plan was thwarted when dozens of Klansmen toting baseball bats showed up. The next day, however, as FBI agents watched, the CORE group returned unannounced to the park with a number of local black activists and successfully made it inside.[10]

In Ferriday, two white nuns arrived to help Father Thompson prepare for the opening of the church youth center. When the Klan threatened a white Catholic in Ferriday with arson for housing the sisters, Thompson moved them to the rectory. Four CORE workers came by the church to introduce themselves to the priest, who had become famous within CORE when he was featured in *Ramparts* magazine in 1963. On the day of their arrival, sheriff's deputies and Ferriday police began to follow their every move.[11]

In the meantime, the *Sentinel* announced that CORE had opened a base of operations in Ferriday. The paper complained that the outsiders were already creating trouble "where none has existed before and cannot possibly give any intelligent and lasting assistance to Ferriday's race relations." Furthermore, the paper charged CORE workers with creating "discord and distrust between white and colored people everywhere they have worked."[12] But it was obvious to any objective observer that there had been trouble in Ferriday for a long time.

Michael Clurman, a twenty-one-year-old white CORE worker from New York, was attacked twice in three weeks. The first beating came when two black men emerged from Frank DeLaughter's patrol car and assaulted Clurman and a colleague. DeLaughter often used others to do his dirty work. Shortly afterward, Clurman's parents called their congressman, who, in turn, contacted the U.S. Department of Justice. By mid-month, an attempt was made to burn the home where CORE workers were staying, while on July 19, Clurman and Mel Atcheson of Iowa, who was also white, were attacked by one of DeLaughter's thugs. Atcheson was beaten and kicked in the face but, as CORE workers were taught, didn't fight back. Clurman ran. When the activists attempted to hail two deputies passing in their patrol cars, neither would stop. By the end of the month, assistant attorney general for civil rights John Doar wrote the congressman who had inquired about the matter: "On the basis of present information the prospect of a successful federal criminal prosecution is not bright. Evidence is lacking that the assailants acted under the color of the law or that they were involved in a conspiracy to deprive citizens of civil rights." In a phone call to Clurman's parents, Doar warned, "Get your son out of there. That's outlaw country."[13]

After the beating of Atcheson, black CORE worker Archie Hunter of Harlem was in a fury that local blacks who had witnessed the crime didn't help the CORE workers. "We come halfway across the country and you stand right here in the middle of your community and don't help us?" Hunter roared.[14] His admonition made a difference. Under CORE's direction, the Ferriday Freedom Movement (FFM) was born on July 27. In its first newsletter, FFM reported that the organization was born to change "police brutality, years of inactivity, years of fear of retaliation from elements of the white community, years of being told we are inferior, years of being exploited, years of being murdered, and years of bondage. Now, today, we bear the burden of having to rectify all of the things that our forefathers tolerated, because we will not tolerate them."[15]

The newsletter also reported that DeLaughter had arrested four black teens for allegedly cursing a white woman, noting he took them to the Ferriday jail and beat all four. One was knocked down, according to the newsletter. "Who told you to lay on the floor?" DeLaughter shouted. When the youth stood up, DeLaughter struck him again: "Who told you to get up?" The newsletter reported that another teen was jabbed with a cattle prod, and one victim was sentenced to thirty days in the city jail without facing his accuser.[16] A short time later, Louisiana CORE field director Ronnie Moore joined 150 youth for a march to town hall. Other marches against police brutality would follow. Soon the Ferriday library was integrated and blacks were accepted into the trade school.

As in Adams County across the river in Mississippi, a drive to register more black voters began in Ferriday. The Klan responded with another smut sheet, criticizing civic groups for not standing up for segregation and claiming the mayor had been tricked by the communists from "Bucktown" for allowing blacks to march. Klansmen also claimed that new federal programs, such as Head Start, were being used to buy "Nigger Dolls and Red Wagons for the colored children."[17]

ONE OF THE LEADERS of the FFM was twenty-five-year-old Robert "Buck" Lewis Jr., who was motivated to action after black homes and businesses were bombed during the summer and fall of 1965. The discrimination that most offended Lewis was having to say "yes sir" and "no sir" to white men his age or younger. He could walk into the front door of a town café to order a hamburger for his white boss, but if Lewis wanted a meal for himself, he had to go through the back entrance. At the Arcade Theater, the change from the dollar he handed over to pay the twenty-five-cent admission fee for a segregated balcony seat was sometimes thrown on the floor by the white woman who sold tickets.[18] When blacks picketed the segregated theater, Deputy Junior Harp assaulted twenty-eight-year-old Roy Twitty, chairman of CORE's branch office in Tucson, Arizona.[19]

Throughout the year, blacks faced daily threats of violence in retaliation against civil rights activities. The SDG bombed the home of Thomas Hart and threw an explosive at the home of the Rev. A. T. White. By year's end, CORE reported fourteen acts of violence against Ferriday blacks, including two instances of shots being fired into homes, two arsons, and five bombings or bombing attempts. These incidents included the firebombing of activist Lucky McCraney's gas station. William Piercefield was shot multiple times and killed after barricading himself in his Ferriday house with two of his children in July. The sheriff's office told the *Sentinel* that Piercefield had argued with his family and retrieved a .22 caliber rifle before locking himself inside his home. Police claimed he refused to come out even when teargas was thrown inside. After exchanging gunfire for more than three hours, police kicked in the door and shot Piercefield in what they claimed was self-defense. Piercefield was even blamed for the shooting injury of his son, despite the fact that police fired more than one hundred rounds into the home.[20]

During the summer, African Americans gathered for a meeting at the blacks-only Sevier High School in Ferriday to discuss fighting back. It was a watershed moment for civil rights in the town. Lewis and others emerged from the meeting ready to take a stand, even though informants for the sheriff's office and town police had reported some of those plans. Lewis not only became the first president of the FFM, he also was elected president of the reactivated NAACP. His actions quickly drew the wrath of the sheriff's office and the Klan. At 9:30 p.m. on the night of November 21, Lewis heard a truck stop and a door open outside his Ferriday home. An explosion suddenly splintered part of the front porch and shattered windows throughout the house. He saw a man jump a ditch and run out of sight. While his neighbors worked to extinguish the flames, Lewis led his wife and five children safely out of the house. He grabbed his shotgun during the confusion but couldn't find the shells. When Ferriday police arrived, Lewis was standing on the porch with the unloaded weapon in his hand. As police rushed him, a neighbor took the gun from Lewis, who was arrested and transported to city jail, where a crowd of white people, including children, had amassed. Lewis was charged with aggravated battery, placed again in a cruiser, and transported by Ferriday officers to the parish jail in Vidalia.[21]

On his arrival at the courthouse, Lewis looked out the car window to see several deputies, including Frank DeLaughter, Bill Ogden, and Junior Harp, waiting for him. Lewis knew there were few things worse than jail time for a black man in Concordia Parish. "It was a dreaded thing," he would recall in the years to follow. At the courthouse door, Harp raised his voice: "We're going to teach that smart nigger a lesson he won't ever forget." DeLaughter glared. But Louisiana state trooper Marion Barnette, who had arrived at the same time as Lewis, rushed to the door. Someone had called Louisiana governor John Mc-Keithen, who had contacted the state police.[22]

"You can't touch him," Barnette told the deputies. "And don't go in his cell." Upstairs, Barnette had Lewis strip and then instructed the jailer, "Write down that there are no bruises on this man's body. And don't allow anyone to go into his cell."[23]

Under $2,000 bond (equivalent to $15,000 in 2015)—a staggering sum for most parish residents to raise in the 1960s—Lewis sat in the parish jail for sixteen days and seventeen nights before he was able to make bail. Because no local bondsman would underwrite his release, Lewis obtained the services from New Orleans. As was typical for black prisoners, his release didn't come until after dark. Lewis had received news to delay his trip home so that the newly formed Deacons for Defense and Justice in Ferriday—formed to defend black neighborhoods from Klan attacks—could ensure his safe return. Word had gone out that Glover and his men would be waiting. Lewis hopped into the bondsman's black Cadillac. They crossed the Mississippi River Bridge, visible from the courthouse, and entered Natchez. After waiting a short time, the bondsman returned to Vidalia and dropped Lewis off at the home of his mother-in-law. Minutes later, five Deacons arrived in a canary yellow 1965 Pontiac Tempest. The car belonged to the brother of Antonne Duncan, who was in the driver's seat. Across town at the railroad tracks, Duncan gunned the Pontiac as headlights from a number of cars flashed on. Traveling at one hundred miles per hour, Duncan watched the pursuing "line of headlights" in the rearview mirror. Because of construction along the Ferriday-Vidalia highway, the car was in a constant zigzag motion. Duncan guided the Pontiac and Lewis safely home, eluding the pursuing Klansmen a few miles outside Vidalia.[24]

ANYONE INVOLVED in civil rights work in Ferriday was targeted, twenty-year-old David Whatley told the *New York Times* in an article about Lewis's arrest. "When we demonstrate, [law enforcement officers] take pictures of the people, and if you've got a job, they show the picture to the men you work for and when you go to work the next day you're out of a job."[25]

By late 1965, Whatley and his family were accustomed to sleeping lightly and standing on guard throughout the nighttime hours. Whatley's grandmother, Alberta Whatley, was one of the few people in Ferriday who would house CORE workers. Klansmen shot holes in her house, shot out outside lights, and threw Molotov cocktails on three occasions. A leader in CORE and the FFM, David Whatley was also one of the youngest members of the Deacons for Defense.[26]

The October 14 edition of the FFM newsletter announced that the group would soon file a court motion to integrate the white high school in town, and it did so in late November. The Concordia Parish School Board submitted a desegregation plan on December 15 to Federal Judge Ben. C. Dawkins Jr. in Monroe. The plan called for incremental desegregation in the 1966–67 school year and full integration by the following school term. The plan also allowed parents to transfer their first-, second-, eleventh-, or twelfth-grade students to the school of their choice for the spring semester of 1966.[27] Following meetings at black churches during the late fall and early winter of 1965, several black children expressed an interest in integrating the white schools. But the white employers of the children's parents indicated that those parents would be fired if they moved forward. Whatley, who knew the white Ferriday High School had finer facilities, modern textbooks, and better-educated teachers, decided he was willing to be the first student to test the integration waters.[28]

That decision soon drew a Klan response. During the early morning hours of January 30, 1966, a Monday, nine people were inside Whatley's grandmother's home, including his extended family, two children, and a civil rights worker. One of his cousins who had been assigned guard duty had fallen asleep. In the past, when Klansmen circled the block where Whatley's home was located at 310 South Fifth Street, the family would illuminate the yard with floodlights, show themselves, and the Klansmen would flee. Beginning in the latter part of 1965, the Deacons for Defense had members hiding at points throughout the black neighborhoods and had encountered Klansmen from time to time. There had been little gunfire, but Klansmen were fearful of an ambush.[29]

Suddenly, during the night, Whatley heard an explosion. A witness saw a man running from the scene. Outside, Whatley found that a detonator—a blasting cap used in oil fields—had ignited, but two sticks of explosives attached to it had not. Had the explosive sticks detonated, there would have been extensive damage to the home. The FBI would later learn that the bombers were Sonny Taylor and James Frederick "Red" Lee, the two men Glover had assigned to perfect the bomb used against Metcalfe five months earlier. Since both Metcalfe and Whatley had survived, it became obvious to Glover that more experimentation with explosives was needed.[30]

While the school board turned down Whatley's admission at Ferriday High due to his age, Judge Dawkins admitted him. Crowds of white men gathered at the school during the first days of Whatley's attendance. Outside his classroom windows, whites lined up and stared. Whatley heard "slurs, slanders, curses, swears, intimidation and threats" on a daily basis. His gym clothes were thrown in the toilet and his books knocked from his hands. This harassment went on for weeks until he was arrested by Ferriday police on a false charge of stealing. For two weeks he was held at the city jail without knowing his accuser's identity. During his incarceration, representatives of the local draft board met with him, and a short time later he was drafted. Police Chief Bob Warren drove him to the bus station and warned him to get out of town. By the spring of 1967, Whatley was a first gunner on a machine gun reconnaissance unit in Vietnam and was injured in a land mine explosion. It took a year to recuperate. "I often thought," Whatley told the *Concordia Sentinel* in 2010, "that I wasn't good enough to attend Ferriday High School but I was good enough to go and fight for my country." But he had opened the door for integration in Ferriday.[31]

IN OCTOBER 1965, Sheriff Noah Cross's top political ally, Blackie Drane, accused William Cliff Davis, a white employee, of stealing an electric motor from a slot machine. An alcoholic and one of many transients who found temporary employment in the parish's illegal gambling and prostitution trade, Davis was suspected of having sold the motor to buy booze. On October 20, Drane, DeLaughter, and Ed Fuller found Davis at the bar in the King Hotel. DeLaughter, who was drinking heavily, brought Davis to the Ferriday jail, handcuffed him, pushed him into a chair, and backhanded him. Fuller and Drane soon arrived. All three questioned Davis about the location of the motor, and all three slapped him several times before Fuller attacked Davis with a cattle prod. Fuller pushed the tip of the prod so deeply into Davis's eye that it caused permanent damage. DeLaughter and Fuller beat Davis until the jailer demanded they leave. The three men transported Davis to Drane's warehouse, where the assault continued.[32]

After Davis passed out for the second time, DeLaughter took the unconscious man to the parish jail. Davis's face was swollen and covered with blood, one eye completely closed and the other almost closed. Bruises covered his body. Witnesses had seen DeLaughter apprehend Davis at the King Hotel, and witnesses had seen DeLaughter, Fuller, and Drane with Davis at the town jail. Worried that Davis might die, DeLaughter called the sheriff, who was sleeping at home. Cross told DeLaughter to get Davis out of the parish and made arrangements for him to be taken to the East Louisiana State Hospital Alcoholic Treatment Center in Jackson, Louisiana. A week later, Cross showed up at the facility, took Davis back to Concordia Parish, and delivered him to Drane.[33]

A headline—"Three Local Men to Be Arraigned"—appeared over a story on the front page of the November 11, 1965, issue of the *Concordia Sentinel*. The new publisher, Sam Hanna, who had bought the paper a few days earlier, wrote the article.[34] A seasoned reporter for a Monroe, Louisiana, daily, Hanna had a reputation statewide for his comprehensive coverage of Louisiana politics and a hard-charging reporting style. Never before had Concordia citizens seen anyone report anything bad about Cross or the sheriff's office. The article explained that DeLaughter, Drane, and Fuller had been indicted by the parish grand jury on charges of aggravated battery. How the matter got before the grand jury remains a mystery. No one remembers. No records exist. But by early 1966, the *Sentinel* reported in another front-page story that the case—delayed twice since the indictment—appeared to be at a dead end. The headline read, "Witness Missing in Concordia Case," and the article explained that Davis had disappeared.[35]

FERRIDAY-CLAYTON KLANSMEN followed the Davis matter with particular interest. Davis's apprehension by DeLaughter at the King Hotel had been witnessed by O. C. "Coonie" Poissot, a transient like Davis, who had arrived in Ferriday in 1964 and had become a close friend of Douglas Nugent, a gambling competitor of Drane's. Nugent operated the King Hotel and had served as Exalted Cyclops of the Ferriday-Clayton Klan in 1963. He recruited Poissot into the Klan. Poissot was a rowdy, tough-talking ex-con with a long rap sheet and had served time in the state penitentiary at Angola. While Ferriday and Clayton Klansmen frequented Nugent's King Hotel, they rarely patronized any of Drane's joints on the Ferriday-Vidalia highway. In February 1965, Poissot and one of Drane's henchmen had helped DeLaughter steal illegal fishing seines and netting that had been confiscated by the Louisiana Wildlife and Fisheries Department and stored at the agency's Ferriday warehouse.[36] Sheriff Cross and his deputies later used the booty to fill their freezers with fish. Drane and Fuller, however, didn't like Poissot because of his association with their rival Nugent.

A few days after the Davis beating, Klansmen witnessed an altercation between E. D. "Big" Morace, the investigator for the Ferriday-Clayton Klan, and James Scarborough, the Exalted Cyclops. Morace accused Scarborough of informing on the klavern. In fact, he claimed Scarborough was divulging Klan secrets to DeLaughter, Drane, and Fuller and that this action had endangered the life of Coonie Poissot.[37]

Scarborough was convinced that violent days were ahead for white people in the South. He blamed the federal government and the menacing influence of communism for the push for integration, and ultimately, he believed, black insurrection and a bloody race war would be the result. Scarborough had grown up in the shadows of one of the meanest Klan groups in the history of the United States; its crimes resulted in the first intense FBI investigation into the KKK. The case had drawn the interest of J. Edgar Hoover, then the number-two man in the bureau.

ON THE AFTERNOON of August 24, 1922, residents of Mer Rouge, located in northern Louisiana near the Arkansas line, were heading home after a barbecue and baseball game in the Morehouse parish seat of Bastrop. At a roadblock midway on the seven-mile highway separating Bastrop and Mer Rouge, hooded Klansmen searched each vehicle passing through. Five white men were detained. Each was bound, blindfolded, and led into the woods. Three made it out alive. Two went missing—thirty-five-year-old World War I veteran Walt Daniels, a bachelor, and his friend, Thomas F. Richards, a mechanic and married father of two. Both had been warned previously by the Klan to stop associating with blacks. Daniel, a womanizer who allegedly liked white and black women, had told the Klan to go to hell.[38]

Both Daniels and Richards were beaten to death, their bodies mutilated, their heads removed, bones broken, and testicles crushed. Soon, tips revealed that their bodies had been dumped into Lake LaFourche. When federal authorities appeared, ready to search the lake, an explosion blew out a sixty-foot-wide, twenty-five-foot-deep hole along the bank. The next morning, the two men's headless bodies floated to the surface.[39]

The murders split Morehouse Parish between pro-Klan and anti-Klan factions. Louisiana governor John Parker soon learned not only that the Klan controlled the parish top to bottom, from courthouse officials down to local justices of the peace, but also that they were interfering with the mail, telegraph, and telephone services in the region. So great was the Klan's influence that Parker asked a reporter for the *New Orleans Times-Picayune* to hand deliver a message to the FBI calling for assistance. The letter was written to the attention of Hoover, then the assistant director of the bureau.[40]

Everyone in Morehouse Parish knew that Klan leaders John J. Skipworth, seventy-four, the former mayor of Bastrop, and B. M. McKoin, a dentist and former Mer Rouge mayor in his late thirties, were responsible for the homicides. Skipworth had waged a battle against bootleggers, moonshiners, "immoral" men and women, and anyone who challenged the Klan. His right-hand man McKoin was a Baptist deacon who was particularly offended by white men sleeping around with black women.[41]

Federal officials in Washington were stunned at the degree of Klan power in northern Louisiana. It included a plot to kill FBI agents, masterminded, in part, by the U.S. attorney at Shreveport. Although two separate grand juries, populated by Klansmen, failed to indict anyone on felony charges in the killings, the state's extensive hearing on the matter provided pages of testimony. This would become one of the most famous murder cases attributed to William Simmons's Klan during the first half of the twentieth century.

BORN IN THE NEIGHBORING parish of Union in 1921, a year before the murders of Daniels and Richards, Scarborough grew up hearing stories about the heroic Morehouse Klan's crusade against immorality and racial mixing. A World War II veteran with an eighth-grade education, he moved to Ferriday in 1951 after transferring to the International Paper Company mill in Natchez. He joined the Concordia Klan at its formation and in late 1964 was elected Exalted Cyclops of the Ferriday-Clayton Original Knights klavern. Known for his marksmanship with an archer's bow, he was called "The Indian" by some of his fellow Klansmen and local hunters. At a Klan meeting in March

1965, Scarborough delivered a passionate speech advocating the formation of armed squads to train for the coming race war.[42] He joined Red Glover and other SDG Klansmen in beatings and arson projects in 1964 and early 1965 and was known to have a cache of explosives.

Morace believed that Scarborough alerted DeLaughter by messenger about the Klan's proposed projects. During his ten years on the ground investigating the sheriff's office, FBI agent John Pfeifer learned that DeLaughter and other deputies rarely attended Klan meetings. They were members mostly to gather intelligence to prevent the execution of any Klan projects that targeted prostitution and gambling enterprises from which the sheriff profited via kickbacks, such as the early 1965 arsons of two parish lounges where both vices flourished.[43]

In early November, a few days after the beating of Davis, Klansmen convened at the meetinghouse in Clayton. Morace collected guns from the arriving Klansmen and hung them on racks along the wall. Within a few minutes, they heard a car drive up. Soon four men wearing white robes and white hoods, each armed with a rifle, walked in and sat at the front of the room facing the gathering. Morace said that Scarborough was to be tried for divulging Klan secrets and that the four men in robes would serve as executioners. They were to carry out the sentence imposed by the Klansmen.[44]

Morace planned to reveal that Drane and Fuller believed Poissot and another Klansman had torched Drane's warehouse that stored, among other things, gambling machines and parts. It was also where William Cliff Davis received his second beating. Drane thought the arson was Nugent's idea. To make matters worse, Poissot had witnessed DeLaughter's apprehension of Davis at the King Hotel, and Poissot knew Fuller and Drane had joined the deputy in beating Davis. A grand jury was investigating the beating. Now, DeLaughter intended to deal with Poissot.[45]

Before the trial of Scarborough began, a handful of Klansmen huddled. When a terrified, newly recruited Klansman stood to leave, the four executioners pointed their rifles at his head. The trembling man returned to his seat.[46] In short order, a deal was cut. Morace agreed to call off the trial if Scarborough was removed as Exalted Cyclops and booted out of the Klan. Morace had stacked the deck against Scarborough.[47]

As the hooded executioners left the building, only Morace knew their names: Glover, Kenneth Norman Head, Buck Horton, and Coonie Poissot. Poissot appeared unhooded at the klavern's December meeting and thanked

Morace and others for protecting him from DeLaughter.[48] Knowing his fate would be similar to Davis's if DeLaughter had his way, Poissot left town. But in two years, the FBI would find Poissot in Texas and secretly bring him back as an informant. Poissot would tell agents that he was with DeLaughter the night before the arson of Frank Morris's shoe shop in late 1964 and that the deputy had previously argued heatedly with the shoemaker over a pair of cowboy boots.

1966

11

"OH, LORD, WHAT HAVE I DONE TO DESERVE THIS?"

IN CONCORDIA PARISH, Sheriff Noah Cross's alliance with the New Orleans mob in the operation of a profitable brothel drew the attention of a young FBI agent. Cross also found himself under attack from several other formidable foes. A confederation of preachers and civic clubs opened a campaign to rid the parish of prostitution and gambling, and sought the help of Louisiana governor John McKeithen. Meanwhile, the *Concordia Sentinel*'s new publisher, Sam Hanna, covered the lack of law and order with fourteen front-page stories detailing the "moral and ethical" crisis the ministerial alliance was addressing. Hanna also extensively covered the race for district attorney, in which vice and corruption became the top issue, setting the stage for Cross's reelection campaign in the year to follow.

The preachers' crusade drew immediate support from civic groups and local governing bodies. The governor met in May with the ministerial alliance and local legislators. McKeithen learned from Assistant District Attorney Roy Halcomb that Cross was stonewalling any efforts to address the vice issues.[1] In June, Louisiana state police superintendent Thomas Burbank met with Cross. "I think we had an understanding," Burbank told the *Sentinel* after the meeting. Burbank advised Cross that if he didn't close the gambling and prostitution operations, the state police would. When, after a month, Cross hadn't moved, Burbank made good on his threat.[2]

State police launched a late-night raid on Saturday, July 30, on three lounges, two of which belonged to the sheriff's political and financial ally Blackie Drane. Three of Drane's employees were arrested, as were a pimp and four prostitutes who worked at the Morville Lounge, a brothel and casino fourteen miles south of Vidalia. Thirteen state troopers confiscated Drane's blackjack and dice tables, as well as an assortment of chips, dice, and cards. At the Morville Lounge, troopers found an arsenal of weapons and ammunition, and observed ten bedrooms used for prostitution.[3] The confiscated gambling material, per state law, was turned over to Sheriff Cross. Although the ministers praised the governor, McKeithen advised the preachers, "Prosecution is local." A few days later, the Morville Lounge was back in operation, Drane had repossessed his property, and bribes to Cross resumed.[4]

In the DA race, Halcomb and Vidalia attorney W. C. Falkenheiner waged a heated run-off battle. Halcomb had worked for District Attorney Wana Gibson for eight years. Gibson hailed from neighboring Catahoula Parish, which shared the judicial district with Concordia. He had served since 1948, but when in Concordia Parish neither he nor the judge typically challenged Cross. The sheriff despised Halcomb, who labeled Falkenheiner as Cross's candidate in the race. Falkenheiner countered that Halcomb held the power to close the vice operations. In fact, such action required the support of Halcomb's boss, the DA.[5] On election day, Falkenheiner was victorious. In December, a month prior to his taking office, the DA-elect said he would fulfill his campaign promise to "carry out the law as written in the statutes."[6] When he took office in January 1967, he padlocked the lounge. The FBI by then had launched a full-scale investigation.

DURING THE EARLY stages of the race for district attorney, two young FBI agents arrived in Ferriday with instructions to put a stop to the violence perpetrated in part (and completely ignored by) the sheriff's office. Born and reared in Ohio, John Pfeifer was an English literature major at Princeton. Honorably discharged from the Marines in 1959, he went to work as an insurance investigator and adjuster in Detroit before he was promoted to bodily injury claim supervisor in Brooklyn, where he reviewed five hundred claims each month. Pfeifer disliked the long commute to work and hated the job.[7] Throughout his life, he had been an admirer of the FBI. He devoured Don Whitehead's book *The FBI Story*, which outlined the bureau's history and some of its most famous cases. While sipping beer with a fellow Marine reservist in 1964, Pfeifer learned that a comrade was joining the bureau. It was a heavy recruiting period for the FBI, which was waging war on the Klan in the South. After learning that he didn't have to be a lawyer or an accountant to become a special agent, Pfeifer decided to fulfill his dream of becoming a G-man. After training, he worked for a few months in Belleville, Illinois, before being transferred to the New Orleans field office in February 1966, just in time for Mardi Gras. Pfeifer was thirty-three.[8]

The office, which handled all of Louisiana, also had been responsible for the southern half of Mississippi until 1964, when the bureau opened a field office in Jackson. The New Orleans office took up two floors in the post office on Loyola Avenue across the street from the new Hyatt and near the future home of the Louisiana Superdome. Space was so limited in the busy office that clerks worked in cluttered hallways filled with desks, filing cabinets, and stacks of papers. Each desk was shared by two agents. Joseph Sylvester, the assistant special agent in charge, headed up one of two squads that operated out of the office. His No. 2 Squad handled police brutality, Klan, and civil rights cases. Sylvester was a short man, fearless, and beloved by agents, who felt he cared about them and their families. But he was a tough boss. Pfeifer described him as the type of father who would take his son to the swimming hole, throw him in, and see if the child would learn to swim on his own.[9]

Sylvester was proud of Pfeifer's work and that of another agent on his squad, twenty-seven-year-old Ted Gardner of Virginia. Like Pfeifer, Gardner had joined the bureau in 1964. In the months ahead, he would become involved in the investigation into the murder of Oneal Moore, a black deputy with the Washington Parish Sheriff's Office who was gunned down by Klansmen in 1965. Pfeifer and Gardner, also a Marine, looked like brothers.[10] Together, the new team investigated several racketeers who worked for the New Orleans–based Carlos Marcello mob. Pfeifer came to believe that gambling was so prevalent in Louisiana that "bookies grew on trees."[11]

Sylvester had visited Ferriday in 1965 when Frank DeLaughter's henchmen attacked CORE workers. He quickly assessed that the parish was a powder keg. Agent Don McGorty (who would soon be transferred to New York) was bogged down in a number of civil rights complaints relating to the sheriff's office and the faltering murder investigation of Frank Morris. Sylvester handed the two new agents the Concordia Parish file, which was so thick they didn't have time to finish reading it before heading to Ferriday. In addition to stopping the Klan violence, they also were to look into the growing number of police brutality cases that had been filed. These had quickly stalled, mostly because witnesses and victims were afraid to testify. Upon arriving in town in March 1966, the agents met with two informants McGorty had developed during the past months. They quickly learned that in January, Klansman

Douglas Nugent, who operated the King Hotel, had died in an automobile accident.[12] The funeral of the former Exalted Cyclops, who was buried in his red Klan robe, was held at the hotel lounge. Among the mourners was DeLaughter, who wore his Klan robe over his deputy uniform.[13]

Soon after their arrival, Sylvester alerted Pfeifer and Gardner that White Knights imperial wizard Sam Bowers of Mississippi might be hiding out with Klan friends in Concordia Parish. Warrants had been issued for his arrest in connection with the murder of African American Vernon Dahmer, a fifty-seven-year-old farmer and businessman who was the NAACP leader in Hattiesburg, Mississippi. Dahmer died on January 11, 1966, as a result of a White Knight firebombing attack organized by Bowers and carried out the night before. Pfeifer and Gardner met an FBI agent in Natchez who provided photos of Bowers, a physical description, and details of the warrant.[14]

They worked into the night, searching fishing and deer camps in the Monterey–Black River area of Concordia. They also took a drive on Highway 15, a lonely two-lane state road that runs parallel at intervals with the Mississippi River outside Ferriday southward to Pointe Coupee Parish. It was common knowledge parishwide that along that route there was a house of prostitution like no other in Louisiana. Spotting lights on the other side of the levee, just north of Deer Park, the agents topped the levee and below saw a single-story building with fifty cars and pickups in a gravel parking lot. A jukebox was blaring, and the voices of partying men and women streamed out. Inside, they saw women in negligees and men, dressed in business suits, work pants, and hunting clothes, three deep at the bar. Nearby, in a cloud of cigarette and cigar smoke, players surrounded blackjack, dice, and poker tables. Slot machines also were in play. Pfeifer and Gardner sidled up to the bar and asked to see the manager, who introduced himself as Curt Hewitt. They showed him photos of Bowers. Hewitt said he had never seen the man before. Neither had any of the lounge's customers.[15]

THE MORVILLE LOUNGE was located in an old country store that had closed in 1960. The owner of the building was fifty-three-year-old J. D. Richardson, a tall, thin, rugged cattle and horse rancher who dressed in western attire and was rarely seen without his revolver secured in a holster at his waist. Richardson had a reputation as a ladies' man and as someone you didn't mess with. With only a fourth-grade education, he could barely read and write. Despite those limitations, he had done well for himself. Among other ventures, Richardson had a stake in the 6,600-acre Morville Plantation along the Mississippi River.[16]

In early 1965, Richardson leased the old grocery building on the property to Curt Hewitt, who had been tapped by the Carlos Marcello mob to manage the prostitution and bar business there in what proved to be a lucrative venture. (The mob had previously sent a representative to Concordia and Natchez to do a feasibility study.) After the deal was made, Hewitt asked Richardson to "fix it" with the sheriff. A short time later, Richardson found Cross at his farm in Ferriday and asked if he would allow Hewitt to operate for $200 a week in protection money. The sheriff agreed, but to insulate himself, he made arrangements for the money to be paid directly by Richardson and not the mob. Later, Cross arranged for DeLaughter to pick up the weekly kickback at the lounge, where Hewitt would hand him a white envelope marked "The Man" with the cash stuffed inside.[17]

As early as 1959, Hewitt had been arrested for employing "b-girls," and he had operated the Peppermint Lounge in Eunice in St. Landry Parish before being tapped for the Morville Lounge position. He immediately plugged into the mob's network of pimps, who delivered the working girls to the lounge. One pimp paid the $100 bond of a destitute twenty-one-year-old named Betty being held in a Shreveport jail on bad check charges. Instead of taking her home, the pimp drove her against her will 182 miles to the Morville Lounge. When she refused to perform, one of Hewitt's associates slapped her several times and threatened her. Eventually, Betty agreed to turn two tricks. She was held in the lounge for six weeks until, on the sly, she reached her mother by pay phone.[18] Around the same time, Methodist preacher Jerry Means, an outspoken leader in the ministerial alliance, was taking a Sunday afternoon drive with his wife near the lounge when he watched in disbelief as a naked teenage girl came running over the levee. She, too, had been forced into prostitution but had escaped. Means drove the teen to Natchez, where FBI agent Billy Bob Williams made arrangements for her safe return home while alerting the New Orleans FBI office of the rescue.[19]

Shortly after Hewitt took over, Blackie Drane and Ed Fuller, both wearing sidearms, paid him a visit. A feared bouncer in Drane's lounges, Fuller was known to use brass knuckles, ax handles, and chains against patrons. Both were believed to have contacts within the Dixie Mafia, a group of conmen who traveled the South committing crimes. They were especially active in the illegal gambling underworld. While the Marcello mob would recruit the prostitutes, Hewitt was informed that Drane would provide the gambling machines and devices used in the operation, as well as the men who operated the games. After the sheriff was provided his protection money, Hewitt agreed to split the remaining gambling profits with Drane. Otherwise, Drane indicated, "The Man" would shut the operation down. Hewitt agreed. Once all the payoffs were made, Hewitt was to split the lounge share of profits with Richardson. In the meantime, DeLaughter demanded that, in exchange for his personal protection, Hewitt help finance a car and a camp lot for the deputy. Of all the players operating under Cross (including Richardson, Drane, Fuller, and DeLaughter), only the Marcello mob's representative, Hewitt, did not belong to the Klan.[20]

When the FBI agents wandered into the lounge in the spring of 1966, Pfeifer spotted on the bar a stack of counter checks "blank and ready to be filled out." He realized that if the lounge owners were accepting checks for prostitution and gambling, they were breaking federal laws. Pfeifer would learn that during an eighteen-month period, the lounge deposited $250,000 in checks alone for prostitution and gambling. Agents never learned how much cash was spent. Obviously, this operation could not have existed unless the sheriff was paid protection money. The agents were standing in a dark corner of the parking lot talking when they observed three scantily clad women and four men in business suits climb into a Cadillac limousine. Pfeifer and Gardner followed the vehicle to Vidalia and watched it turn right onto the bridge and cross the river into Natchez and the state of Mississippi. To both men, it was obvious that the Morville Lounge was a sophisticated operation that violated the federal Interstate Transportation in Aid of Racketeering statutes.[21]

To help make a case, Pfeifer first looked for a mole within the sheriff's department, particularly a deputy who would have firsthand knowledge of Cross and DeLaughter's criminal operations. He settled on Ike Cowan Jr., a short, stocky father of four who had served in World War II and Korea. Cowan had been implicated in a beating in 1962, but his record was clean when compared to DeLaughter's and Deputy Bill Ogden's. One day Pfeifer surprised Cowan with a visit to his home. He told the deputy this would be a good time for him to get on the right side of the fence and perform a beneficial service to the community he was sworn to protect and serve.[22]

To Pfeifer's astonishment, Cowan began to talk, explaining how Cross had made the gamblers his solid allies in the 1950s in exchange for kickbacks. In the past, Cross had often sent deputies to various clubs to order them to stop gambling activities when there was a possibility of state police raids. But since the opening of the Morville Lounge, Cowan said, the sheriff had "gone to extremes to keep it operating." The deputy said he had been to the lounge with the sheriff and other deputies and that he once watched a local gambler who operated an extensive burglary ring pay Cross "a stack of money" to look the other way. Pfeifer left Cowan's home late that night after hours of conversation. He had picked Cowan's brain clean, garnering information connecting the sheriff to the lounge. But would Cowan agree to testify against the sheriff in court?[23]

Two days later, while driving along the Ferriday-Vidalia highway, Pfeifer observed the sheriff in his Cadillac with Cowan and two other deputies. "They're all pointing at me like there's that SOB!" Pfeifer recalled years later. Continuing on his way, the agent stopped at the King Hotel to ask the bartender for help in locating someone he needed to interview. Suddenly, Cowan burst through the door into the lounge, well populated by pulpwood haulers and oil-field workers. The uniformed Cowan had his sidearm prominently displayed, while Pfeifer, dressed in a white shirt and slacks, had his revolver in the usual place—in a briefcase he always carried with him.[24]

"The Man wants to see you outside right now!" Cowan shouted.

Despite the tense situation, Pfeifer's sense of humor quickly surfaced: "Well, Ike, I see you apparently do not stand up very well under interrogation!" Then he continued, "If Noah wants to get a hold of me, he should call me at my office, explain what he wants over the phone, and if it's real business, I'll make an appointment to see him then."

Cowan's face reddened when he realized Pfeifer was not going to adhere to the boss's demands. The patrons in the bar couldn't believe their eyes or ears. Never had they witnessed anyone stand up to the high sheriff. That was the last time Cross made any effort to talk to Pfeifer, who afterward occasionally dropped by the sheriff's office and, with the secretary's permission, sat at Cross's desk and made a collect phone call. If the sheriff had studied his phone bill, he would have seen that periodic calls were being made to the FBI's New Orleans field office.[25]

WHILE THE KICKBACK CASH poured in throughout 1966, Sheriff Cross also shored up his close relationship with the Klan. On March 19, in a field near the outskirts of Ferriday, the United Klans of America held a nighttime rally sponsored by the Louisiana and Mississippi Realms. An estimated one thousand people attended, mostly spectators, as well as fifty robed Klan members, including eight women and a number of children, plus a dozen UKA security guards. Cross assigned DeLaughter and five other uniformed parish deputies to assist Klansmen in parking their cars.[26] Louisiana UKA grand dragon Jack Helm of New Orleans, nursing a bad case of laryngitis, along with Mississippi grand dragon E. L. McDaniel, were the featured speakers. Helm, who had recently lost his New Orleans Selective Service Board seat because of his Klan affiliation, claimed that homosexuals had corrupted the federal government. He also urged white citizens not to register their guns.[27]

At the UKA rally at Liberty Park on May 7, DeLaughter was among a handful of UKA dignitaries recognized by McDaniel, who had sworn the deputy into the Klan months earlier. McDaniel could turn to DeLaughter when he needed help in Concordia Parish.[28] In February, McDaniel's friend Jack Seale had been arrested in Ferriday after an officer spotted a car speeding and weaving through town. After pulling the car over and identifying Seale, the officer noticed a typewriter in the back of the car. Recalling that some typewriters had recently been stolen, the officer obtained a search warrant. While no typewriters were found inside the trunk, the policeman did find more than six hundred rounds of ammunition, four loaded ammo clips, a .38 snub-nosed pistol, two rifles, two traffic blinker lights, and two walkie-talkies.[29] Before daylight, Ferriday mayor Woodie Davis heard a knock on his door. Outside was SDG Klansman James Scarborough, who wanted to pay Seale's bond for DWI but couldn't come up with the $250. A short time later, Davis was awakened again by DeLaughter and McDaniel. DeLaughter wanted Seale released without bond. The mayor refused, so McDaniel returned with the money a half hour later, and Seale was freed.[30] Imperial Wizard Robert Shelton heard a few days later about Seale's arrest. There had been rumors that McDaniel was keeping two sets of books, and Shelton, knowing his reputation for mishandling money, wondered if the second set had been in Seale's trunk.[31]

After the rally at Liberty Park ended, two Louisiana UKA officers from Monroe stopped to visit DeLaughter at his home in Ferriday. Later, DeLaughter drove the Klansmen to the sheriff's home, where Cross promised his continued cooperation. The Klansmen responded by providing Cross a card declaring his honorary membership in the UKA.[32]

Also on May 7, McDaniel convened the Mississippi UKA annual convention, held at the Natchez Eola Hotel. Shelton, recognizing that an anti-McDaniel faction was growing within the UKA, urged members to settle their differences and stop fighting. McDaniel reported that for the year 1965, the UKA in Mississippi had collected $19,800 from dues, rallies, and the sale of literature. He had been paid $4,800 in salary, amounting to a quarter of the state organization's reported total income for the year, and had spent $1,600 for office rent in Natchez. Many Klansmen had long contended that McDaniel was only in the Klan to line his pockets, and this report on spending set his opposition to yelping.[33]

By mid-September, anti-McDaniel sentiment had reached a boiling point. On the eighteenth, the UKA held an emergency state meeting at a shed in the woods near Natchez to elect a grand dragon. Thirty-two UKA units, totaling 120 men and 96 voting delegates, were represented. McDaniel and Durrell Fondren from Columbus, Mississippi, were nominated. (Fondren led the anti-McDaniel faction.) On the first two rounds of voting by raised hands, Fondren won by fifteen to twenty votes, but on the third round, McDaniel's supporters claimed, their candidate won, fifty-seven to thirty-three. When the Exalted Cyclops from the Puckett, Mississippi, klavern, asked if the organization was to be operated "by lies," McDaniel told the man to "hit the door." That remark almost ignited a brawl. After McDaniel took the chair, several delegates complained that the election was rigged and walked out, including some members of the Natchez UKA klavern.[34]

On September 27, McDaniel and Fondren, along with Jack Seale and three other Klansmen, met with Shelton at the Airways Inn Motel in Jackson. Before anyone could make their case, Shelton advised that the state officers were not doing their jobs and was furious that McDaniel, on his own, had revoked the charters of seven UKA units whose Klansmen had walked out during the disputed election. Additionally, Shelton reported, he had learned that McDaniel, a married man, was "dating" prostitutes in Concordia Parish and had girlfriends. Shelton also said that L. C. Murray, an SDG Klansman and McDaniel's UKA secretary, was rude to members who called the state office in Natchez.[35]

Then Shelton made a startling announcement: He was dissolving all state positions and would personally operate the Mississippi UKA from his office in Tuscaloosa. Shelton told McDaniel he couldn't soften the blow by giving him the balance of UKA funds because there was no money in the state treasury. McDaniel was out of a job and without a Klan to call home. He had been booted out by the Original Knights, deceived the White Knights during his membership by secretly recruiting for the UKA, and now was ousted by the

UKA. By December he was flat broke, unemployed, and had no money to buy Christmas presents for his family.[36]

ON NEW YEAR'S DAY in 1966, FBI agent Williams and Natchez police officers arrived on the scene of a fire at one of Mayor John Nosser's stores. A group of Klansmen, including Jack Seale, had gathered there. Bone tired from months of dealing with Klan violence, Williams was in no mood for the usual banter with Seale.

"Where's your camera?" Seale yelled as Williams walked by him.

"Jack," he answered, "I came directly from home, and my camera is at the office."

"Well, if this was a nigger joint you'd have it," Seale smirked.

Without thinking, Williams punched Seale in the jaw. Seale struck back, but before the two could exchange many blows, police officers and Klansmen pulled them apart. Williams hated that he lost his cool but acknowledged that punching one of the Klan's most brutal predators felt good.[37]

A few days later, Seale and other Klansmen were in Washington testifying before the House Un-American Activities Committee. The committee had exposed dozens of local Klansmen throughout Concordia Parish and southwestern Mississippi, particularly those who worked at the International Paper Company. Their names were printed in the *Natchez Democrat.* Many were embarrassed and feared they might lose their jobs. As a result, Klan membership plummeted. Among the local men called to testify before the HUAC were McDaniel, Murray, Ernest Avants, Ed Fuller, Ernest Parker, and Clyde, Jack, and James Ford Seale. James Ford Seale reportedly chewed on a cigar during his testimony. All took the Fifth Amendment. Of the eight subpoenaed, only McDaniel and Murray were not implicated in a murder, but they were leading suspects (along with the Seale brothers) in the bombing of Mayor Nosser's house in 1964.[38]

In many ways, 1966 marked the last stand of the traditional Klan in the region. Only the Silver Dollar Group remained firm and continued to attack. Some of the men who had spent all of their energy in fighting civil rights were having a hard time earning a living. Just as McDaniel's Klan life was spiraling in 1966, so was Jack Seale's. Seale's record of trouble was longstanding. When he had enlisted in the Navy in 1944, he had immediately showed contempt for authority and a dependence on alcohol. He was convicted in June 1946 of failure to report to duty without leave, falsification of records, and abusing a private citizen onshore. Two months later, he was convicted of threatening masters-at-arms while onshore and insolence to a petty officer. Punishment was five days' solitary confinement with bread and water.[39] Years later, Seale bragged at the White Knights klavern that he had served prison time in the Navy for running over "some Chinaman in a jeep."[40]

Since 1955, Seale had been charged with a number of offenses in Natchez, including public drunkenness, two charges of drunk driving, disturbing the peace, and speeding. He was prosecuted and convicted in 1959 for drunkenness and disorderly conduct at the G&J Lounge but not prosecuted for pointing a .22 caliber pistol at Ed Fuller and another man that same night. In 1962, his third DWI charge, involving an automobile accident, resulted in a $100 fine that was suspended.[41]

After Shelton ousted McDaniel from the UKA, Seale, the nighthawk, and Murray, the secretary, now were also without a traditional Klan home, although both remained in the SDG. Afterward, when Seale provided a few scant details on Klan activities and membership, the FBI considered paying him as an informant. But the bureau ultimately rejected him as a snitch because of his violent background and the continuing probes into the crimes in which he was believed to be involved. By November, as his garbage disposal business failed and he teetered on financial collapse, Seale went out drinking with Klan business on his mind. As an SDG member, he didn't have to go through a channel of authority to commit a crime, as was required officially (but not always followed) in the traditional Klans. Now free of any binding oath or rulebook, Seale could act on behalf of himself and the SDG when and where he wanted.

At 1 a.m. on November 19, he threw a grenade on the lawn of June Callon, a member of the board of supervisors in Adams County. Although the explosive landed within six feet of Callon's home, there was no damage. Twenty-seven minutes later, a second grenade exploded at Jerry Oberlin's Ritz Jewelry Store on North Commerce. The explosion damaged goods and broke windows. Three witnesses, including two recently hired black policemen, observed a red Volkswagen without a rear bumper racing from the scene. The car was later spotted in the parking lot of the Fountain Lounge. Grenade fragments were embedded in the metal. When Seale came out of the lounge and got in the car, he was arrested on charges of public drunkenness and carrying a concealed weapon. On December 5, he was indicted by a grand jury on the charge of unlawful use of explosives in the jewelry store bombing. The MHSP believed that Oberlin was targeted because he had attended an NAACP meeting the week before.[42] Seale pled guilty and paid a $16.50 fine on the charges of public drunkenness and carrying a concealed weapon. His trial for the explosives charges was set for early 1967.[43]

The FBI knew that Jack Seale would never be convicted in the jewelry store bombing. By the end of 1966, fifteen area Klansmen, including DeLaughter, had been arrested or indicted. In all but one case, however, the charges were either dropped or silently went away. Only two men faced jury trial, but neither was convicted.

CLAUDE FULLER WAS a Klansman without a home until he found shelter with Red Glover's Silver Dollar Group. His welcome came after June 1966, when the forty-three-year-old mill worker, with two accomplices, committed a crime that made as much sense as a man stomping a puppy to death. Prior to that, Fuller had been booted out of the White Knights after months of marauding with the renegade Sligo klavern. Fuller was never implicated, but he was almost certainly involved in the shooting of Richard Joe Butler. Claude's brother, Ed Fuller, Blackie Drane's associate, had been considered a suspect, and there's little chance Claude would not have been part of the attack. Klansmen had gone after Butler because they believed he was spending too much time with the Fuller brothers' niece. After the White Knights hierarchy came down hard on the Sligo group for acting without authority, Fuller went through proper channels with a request to kill a black preacher. He was furious when permission was denied.[44]

In 1963, Fuller had made the runoff for constable of the Kingston area but lost. Two days later, Fuller reported to the sheriff's office that six black males had passed him on the road and fired buckshot into the front fender of his 1958 Ford. Fuller claimed he was so terrified that he stopped and fled into the woods, then watched as the black men returned and torched his car. Then-sheriff Billy Ferrell reported to the FBI that his investigation had determined that Fuller had burned the car himself with two likely purposes: first, to collect the insurance money (Fuller was behind on the payments), and second, to create fear within the white community that gangs of blacks were indiscriminantly attacking white people. On the Saturday after the car was burned, Douglas Byrd, then the grand dragon for the Mississippi Realm of the Original

Knights, asked Ferrell why he had not released news of the arson to the local newspaper. Byrd and Fuller wanted publicity.[45]

One of Fuller's surviving coworkers at International Paper Company, speaking to the *Concordia Sentinel* in 2014 on the condition of anonymity, described Fuller as a frail, withered man who, when he wore a cap, looked like a rat peeking from beneath a collard leaf. To get attention, Fuller felt he needed to establish his own Klan, come up with a grand scheme, and kill a black man. He wanted to do in a big way, to prove himself and make his mark. In late May 1966, he found his target: Ben Chester White, a sixty-seven-year-old farmhand who worked for an Adams County government supervisor. White was known as a gentle, kind, timid man who would never challenge the authority of a white man, the perfect target for Fuller. Along with an IP coworker named James Lloyd Jones and two brothers, one being James Howard Jackson, Fuller went to White's house with the intention of killing him. During the drive, Fuller gave Jones the oath into his Klan, which he called the Cottonmouth Moccasin Gang. Retribution for violating the oath, Fuller warned, would be as fierce as a bite from a cottonmouth.[46]

Fuller called White to come outside to his car. Armed with two automatic pistols, he baited White by asking if he agreed that it was all right for blacks and whites to go to school together, swim in the same pool, and use the same public facilities. White said he guessed it would be okay. When witnesses were spotted, Fuller postponed the killing. Afterward, he told his companions, "See, he is really involved deep in civil rights; he's got to be got rid of."[47]

Two weeks later, on Friday, June 10, Jones arrived as planned at Fuller's house in Kingston. Divorced from his wife, the fifty-seven-year-old Jones had served in the Army during World War II and had done time in the state pen in Mississippi for stealing a car in Port Gibson and in the Louisiana pen for stealing a shotgun in Winnsboro.[48] From his bedroom, Fuller retrieved an M-13 carbine and shotgun. Jones loaded the weapons into his new four-door 1966 Chevrolet Bel Air. Fuller told Jones that Martin Luther King was involved in a march to Jackson and that he intended White's murder to lure King to protest in Natchez. (James Meredith, who had integrated Ole Miss in 1962, had been leading the march from Memphis to Jackson when he had been shot four days earlier. He survived.) If King took the bait, Fuller boasted, the Klan would assassinate the preacher in Natchez. Fuller also claimed that he was leading the mission on the orders of Klan higher-ups; this was a lie.[49]

A short time later, Avants, also an IP employee, arrived. Avants was an overbearing man who once during a gathering shot a black man's cow over an alleged unpaid debt. He had been involved in the beating of Earl Hodges in Franklin County in 1965 and, like Fuller, had been booted out of the White Knights. An alcoholic, Avants had been labeled by Sheriff Odell Anders as crazy and dangerous. In 1965, Avants was so drunk on Jax beer that residents of a fishing camp outside Vidalia ran him off after he strapped a holster on his seven-year-old son and let the boy use a .22 pistol to shoot at logs in the river.[50] Fuller introduced Jones and Avants, who had never met. Avants bragged that he had been to Washington (in January) and had "outsmarted the FBI" during congressional hearings on the Klan.[51]

The three stopped at two country stores along the way to White's home. Jones drank a Coke and ate a pickled sausage, while Fuller and Avants drank more beer. Once at White's, Fuller called the old man outside. Fuller said he would pay White two dollars to help him find a dog. Reluctantly, White got into the car. By then, Fuller and Avants were drunk. As if they had not left a long enough trail of witnesses, they stopped again at a store, got more beer, and bought White a soda pop. Jones was driving and Fuller riding shotgun. White was in the backseat behind Fuller, and Avants was behind Jones.[52]

On Fuller's orders, Jones stopped atop the Pretty Creek Bridge in the Homochitto National Forest. It was dusk. Immediately, Fuller grabbed the automatic carbine, and Avants grabbed the shotgun. As Fuller opened White's door, Avants came around. Fuller told White, "All right, Pop, get out." White said, "Oh, Lord, what have I done to deserve this?" and slumped on the seat. Impatient to kill, Fuller unloaded seventeen rounds into White and the car. Then he told Avants, "Now you shoot him." Avants aimed the long-barreled shotgun and pulled the trigger, releasing a fireball that blew White's brain matter throughout the car and onto a terrified Jones, who was still sitting in the front seat: "I had brains splattered all over me—a piece hit me on the neck. I reached up there with my hand and felt it. I thought I was shot. A big piece, as big as the end of your finger, and there was big spots all over the front of my shirt."[53]

Fuller was too weak from drinking to help dispose of the body. Jones grabbed White's feet while Avants took his hands, and they lifted him over the bridge and dropped him below to the bank of Pretty Creek. They returned to Fuller's shortly after 8 p.m., went inside, and washed their hands. Jones took off his brain-splattered shirt and put on one given him by Fuller. They sat around for an hour without comprehending what fools they were. Jones car, now a crime scene, was too full of bullet holes, blood, guts, and brains to clean. Fuller decided to burn it.[54]

They left at 9 p.m. Minutes later, Fuller parked Jones's car at the Braswell store on Liberty Road before joining the others in Avants's car. The three went to Tiny Lewis's barbecue pit in Natchez. Avants and Fuller each drank yet another beer, while Jones nervously waited in the car for twenty-five minutes. When the two returned, they put a gas can in the trunk. They took Jones to work at the IP plant at 10 p.m. He was instructed that when his shift ended the next morning, he was to walk around the parking lot and pretend to search for his car before reporting to the guardhouse that the vehicle was stolen. "If you sell me down the river, the same thing can happen to you that happened to the old darkey," Fuller warned.[55]

Two hours later, shortly after midnight, Boyd Sojourner called the Adams County Sheriff's Office to report that a car was on fire in front of his home on Upper Kingston Road. At 7:45 a.m., a Natchez telephone operator notified the sheriff's office that an unknown party had called to report that Sojourner had killed a black man at the Pretty Creek Bridge near Kingston. She traced the call to the Billups gas station on US 61 south of Natchez. Sheriff Anders was immediately suspicious. Sojourner was a well-respected farmer and community leader. Anders raced to the station and learned from the attendant that the only person who had used the pay phone had been Claude Fuller, whose wife and son had been sitting in his car at the time. Fuller had left the station just thirty minutes before the sheriff's arrival. Apparently, he was trying to use the same ruse that had failed three years earlier when he burned his own car and blamed others. He had also reportedly threatened Sojourner a few weeks earlier, telling Sojourner "to get the Negroes off his place."[56]

The next day James Carter, a county official and farmer, reported that his employee Ben Chester White had not been seen since 7 p.m. Friday. Mid-afternoon on Sunday, a woman reported that she and her children were wading in the shallow, clear water by the bridge at Upper Pretty Creek near Kingston when they discovered the body of a black male.[57] White lay on his stomach, his body on the sandy bank and his head in the water. A deputy found in his left shirt pocket a wallet containing White's Social Security card and twenty-nine dollars in cash. Fifty-six cents were found in his right rear pocket. Dr. Leo Scanlon's autopsy revealed that White "was in a state of abject poverty." He was wearing no socks. A hole in the toe of one of his boots had been patched with small twisted wires. The upper portion of his face and skull were missing. He had been shot in multiple places, including the heart. His liver was shattered. His aorta had been perforated several times. The top of his head had been blown away.[58] In mid-July, *Jet* magazine ran a photo of White's hideously disfigured face with the caption: "The grisly remains of White at funeral last week tell grim story of horror Mississippi Negroes face day after day."[59]

WITHIN HOURS, Jones simultaneously got scared and got religion. He went to the sheriff's office, and over the days to come, he gave several statements confessing the whole senseless scheme: "I was just as deep in sin as anybody that ever was. I have read the Bible and I have prayed and I had the blood on me and I knowed that I could never enter the Kingdom of Heaven. So I'm telling, and if it costs me my life, this old body of mine, I believe my soul will be in Heaven." After learning that Jones was to be given a polygraph, Fuller checked into a Natchez hospital, suffering from "a nervous attack."[60] Avants called Sheriff Anders one day, stating that he needed to be locked up because he feared he was going to kill somebody. He discussed the White case with FBI agents: "Yeah, I shot that nigger . . . I blew his head off with a shotgun." He insisted that all he had done was "shoot a corpse."[61]

All three men were arrested and charged with murder. Although the eyewitness and physical evidence against the three was overwhelming, Avants was acquitted in a jury trial, Jones's trial ended in a hung jury, and Fuller was never tried. On June 11, 1968, county attorney Edwin E. Benoist Jr., who fought hard for Klan convictions and worked tirelessly to help the FBI in its investigations, informed the bureau that Jones and Avants would not testify because each feared that Claude Fuller's brother, Ed, would kill them.[62] Jones, despite his confessions of being a tortured soul longing to get right with Jesus, obviously feared Ed Fuller on earth more than an afterlife with Satan. On August 15, District Attorney Lennox Forman said he was closing the case against Fuller because of Jones's and Avants's refusal to testify. He added that the Klan had so many connections in Adams County that it would be impossible to convict Claude Fuller. During Avants's trial, the prosecution went through 211 prospective jurors before seating twelve men who quickly acquitted him.[63] Among them were two Klansmen, including John Dawson, who had been a UKA state officer when McDaniel was head of the Mississippi Realm.

As a reward for their efforts to kill a black man, Red Glover accepted Claude Fuller and James Howard Jackson, who had been with Fuller on the first attempt on White's life, into the Silver Dollar Group. This 1967 induction connected the SDG to yet another murder and once again gave Fuller a Klan home.[64] In 2000, ABC's *20/20* reported that the crime had been committed on federal government property. Avants, the only perpetrator still alive, was indicted on federal charges in June, thirty-four years after the murder, and convicted in February 2003. His sentence was life in prison. He died at the age of seventy-two on June 14, 2004, having served more than four years after his arrest.

1967

12

CODE NAME: WHARBOM

BY 1967, THE NATION'S interest in civil rights in the South was fading as riots broke out in the big cities in the North and protests against the Vietnam War raged on. At the same time, President Lyndon Johnson promoted his program to end poverty and pushed to abolish discrimination in the selection of juries and in housing sales and rentals. His supportive majority in Congress that had passed the Civil Rights Bill of 1964 and the Voting Rights Act of 1965, however, had vanished. Elsewhere, young leaders in the "black power" movement created a schism within the traditional civil rights structure that Dr. Martin Luther King feared would stop the momentum.

One of the emerging black leaders, Baton Rouge native H. Rap Brown, a twenty-three-year-old who thought the United States should be split into two racially divided territories, chilled white people when he warned that if "America don't come around, we've got to burn America down, brother." Brown had followed Stokely Carmichael as chairman of the Student Nonviolent Coordinating Committee. As Carmichael moved toward the Black Power Party, whose members declared war on police, SDG Klansmen considered Brown and Carmichael the new enemies. When the FBI questioned an SDG member in Vidalia about Klan violence, the Klansman was incensed that agents weren't harassing Carmichael, who he believed was as responsible for the unrest in America as the NAACP and the communists. The Klan's war against the integration of schools, neighborhoods, and public buildings was far from over.

WHARLEST JACKSON wanted nothing more from this world than to be treated like a man and to be allowed a fair chance to give his family a good life. He was willing to outwork and out-sacrifice anybody for the opportunity. A native of DeLeon Springs, Florida, twenty miles inland from Daytona Beach, Jackson had moved to Natchez in his youth. His father was a minister. When serving in the Korean War, Jackson risked his life to push a comrade into a fox-hole and out of the way of an enemy shell. Although he returned home a hero, that label embarrassed him. In Chicago in 1952, he met the girl of his dreams on a blind date. Exerlena, a fifteen-year-old Natchez native, had moved to the big city with a girlfriend to find employment and was working in a factory, making bulletproof jackets for American soldiers. From the beginning, Exerlena called him by his last name, "Jackson." His humility and selflessness appealed to her.[1]

After marrying in 1954, they moved to Natchez. The family attended church every Sunday at St. Paul African Methodist Episcopal Church and returned home afterward for a feast. Jackson raised hogs, loved to hunt and fish, played jacks with his four daughters on the front porch, and wrestled with his son. He worked at Armstrong Tire, where his best friend was George Metcalfe, twenty years his senior. The two were elected officers of the reactivated NACCP in Natchez, with Metcalfe serving as president and Jackson as treasurer.[2]

Their friendship intensified following the attempt on Metcalfe's life in 1965. Both Jackson and Exerlena cared for Metcalfe during his year of convalescence, and Jackson's work at the NAACP increased. Jackson became so protective of his best friend that he insisted on chauffeuring him to work. In effect, he became Metcalfe's bodyguard. The two developed a habit of checking Jackson's pickup for bombs. Jackson routinely looked under the hood, and Metcalfe checked beneath the seat. They carried their lunches from home and ate together at the plant. By late 1966, Jackson had decided to step down as treasurer of the NAACP to have more time for his ailing wife, who had been diagnosed with lupus, but he remained on the board of directors.[3]

In early 1967, Armstrong Tire created a third "chemical mixer" position to handle an increase in production. The position was dangerous because it required the blending of raw rubber with a high-octane gasoline that was used to cut the material into a liquid, manageable form. Even so, Jackson wanted the job. All of his working life, he had held as many as three jobs at a time to support his family. In 1967, in addition to his job at the plant, he cut hair part-time at a barbershop and served as assistant director and collected burial insurance premiums for Archie Curtis's funeral home. (The Klan had beaten Curtis in 1964 because of his civil rights work.) The Armstrong mixer position paid seventeen cents more per hour than the $2.90 an hour Jackson was earning in the refine mill.[4] The additional $6.80 per week would increase Jackson's annual salary to $6,385.60 (approximately $44,000 today), and the extra income would mean that Exerlena could quit her job as a cook at nearby Jefferson College.[5]

Jackson was one of 127 men eligible for the job, which had previously been held only by white men.[6] He and two white men were the only employees to apply. Because of his seniority, Jackson got the promotion. He talked to Metcalfe and Mississippi NAACP field secretary Charles Evers about whether accepting it would cause him trouble with white employees. Evers predicted it would but advised Jackson to take the job, despite rumors circulating at the plant that any black man who took a better job traditionally held by a white man would be taken care of by the Klan. Jackson, however, expressed no fear of reprisal.[7]

Jackson's white coworkers liked him. Though he was taciturn, they found him cooperative and dependable. Jackson didn't have a troublemaker reputation, as Metcalfe did, among the white employees. Only one person he knew was upset over the promotion—his wife. Exerlena had long been bothered that Jackson drove Metcalfe to work after the car bombing in 1965. "George didn't have a house full of children like Jackson," she would tell the *Concordia Sentinel* before her death in 2009. "But Jackson didn't pay me no attention. He was quiet and determined to live his life." Although Exerlena was consumed by fear over the danger she felt her husband faced by taking a job over two white men, Jackson appeared unconcerned and told her he had amiable working relationships with the white men on his shift.[8]

He began training for his new job on February 20, 1967, working his regular 4 p.m. to midnight shift, with Metcalfe still sharing a ride to work. But on February 27, Jackson was moved to the day shift, and for the first time the friends went to work separately. At 3:15 p.m. that day, forty-five minutes before his shift ended, Jackson and a white coworker agreed to work four hours overtime. Jackson clocked out at 8:01 p.m. It was dark and raining. He walked a half-block to his pickup, a 1958 green half-ton Chevrolet, parked west of the plant where Concord Street, Kelly Street, and Brenham Avenue converged. After traveling two blocks west on the winding avenue, Jackson turned north onto Minor Street. He had crossed three streets when, at a point a half block from Pine (Martin Luther King Street today), he switched on his left turn blinker. A thunderous boom jarred Natchez, shattering the windows of nearby homes. The pickup veered to the right and splintered a utility pole. Two and a half blocks away at No. 9 College Drive, Exerlena heard the deafening roar and bolted up from her sickbed. Somehow she knew. "Oh, Lord, that's Jackson!" she wailed. "That's Jackson!"[9]

A minute later a Natchez patrolman was on the scene as residents throughout the black neighborhood near the tire plant emerged from their homes into the rainy, cold night. It took a few minutes before anyone could figure out whose lifeless body rested on the slick pavement of Minor Street. As an ambulance arrived, the identity of the dead man became known. Exerlena, joined by friends, raced to the hospital. She followed a blood trail from the ambulance into the emergency room, where she saw her husband's body lying on a gurney with no medical personnel in sight.[10] She was unaware that Jackson was already dead. She would tell *Jet* magazine a few days later that, as she pleaded for a doctor, Sheriff Odell Anders, standing nearby, told a deputy, "Get her out of here. She won't be no help; all she's gonna do is holler."[11]

At 9:15 p.m., Natchez Police Department detective Charles C. Bahin notified the FBI office at Jackson of the bombing. At 11:35 p.m., acting attorney general Ramsey Clark in Washington requested a full FBI probe. A short time later, Special Agent in Charge Roy K. Moore of the Jackson field office rushed to the scene with a squad of eighteen agents. J. Edgar Hoover ordered Inspector Joseph A. Sullivan to spearhead the probe, which was given the code name WHARBOM. Two lab experts were dispatched from Washington to process the crime scene.[12]

The explosion had separated the roof of the cab, the hood, and the driver's door from the main frame, while the passenger door remained attached by one hinge. All of the window glass was shattered. Bits of Jackson's flesh were found in the wreckage and on neighboring lawns, and one of his shoes was blown fifty yards away into a ditch. Inexplicably, all four tires and the spare remained inflated and attached to the crushed frame.[13]

Jackson's body was taken from the hospital to Curtis Funeral Home. Pathologist Dr. Leo J. Scanlon, who eight months earlier had performed the autopsy of Ben Chester White, disclosed after his examination that death had been instantaneous. Jackson's buttocks and abdomen were ripped open, his aorta severed. Scanlon noted there was a "complete divergence of the mesoteric root from the intestine."[14] In 1965 and 1966, *Jet* had published pictures of the injured Metcalfe in his hospital room and the disfigured face of the murdered White. In 1967, the magazine published two graphic photographs—one from the back and one frontal—of Jackson's body lying on its side atop a table at the Curtis Funeral Home. His buttocks appeared as a mass of chunky flesh torn to bits.

FBI lab experts discovered only one significant piece of evidence—a leg wire from an electric blasting cap used for seismographic work in oil-field exploration and production. The cap was used to charge what was obviously a significant amount of dynamite or a form of nitroglycerin, but the explosive material was water soluble, and all evidence had been washed away by rain.[15] The investigation determined that a high-explosive charge had been placed under the truck's cab outside the frame directly below the driver's seat. But what had the bomber used to activate the blasting cap that detonated the nitroglycerin? Immediate interest was focused on the wiring of the taillights, brake lights, and left rear turn indicator. The taillights had been activated when Jackson turned on his headlights for the short ride home, while the brake lights would have been used any number of times before he came to the point on Minor Street where the explosion occurred. Evidence indicated that at that location, Jackson would have as a matter of routine turned on his left turn signal for the upcoming turn onto Pine Street. Lab experts surmised that an "electric blasting cap could be caused to detonate when the left turn signal was turned on by stripping insulation from the turn signal wire, attaching one wire of the (blasting) cap to the turn signal wire and other wire of the cap to ground." It was a simple but deadly procedure that would have taken less than five minutes to execute.[16]

The night after the murder, Evers led a meeting at Rose Hill Baptist Church. The next day, two thousand blacks marched to the Armstrong parking lot to protest the employment of Klansmen at the plant. Natchez police chief J. T. Robinson called the murder "low, low, low." He predicted an arrest, but blacks were not convinced. Mississippi governor Paul Johnson called the killing "heinous and senseless," while Mayor John Nosser described it as "a wanton slaying." Local white legislators also publicly condemned the murder, while a $35,000 reward—$25,000 from the City of Natchez and $10,000 from Armstrong—was established for the arrest and conviction of the killers. At a meeting on the courthouse steps, Evers told the crowd that the gathering was in part a protest of "the social inertia of our white brothers who piously condemn violence after it occurs and refuse to work for democracy in the absence of violence." A grief-stricken Exerlena held her five children close in the days to follow and wondered why her husband had been killed over something as simple as a promotion.[17] But was her husband the main target?

IN ADDITION TO analyzing the crime scene, the pickup, and the Jackson autopsy, the bureau launched an investigation that eventually would involve 180 agents following leads throughout the South. Unpaid overtime hours reached 8,396. Bureau automobiles were driven more than 200,000 miles. By the end of 1967, the expense of the probe reached $300,000, the current equivalent of $2 million.[18] WHARBOM brought the bureau to the realization that though Natchez was the heart of Klan violence, Concordia Parish was its soul. While Natchez was the center of general Klan communications through the Armstrong Tire and Rubber Company plant and the International Paper Company mill, Concordia was the Klan's protective den, the sheriff's office its protector. The only exception was when a segment of the Klan world intolerant of drinking, gambling, and prostitution attempted to shut down the Morville Lounge and the bawdy houses that were paying the sheriff piles of cash to operate. Otherwise, deputies joined the Klan in its projects and informed individual Klansmen when the FBI was asking questions about them.

In 1967, Concordia sheriff Cross needed the Klan's political support more than ever as he faced three formidable opponents in his reelection bid. There were elections in Mississippi, too, but every county there was guaranteed a new sheriff, since the incumbents could not serve two consecutive terms. In addition to the Jackson car bombing, the FBI was intensively investigating a number of other cases, including its first probe into the killing of Joseph Edwards and a second look at the three-year-old murder of Frank Morris. A number of beatings and arsons, most in Concordia Parish, were also reviewed. The bureau placed the ongoing probes into the Morville Lounge and the 1965 beating of William Cliff Davis in the Ferriday jail under its WHARBOM umbrella. The FBI was now certain that the violence would never end until its agents talked to every known Klansman, rooted out their hiding places, and infiltrated the SDG so thoroughly that Red Glover's growing paranoia would stop him from acting and break up his terrorist cell.

In the first days of the investigation, agents interviewed 334 persons living in a 15-block area along Jackson's 6-block route from the plant to the site of the explosion. No one reported seeing anything suspicious. Most people had been inside their homes since it was dark, cold, and raining.[19] After reviewing personnel records of current and former Klan members at Armstrong, agents followed up with interviews of every known Klansman, especially those with violent tendencies and backgrounds. The prime suspect was Red Glover. In the days ahead, informants pointed to other suspects as well, and agents set out to account for their whereabouts at the time of the bombing. Agents were most interested in interviewing members of the SDG.

E. D. Morace, who had implicated Glover, James "Red" Lee, and Sonny Taylor in the Metcalfe bombing, was among the first to be contacted. Morace provided one of the first big leads when he reported that in early December 1966 he had accompanied Glover to the home of Elden Hester, known by SDG Klansmen as the "Junk Man" (his code name as the handler of explosives). Hester was a quiet man considered peculiar by many of his Armstrong coworkers. He lived in Franklin County, Mississippi, and had been a member of Clyde Seale's White Knights klavern and a customer of the mechanic Earl Hodges. Inside his home, Hester had shown Morace a number of canisters he was storing for Glover. They were labeled Nitramon S and Nitramon S Primer, powerful explosives manufactured by E. I. Dupont and used locally for seismic work in the oil field. Hester also showed Morace a portrait of Confederate States of America president Jefferson Davis that had been stolen from the lobby of the Natchez hospital bearing his name. The painting had been stolen, Hester said, so that Davis would not have to look down at the "mixed racial status of the hospital" following integration.[20]

THE BUREAU HAD LOOKED at developing E. L. McDaniel as an informant as early as 1965, but he was considered completely untrustworthy. However, by late 1966, after his ouster as grand dragon of the Mississippi UKA, McDaniel was unemployed and broke, and he became an informant. Anything McDaniel said was likely taken with a grain of salt, but the FBI had to consider the information. Contacted a few days after the Jackson bombing, McDaniel claimed that he had been approved for membership in the SDG but declined to join, an obvious lie since the bureau was beginning to understand that admission into the terrorist Klan unit came only at the invitation of Red Glover. Secondly, McDaniel claimed that in late December 1966, SDG members were told to establish alibis because "something was going to happen" to Metcalfe in early January 1967. To thwart an attempt on Metcalfe's life, McDaniel said that he took it upon himself to call the men he considered the likely suspects (without identifying them to the bureau). He claimed he disguised his voice and said that if anything happened to Metcalfe, "We are going to arrest you." McDaniel told his FBI handler, special agent Benjamin Graves, that he was satisfied that this deception had ended the plot against Metcalfe. A furious

Graves, who had contacted McDaniel in mid-December, twice in January, and twice in February prior to the Jackson bombing, asked, "Why are you just now telling me this?" McDaniel answered, "It just slipped my mind."[21]

Later, as the bureau's second probe into the Morris murder intensified, McDaniel had another "Oh, by the way" moment. For three years, Frank De-Laughter and law enforcement in general had been the main suspects in the Morris arson. But McDaniel had another story to tell the bureau that may have been designed to take the heat off his friend DeLaughter and place the focus on a group of Silver Dollar Klansmen who paid no attention to McDaniel's Klan authority. McDaniel claimed that Morace, James Scarborough, Tommie Lee Jones, and T. L. Torgersen had committed the arson. McDaniel's dislike for Jones dated back to 1963, when Jones had launched a wrecking crew attack on his own without seeking McDaniel's authority. McDaniel said Morace had asked him to authorize Jones and Torgersen, now UKA members, to come to Ferriday and whip Frank Morris for flirting with white women. He also claimed that Morace had requested that if the four men were ever arrested, to rush to Concordia and get them out of jail. When asked why he didn't tell the FBI this three years earlier, McDaniel answered that he feared those Klans-men would harm him if he talked. For a man who counted as a close friend murderous Jack Seale—feared by other Klansmen—the claim seems suspect.[22]

Morace's FBI handlers eventually asked him whether he was involved in the Morris arson. He acknowledged that during 1964 Ferriday Klansmen had made allegations against Morris, including that he was flirting with white women, that he was allowing interracial liaisons between white women and black men in the back of the shop, and that Morris had insulted Frank De-Laughter's wife by trying to make a date with her, a story the FBI had dis-counted. As investigator for the local Klan klavern, Morace said he found the allegations to be untrue and that a project to whip Frank Morris had never been approved. Yet he did offer one possible motive for the arson—that "hard feelings" had resulted between Morris and the deputy over a pair of cowboy boots and DeLaughter's pattern of not paying Morris for his work. Morris certainly was not the first merchant to be stiffed by the deputy, who was well known in the parish for his bullying tactics, including taking whiskey or stock off a merchant's shelf without paying.[23]

Another informant corroborated Morace's story. Convicted felon Coonie Poissot, the Klansman DeLaughter had run out of Ferriday in late 1965 af-ter Poissot witnessed the deputy's apprehension of William Cliff Davis prior to his beating, was secretly returned to the area, where he showed the FBI Klan haunts and outlined several projects in which he was a participant along with Red Glover. Poissot said that before he fell out with DeLaughter, he had spent time riding with him in his patrol car. During those rides in late 1964, he said DeLaughter claimed to have beaten Morris because he "wasn't acting right." On the night prior to the arson, again on a ride in the patrol car, Poissot said the deputy was furious with Morris because he had refused to extend DeLaughter any more credit and failed to repair a pair of shoes without payment in advance. Poissot also told agents that two months later in February 1965, DeLaughter recruited him and Preston Conway, a dealer and bouncer for Blackie Drane, to steal fishing seines and netting from the Louisiana Wildlife and Fisheries Department warehouse in Ferriday.[24]

There was more. Poissot said that in late November 1965, he had been riding with Glover and Kenneth Norman Head when Glover bragged about the Metcalfe bombing three months earlier. In a signed statement, Poissot said, "I recall saying something to the effect that it wasn't a good job and Red Glover said, 'If I had wanted to kill him I would have put the thing under the dashboard instead of under the hood,' or words to that effect. I recall that at this point Kenneth Head spoke up and said something about Red Glover being an expert in explosives. Head said further that he and another Klansman acted as lookouts while the explosives were being placed in Metcalfe's car."[25] While no mention was made of Sonny Taylor, who as an informant later acknowledged his involvement to the bureau, Poissot's statement corroborated that Glover was the mastermind. Such statements, however, pointed to the problem with informants: They were often self-serving and rarely incriminated themselves in acts of violence. Additionally, their identities are protected, and they can't be forced to testify. Jim Ingram, the legendary FBI agent involved in many major Mississippi cases, from the Neshoba County murders, known as Mississippi Burning (MIBURN), to WHARBOM, said that SDG informants would "only lead you to a certain point and stop there." More importantly, there was a line of incrimination involving murder that no SDG Klansman, unlike those involved in MIBURN, would ever cross.[26]

FROM MORACE, the FBI learned that eight Klansmen met for coffee at the Chef Truck Stop Café in Vidalia on February 20, 1967, one week before the Jackson bombing. In addition to Glover and Morace, those in attendance included Head, Scarborough, Hester, and Donald Holland, a feed mill operator from Meadville. Morace said the other two men in the group were both Armstrong employees, but he didn't know their names. One was in his early twenties. During the meeting, Glover informed Morace that the turn signals on his GMC pickup were faulty and needed repair before he could get an inspection sticker. He asked Morace, who was a mechanic, how the turn signal wiring worked. Morace told him. He also told agents that six or seven months earlier Glover and Jones had suggested that someone shoot or bomb the black man driving Metcalfe to work. Jones had just returned home from back surgery at the time of the Jackson bombing and seemed an unlikely participant.[27] In the thousands of pages of FBI documents on the case, there is no other mention of Jackson being specifically targeted, whereas Glover's passion to kill Metcalfe never cooled.

In May 1967, Taylor asked Glover about the Jackson bombing; specifically, he wanted to know how the bomb was timed to go off. Glover answered it was "no problem," that by connecting the bomb to the turn signal wire, the explosive would not detonate until the turn signals were used. This was information that only the killer would know.[28]

Three days after the bombing, Roy Moore relayed to headquarters that agent John Pfeifer, still hot on the trail of Cross and DeLaughter in the Morville Lounge case, had advised Natchez resident agent Clarence Prospere about Hester. Prospere told Moore that if agents could confirm the description of Hester's home as described by Morace, then maybe the bureau could obtain a search warrant.[29]

On March 16, a source told the bureau that Glover's daughter-in-law, the wife of his stepson James Watts, had confided to a girlfriend that a large quantity of nitroglycerine and a painting of Jefferson Davis had been stored in the attic of the Wattses' Vidalia home a short time prior to the Jackson bombing. That information indicated that the cache seen in Hester's home in early December might have been moved. Inspector Sullivan immediately asked Hoover for a search warrant of the Watts and Hester homes. "It is entirely reasonable to presume," Sullivan wrote the FBI director, "that a portion of these explosives could have been used in the preparation of a bomb placed under Jackson's truck."[30] Hoover rejected the requests, stating that in the Watts case the bureau could not establish probable cause "that the instrumentality of the crime, the fruits of the crime or contraband, is presently at the place to be searched." Hoover also advised there was no evidence the material had been transported interstate, nor that it was connected to the bombing. Even if the explosives were in the attic, they "would constitute neither an instrumentality nor a fruit of a federal crime. Explosives are not contraband under Federal law." He suggested that local authorities were in the best legal position to pursue the matter, adding that the theft of the Davis portrait was a state crime.[31]

In connection with the Hester matter, it was also surmised that there was insufficient data to obtain a search warrant. District Attorney Lennox Forman in Meadville took the same stand on behalf of the state. But in Vidalia on April 17, a month after the search warrant request was denied, FBI agents Reesie Timmons and Benjamin Graves received permission from James Watts to search his attic. They found a .32 caliber Smith and Wesson hidden in a white sock but nothing else.[32]

The next day, at Harrisonburg, Louisiana, Glover picked up Taylor at his home for a drive to rural Franklin Parish. Of average height but stout and strong, Taylor was an Original Knight when taken into the SDG in 1965. He earned his living in logging and road construction and would lose the use of his right eye following a chainsaw accident. Prone to heavy drinking, he was a mean drunk, and deputies with the Catahoula Parish Sheriff's Office always approached him in pairs when he was causing trouble. His stepsister recalled a day when Taylor beat his own son with an automobile fan belt after the child accidentally cut down a potato plant while hoeing the family garden. He was known to hoard whole milk in the refrigerator while making his children drink a mixture of powdered milk and water.[33]

Fearing the FBI was following him and that agents had "bugged" his vehicle, Glover steered his pickup along an evasive route to a farm in the community of Baskin on Louisiana Highway 15, thirty-five miles southeast of Monroe. Glover pulled into the graveled drive of a vacant house owned by Hester and handed Taylor his sawed-off sixteen-gauge shotgun to guard them as they entered the house. From a corner of the attic above a storeroom in the back, Glover retrieved five boxes. When Taylor prepared to open one, an army ammunition box, Glover snapped, "Don't look in the boxes and you won't know anything." One box contained railroad fuses like one found outside a Concordia Parish nightclub burned by a Glover wrecking crew in 1964. (The club's owner, Reef Freeman, had made the mistake of doing business with someone other than Blackie Drane.) Glover also handed Taylor a child's toy drum— colored red, white, and blue—containing primer cord. Wrapped in a tarpaulin were eight to ten old shotguns Glover called "nigger guns" (he and Hester had stolen them in previous months from the homes of African Americans), along with shovels, axes, and tools. Glover told Taylor a seismographic company employee had obtained the "stuff"—meaning explosives—but offered no other information. They loaded the material into Glover's truck and returned to Harrisonburg. Taylor never knew where Glover relocated the cache.[34]

A key piece of information determined early in the probe was that the blasting cap's leg wire found at the Jackson crime scene—a twenty-gauge duplex copper wire with yellow insulation—was manufactured by the Hercules Company in Wilmington, Delaware. It was used primarily with seismographic electric blasting caps. The bureau learned that this particular wire was produced prior to the summer of 1965. In Brookhaven, Mississippi, agents learned that the Southwestern Pipe Corporation had employed Robert Luther Hart as facilities manager from 1965 until November 1966, giving him daily access to thousands of explosives and Hercules blasting caps identical to the one used in the Jackson bombing. Agents also identified Hart as a Klansman who had attended SDG meetings in Mississippi in the months prior to the bombing.[35]

ON MARCH 4, 1967, five days after the bombing, Pfeifer and fellow FBI agent John Brady pulled into the driveway of Glover's home on Lee Avenue in Vidalia. This was the first interview with Glover following the bombing and the first of many to be conducted by Pfeifer over the next four years. Glover said that after he completed his midnight to 8 a.m. shift on February 27, he might have stopped for milk before returning home, as he often did. He ate breakfast, read the paper, and went to bed. While he was asleep, his wife went to work at noon at a five-and-dime store in Natchez. He awoke at 2:30 p.m., hung out, and later ate supper with his elderly mother, who resided in his home. He wasn't certain but thought he might have visited with John Henry, a former Vidalia policeman, that afternoon. At 9 p.m., his wife returned from her job. He dressed and went to work at 10:45. As he approached the plant, he observed a roped-off area on Minor Street, where he later learned Jackson had been bombed almost two hours earlier.[36]

The next day, as Pfeifer and Brady drove a bureau car along Lee Avenue, they were hailed by Glover, who wanted to let them know that in his opinion blacks might have been involved in the Jackson bombing. On March 11, Glover told the agents he had forgotten to mention that on February 27 on his way home from work he stopped at an auto parts store in Vidalia at 8:30 a.m.

to buy a wheel cylinder kit. Additionally, he said that at 7 p.m., an hour before the bombing, he had driven by Head's house for a brief visit.[37] As Glover's story evolved, it became obvious not only that was he trying to cover his tracks but that he had several opportunities to plant the bomb in Jackson's pickup. The bureau, however, would never find an eyewitness.

In interviews with Pfeifer and other agents in the months ahead, Glover, unlike the other SDG members, would never even admit to being in the Klan. He denied having heard of the SDG and denied knowing many of the Klansmen he had recruited. During the summer, Glover told agents the man who killed Jackson was a "nut" and advised them to "keep looking for that maniac." Pfeifer would recall in 2011 that Glover "was the kind of guy you would pass and never remember . . . But he was in absolute and total emotional control of himself, as if he were standing 200 yards off and studying you. It was like talking to the great stone face. You could tell he was analyzing each question we would ask him and wonder where did these guys get this question from."[38]

Throughout 1967, Glover's closest associates would find him happy one day, consumed with hatred the next, and almost suicidal another. Pfeifer believed this unevenness displayed a schizophrenic personality. "I have lived a full life," Glover once said, lamenting that the FBI was on his tail from daylight to dark and predicting that the bureau would frame him for a crime. Indeed, agents were following his every move and that of other SDG Klansmen. Glover observed agents taking photos of him in his pickup at a traffic light in Natchez. Agents visited his home constantly, and neighbors, friends, and Klan associates informed him that bureau men were asking questions about him.[39]

Glover was by nature suspicious, and by the spring he knew some of his own men were talking to the FBI. How else did the bureau learn about the SDG meeting in Lismore two months prior to the Metcalfe bombing? By what other means would agents know to question him about the murder attempt? Pfeifer's arrival in March of 1966, two months after the failed bombing of David Whatley's home, had coincided with an end to Klan beatings and murders in Concordia Parish. From that point on, Glover's primary interest was to redeem himself in his own mind by seeking vengeance against Metcalfe, whom he despised with an unyielding passion. And if he got Jackson, too, that would be a lesson to other blacks who dared take what had been traditionally been a white man's job at the tire plant. Pfeifer believed until his death in 2012 that Glover's determination to kill Metcalfe and his growing paranoia concerning his subordinates led Glover alone to plant the bomb under Jackson's truck. Seasoned FBI agents thought the same thing. Police Chief Robinson, who had known Glover most of his life, also was convinced that Glover acted alone.[40]

There was no discussion of explosives at the meeting Glover convened at the truck stop in Vidalia a week before the Jackson bombing. By then, he knew all he needed to know about explosives, and from Morace he learned how to wire the turn signals. In the Metcalfe bombing, the explosion had almost injured white employees leaving the plant, a possibility Glover had not considered. He had followed Jackson's route home so many times that he knew precisely when Jackson would engage the left turn signal, and he knew that the only potential collateral damage would be the black residents who lived along the street. As the lone bomber, Glover would eliminate the possibility of loose tongues.[41]

The FBI's surveillance soon prompted members of Glover's inner circle to come clean—to a point. Many SDG members suspected in murder cases admitted their Klan affiliations and that they had attended the SDG fish fry in Lismore, but, out of loyalty and fear of violating their Klan oaths, none admitted to murder nor implicated others. So successful, however, was the FBI's infiltration into the SDG that Jack Seale and L. C. Murray, McDaniel's best friends and members of his UKA cabinet, became informants. Like McDaniel, both Seale and Murray were financially destitute and out of work by early 1967. Seale's financial condition was so fragile that his utilities had been disconnected over nonpayment. For some time, the FBI was hesitant to pay Seale and Murray to inform. At the time, Seale had yet to be tried for the bombing of Oberlin Jewelers, and he was known to be involved in the murders of Henry Dee and Charles Moore. Agent Prospere and Chief Robinson considered Murray a suspect in the 1964 bombing of Natchez mayor Joe Nosser's home. In a memo to FBI assistant director Alex Rosen, Inspector Sullivan wrote that the two Klansmen "have been moving forces in Klan and SDG activities in the Natchez-Vidalia area since these groups initiated their activities." Their social status in the communities where they lived, however, had deteriorated to the point that "they are regarded as undesirables," Sullivan noted, adding that Seale "is down and very nearly out." During the previous weeks, each had provided the FBI with histories of the SDG's origin and activities but now faced leaving the area to find employment. The only way they could remain locally would be as paid informants.[42]

"We have, however, never really convinced them that there is a quid pro quo potential in dealing with the FBI," Sullivan continued. "They have done some work for us but they keep expecting trouble for their efforts or, at best, to be paid off in chitchat, which, however pleasant, is hardly edible." Pointing out that more than a half dozen murders, a series of bombings, and numerous beatings, shootings, and arsons were suspected SDG projects, Sullivan advised that it "would be naïve to anticipate that these men will involve themselves in the things they tell us. They will, we feel sure, tell us of other important things they know. If their disclosures lead ultimately to their own exposure, as may well happen, they are willing to face these problems when they arise." Sullivan concluded: "Unusual situations call for different treatment than the flow of our regular business is afforded. Our crimes here are wanton and senseless products of a violent apparatus that is motivated by hatred and bigotry. This is a major apparatus in stature and will require special handling to overcome."[43]

In another memo to Rosen, Sullivan addressed a question of immunity. Sonny Taylor, as a paid informant, told the bureau about Glover's journey to Baskin, Louisiana, to retrieve and relocate explosives and weapons. Taylor would later admit his involvement in the Metcalfe bombing, but he wanted a letter stating he wouldn't be prosecuted. Attorney General Ramsey Clark ultimately denied Hoover's request for immunity for Taylor. Despite that, Sullivan held out hope that Taylor would agree to be a witness in the Metcalfe case if it were prosecuted. Additionally, Sullivan advised, the bureau had used Taylor to create conflict within the SDG. He had loaned a chainsaw to Glover, who had given it to Hester. When the bureau found out about it, agents asked Taylor to make a stink about it within SDG circles. Taylor called Glover a thief, and SDG members took sides before Glover ultimately admitted Taylor's accusation was true.[44]

Informants like Taylor, despite their own sins, could be used to "neutralize the apparatus behind our crimes," Sullivan wrote Rosen. "The deterrent effect of solving these crimes even without immediate prosecution would be enormous." Sullivan also reminded Rosen: "We know that Raleigh Jackson Glover has plans for future violence that will bring us back again into the Natchez area with problems of such gravity that further specials will be necessary. This is about the fifth occasion we have required a special at Natchez."[45] While no one was ever arrested and prosecuted in the Metcalfe bombing or the Jackson, Morris, or Edwards murders, the FBI did effectively neutralize the SDG by the end of 1967. Informants were the key. At one meeting for coffee in Ferriday, four SDG members were in attendance. Later, when all four reported to their handlers, the FBI had a view of the meeting from all four perspectives. But none of the Klansmen reported admissions of murder on the others' part.

Glover's thievery contributed greatly to the SDG's demise. He had stolen liquor from the Bonanza Club at Ferriday at a time when Morace was working there as a bouncer. When Morace confronted him about it, Glover initially lied but later confessed. Glover had also convinced a number of SDG Klansmen to purchase automatic rifles from him as part of the offensive on the looming race war. But in 1967, those who had purchased the rifles or automatic conversion kits learned that Glover was making a profit off of his Klan brothers. Many of his closest associates were upset by the news, but Glover slowly regained the confidence of some. All the while, the constant pressure of FBI agents tailing their every move put most into retreat for good.

During the spring of 1967, Glover's wife learned of his longtime affair with a female coworker at the Armstrong plant and threatened to kill the woman. Glover quickly gave in to his wife's demands to move to Kentwood, in southeastern Louisiana, where many of her relatives lived. Glover bought a house there but continued to work at Armstrong; he lived in various rentals and went to Kentwood on his days off. His paranoia reached a fever pitch during the summer, when he was arrested for the theft of a pasture mower in Jefferson County, Mississippi. A newspaper story about his booking caused him great embarrassment. Even though an FBI agent discovered the mower on Glover's property in Kentwood, District Attorney Forman failed to get a grand jury indictment in the case, reporting that there was no eyewitness to the crime.[46]

By late summer, several SDG members, including Glover, were convinced that Tommie Lee Jones, by now one of four new suspects in the Morris murder, was informing on the Klan. His propensity for talking too much while drinking was a concern to all. In August, agents confronted Jones with their knowledge of his involvement in the attempted kidnapping of Morris's friend James White in February 1964, as well as other acts of violence. Jones had initially been hostile to agents in early interviews, but the details they had gathered clearly stunned him. He admitted he had committed violent acts but said they all fell short of murder. He refused to name any participants in any crimes and refused to admit or deny any involvement in the Morris murder, claiming that the FBI could never arrest him in that case without also arresting DeLaughter, a man Jones said was more involved in the Klan than the FBI realized. A few days later, Jones hired a lawyer and quit talking. By September, a handful of SDG members met along the riverfront park atop the bluff at Natchez to decide whether to kill Jones. While there was strong support for his murder, especially from James "Red" Lee, Glover nixed the idea.[47]

By the end of 1967, the FBI had reached a dead end in the Jackson, Morris, and Edwards murders. The bureau had located no eyewitnesses and, despite tantalizing physical evidence, could not link the murders to the killers or build an evidentiary trail. Plus, none of the informants would have been willing to testify in court. In October 1967, assistant attorney general for civil rights John Doar called two informants to testify during the federal trial of the killers of Michael Schwerner, James Chaney, and Andrew Goodman. "All of you probably have an initial resentment against paid informers," Doar told jurors during his closing argument. But he pointed out that without informants, no arrests would ever have been made in the 1964 murders.[48]

While the WHARBOM murder investigations fizzled, the probe into the Morville Lounge gained momentum. At the same time, Pfeifer drove to Natchez to talk with Sullivan about the potential of a federal prosecution in the 1965 William Cliff Davis beating by DeLaughter, Drane, and Fuller. Pfeifer suggested that because DeLaughter was a sworn deputy, he could be charged under federal statues regarding police brutality. Sullivan discussed the matter with Justice Department lawyers in Washington, and soon that case, too, was placed under WHARBOM. However, the results of the presidential election of 1968 slowed the investigations. Republican Richard Nixon replaced Democrat Lyndon Johnson in January 1969, which meant there would be new U.S. attorneys appointed throughout the country. Pfeifer said the transition of the cases within the U.S. Attorney's Office in Shreveport slowed but did not hamper the Morville case.[49]

In 1970, DeLaughter, Drane, and Fuller were tried for the Davis beating in federal court in Monroe. All three defendants seemed smugly unconcerned with the government's case until prosecutors called William Cliff Davis to the stand. Since he had disappeared from Concordia Parish in 1965, the trio never expected to see Davis again, but the FBI had found him in Chicago and escorted him to Louisiana to testify. Pfeifer watched DeLaughter's eyes grow wide in disbelief as Davis walked into the courtroom. It was a moment Pfeifer would never forget. All three men were convicted for violating Davis's civil rights, and each served more than a year in prison.[50]

IN DECEMBER 1967, Noah Cross was reelected sheriff by fifty votes in a run-off with former state trooper Marion Barnette. One of Cross's ex-deputies, Raymond Keathley, a friend to the FBI, and former state representative and future sheriff Fred Schiele were eliminated in the first round. "I am proud that intelligent citizens saw through the recent political smear tactics used against me," Cross said after the election. All three of his opponents had promised to rid the parish of gambling and prostitution.[51]

Although deputies in the past had harassed voters at the polls and bullied every transient passing through Concordia to vote for Cross, either in person or by absentee ballot, a new clerk of court ended much of that practice. The former clerk, Victor Campbell, who had been removed from office on charges of corruption, had been conditioned by Cross to hand over unsealed envelopes containing absentee ballots before the election results were announced. The envelopes were supposed to have been licked and closed after the voters filled out the ballots. If Cross needed more votes to secure his reelection or to elect a candidate of his choice in another race, he exchanged the ballots with his own and then personally sealed the envelopes. Campbell's role in the absentee voting scam became so well known that it earned him the nickname "No Lick Vic."[52]

Few people were happier with Cross's reelection than Red Glover, who had urged all Klansmen to support the sheriff. He reminded the SDG that Cross was a friend of the Klan, adding that the sheriff had protected him when the bureau was investigating Glover's alleged break-in of a liquor store in Ferriday. The FBI, however, was disappointed in the results, having noted prior to the runoff that the defeat of Cross and the "presence of responsible law enforcement in Concordia Parish would be a great boon to the cause of law and order in the Natchez-Vidalia area."[53]

Morville Lounge owner J. D. Richardson, manager Curt Hewitt, two pimps, a bookkeeper, and two prostitutes were indicted in 1969 and later pled guilty to violation of the Interstate Transportation in Aid of Racketeering Act. Cross and DeLaughter were indicted in 1971. Initially, Richardson refused to testify against Cross, but after a few months in the federal prison in Atlanta, where his job was to wash dishes alongside a malicious murderer, he changed his mind and outlined Cross's involvement. A series of grand juries, a hung jury, and other proceedings followed, but the sheriff's lies were eventually his downfall. He pleaded apathy to the illegal prostitution and gambling that financed the Morville Lounge, adding that he simply followed the unwritten customs of the parish, not the written laws of the state.[54] "If you followed every law that is in the constitution of the state, you would never be elected anymore, I will put it that way," Cross said during trial proceedings. He claimed that he went to the lounge: "I didn't see nothing. It wasn't none of my business to stay down there and watch. I got a family that I stay with at night." He also claimed he never witnessed any prostitution.[55]

When, during a federal grand jury proceeding in 1972, Cross was asked about the ministerial alliance that asked him to close the Morville Lounge, the sheriff was indignant: "That was a Baptist preacher and the Methodist preacher, the priest and the president of the nuns came up there and they organized a ministerial alliance. They told me, 'They are running a [whore] house down there.' And I said, 'Well, I don't know nothing about it.' They said, 'Well, you go down there and close it or we are going to beat you . . .' and I said, 'You all just go ahead and beat me, by God.'"[56] When asked about the Klan exchanging gunfire with lounge operators, he claimed that could not have happened: "I couldn't tell you one Klan member in the parish of Concordia," he said, although he himself was an honorary member of the UKA.

Cross also denied he had hosted a party for other sheriffs at the lounge, an event everyone in Concordia Parish knew about. Later, Pfeifer learned from two serving sheriffs that Cross had sought their influence from residents in their parishes selected to the federal jury hearing his case. At Cross's second trial (the first ended in a hung jury), two of the sheriffs met with him privately in a vacant room at the courthouse. They notified the sheriff they intended to tell all.[57] Margaret Johnson Mulligan, a black woman from Ferriday who cooked at the lounge in 1965, was the most effective witness. She testified to watching the sheriff's lounge party and said that Cross lost playing blackjack. Drane's dealer, known as "Big," complained when he had to reimburse the sheriff for his hefty losses.[58]

Despite all of the controversies surrounding him, Cross was reelected in 1971 by more than 2,100 votes. On July 1, 1972, he began his eighth term in a ceremony on the courthouse grounds. He had been in office longer than any other sheriff in Louisiana at the time. DeLaughter, who had previously pled guilty to involvement in the promotion of prostitution at Morville, was already in federal prison. His wife, Lula, now on the sheriff's staff, and deputies and members of the office staff took their oaths as well. Fifty spectators watched as Cross wept afterward.[59] Eight months later, he was in federal prison in Fort Worth when his convictions on two counts of perjury and one count of jury tampering were affirmed on appeal. Due to illness, he was pardoned after serving more than a year of his six-year sentence. DeLaughter also served slightly more than a year in federal prison. Neither man would ever wear a badge again. Cross died in 1976 at the age of sixty-eight.

Although a number of federal prosecutors pursued the Morville case for six years, it was Pfeifer who made it happen. Pfeifer later received a letter of commendation from his boss. "I am appreciative," J. Edgar Hoover wrote. The cases involving Morville and the Davis beating resulted in the only convictions in the massive WHARBOM probe, although hope would arise again in 2007, when a new generation of Justice Department lawyers and FBI agents reopened the files in the wake of the indictment of James Ford Seale in the Dee and Moore murders.

EPILOGUE
New Investigations

THE EMMETT TILL Unsolved Civil Rights Crime Act of 2007, named after a fourteen-year-old black child murdered in 1955 in Money, Mississippi,
was signed into law by President George W. Bush in 2008. (After a white male
jury found them not guilty, Till's killers confessed to the homicide to a *Life*
reporter.) As a result of the Till Act, the Department of Justice and the FBI
were directed to investigate and coordinate prosecution with state and local
law enforcement of the civil rights–era murders that happened on or before
December 31, 1969. By May 2015, the FBI had closed 105 of 113 cold cases involving 126 victims. In June 2016, the bureau closed its Mississippi Burning
investigation.

During the spring of 2007, Janis McDonald, a professor at the Syracuse
University School of Law, visited the *Concordia Sentinel* office. She was re-
searching a book that had a Concordia Parish connection, and someone had
sent her to me because of my interest in local history. After we began talking,
FBI agent Sheila Thorne, who handled the bureau's community relations
for the New Orleans division office, called me. As I questioned her about the
Frank Morris case, McDonald listened. When I hung up, she asked me about
Morris. A former civil rights lawyer, McDonald was intrigued by the murder.
She left me her card and expressed a keen interest in keeping up with the case.
A few days later, I called her and asked for help. She told Paula Johnson, a col-
league at Syracuse who also taught criminal law, about her visit to Ferriday.
Johnson immediately agreed to work with us. The two professors quickly en-
listed twenty-five criminal law students who volunteered to do research.

In a short time, they began sending paper gold, including copies of the
House Un-American Activities Committee hearings involving local Klansmen. They sent Don Whitehead's 1970 book, *Attack on Terror: The FBI against
the Ku Klux Klan in Mississippi*, which made the earliest public mention of

the Silver Dollar Group and connected this Klan cell to the murders of Morris and Wharlest Jackson. The professors also sent newspaper articles, including one on the Morris murder by John Herbers of the *New York Times,* the first of many 1960s journalists I had the honor of getting to know. Before long, the professors got approval from the law school dean to teach a course on investigating real civil rights–era murders, with the Morris case as the centerpiece. In the meantime, they made several trips to Louisiana, and their interest spread to cases in other states, resulting in their cofounding the Cold Case Justice Initiative at the university. Over the years, they have held events for the families of victims and have linked them with many big names in the civil rights movement. Thanks to McDonald and Johnson, I met Rosa Williams, Frank Morris's granddaughter, in person at a program at Syracuse. Later, I experienced the joy of seeing Ferriday's Robert "Buck" Lewis recognized for his years of activism as president of the NAACP and the Ferriday Freedom Movement. Although his home had been bombed in 1965 and he had faced months of harassment and death threats by the Klan and local police, he had survived and persevered. He shared his experiences before an audience that included civil rights icons Diane Nash and the Rev. C. T. Vivian. Lewis was so happy, he burst out into song.

IN JANUARY 2008, U.S. Attorney Donald Washington of Lafayette visited the *Concordia Sentinel* office with a team of lawyers, two FBI agents, and Paige Fitzgerald, deputy chief in charge of the Cold Case Initiative at the Department of Justice (DOJ). Fitzgerald recently had been involved in the prosecution of James Ford Seale, and Washington had been unfairly vilified in some circles in the racially charged Jena 6 case in LaSalle Parish, Louisiana, that resulted in a march of more than 15,000 people on the town of 3,400. Demonstrators claimed that six black teens were treated unfairly by the local justice system.

In 2001, President George W. Bush had appointed Washington, who is black, as the U.S. attorney for the Western District of Louisiana, which includes forty-two parishes west of the Mississippi River. The choice of the West Point graduate to spearhead the Morris probe could not have been better—his heart was in it. After the DOJ/FBI initiative was announced, Washington eagerly awaited word of what cases his office would be assigned. The FBI and lawyers in the DOJ Civil Rights Division criminal branch made the assignments. Washington intended to push his cases with urgency and with appropriate manpower. I was later surprised to learn that when FBI director Robert Mueller announced the initiative, the DOJ and the bureau were only beginning the process of obtaining the old case files of the victims. Not only is getting the documents a time-consuming chore, but someone has to read them. In June 2009, the Syracuse professors handed me several disks containing seven thousand pages of unredacted pages of the WHARBOM file that included documents on the 1960s FBI investigations of the Jackson, Morris, and Joseph Edwards cases. Students from law schools at Syracuse, Howard, and Catholic Universities spent three weeks using digital cameras to photograph the file. When McDonald and Johnson showed Washington some of the documents on Edwards, he excused himself from the room. He was furious with the FBI. The bureau had told him there was no Edwards file. A few months later, McDonald was back at the archives and was astounded to find that the WHARBOM pages had been heavily redacted since the students had photographed them.

A key to success in a civil rights cold-case murder investigation is a U.S. attorney who personally pushes the case forward. U.S. attorneys have a lot of leeway. Early on, Washington realized that if the Justice Department did a standard investigation, valuable time would be lost. The witnesses and perpetrators in these cases were aging and dying off, so it was important to move forward as quickly as possible. He wanted to generate public interest in the Morris case and liked the fact the *Concordia Sentinel* was publishing stories about Morris and other cold-case murders almost every week. As a result, his office and the FBI were getting leads. A visit to the newspaper made sense to him, but he later told me that Fitzgerald was not happy with the visit. The department had concerns about a third party impacting the investigation in an adverse way. Also at the meeting was Syracuse's McDonald, yet another outside party the DOJ lawyers weren't comfortable around.

Fitzgerald was a proven cold-case prosecutor, and Washington found her generally cooperative and quick to respond. He also liked Cynthia Deitle, whom Mueller named to head the FBI's cold-case unit. Deitle met with the New Orleans special agent in charge and worked closely with the office in getting the cases investigated. Although Washington thought a good effort was initiated, he realized that "if you don't stay on top of it, a month can pass in the blink of an eye and nothing gets done."[1] He found some agents more energetic than others and personally requested the transfer of one agent who wanted to close the Joseph Edwards case before much work had been done. Washington was aware, too, that agents typically spent eighteen months to two years in one office. Heather Koch, a young agent from a small town in Illinois outside Chicago, was one of several case agents to investigate the Morris case. She felt privileged to be involved in the historic investigation and devoted personal time to studying the case. When it came time to transfer, her request to remain in Louisiana to complete the investigation was denied. While this may be bureau policy, sending off a dedicated on-the-ground agent knowledgeable about a fragile case made no sense.

Washington called a meeting to figure out a way for government investigators and lawyers, a weekly newspaper, and a university lawyer to work together in the race against time to solve an aging murder case. The meeting was held in the *Sentinel's* break room. When the delegation of federal officials arrived with their umbrellas on a nasty winter day, I was overwhelmed and nervous, a novice in dealing with the FBI and DOJ, and I was glad McDonald was there. Washington was absolutely sincere, but the DOJ and FBI didn't buy in. Their terms are a one-way street: You tell all, and they tell you nothing. I came to believe that it is impossible for a journalist to work with a government bureaucracy. There are ethical issues as well. But I trusted Donald Washington, and he trusted me. He came to Ferriday dragging along everybody he could find, willing and unwilling, because he wanted to solve Morris's murder and knew that it and other cold cases needed an innovative and aggressive approach. From that day until he stepped down from his position in 2010, we quietly and confidentially worked together to solve the murder. When Washington left, the DOJ and the FBI for all practical purposes yanked the case from the U.S. Attorney's Office and oversaw it at headquarters. Unfortunately, Louisiana and Frank Morris's family lost a most passionate government advocate.

IN MARCH 2008, Canadian filmmaker David Ridgen of Toronto, spearheading a new investigative initiative, wanted to know if I would be interested in collaborating with other journalists independently seeking justice in civil rights–era cold cases. He had worked on an investigation that had resulted in the 2007 arrest and conviction of James Ford Seale. One of Seale's victims, Charles Moore, was the younger brother of Thomas Moore, Ridgen's investigative partner. Their work bonded them like brothers.

During Seale's trial, Charles Edwards, in exchange for immunity, testified against his old White Knight comrade. Edwards also did something few Klansmen have done: He asked the victims' families to forgive him. His courtroom request stunned Moore, who was sitting only a few feet away. In the previous years, Moore and Ridgen had confronted Edwards, who had steadfastly denied having been involved in the crime and had run them off his property and the church property where Edwards was a deacon. Charles Moore's murder had filled his brother with a hatred of white people that had consumed him for a lifetime, and Edwards's testimony and his plea for forgiveness left Thomas Moore speechless.[2] The next day, Moore forgave him.

In 2011, Moore and Ridgen returned to Franklin County to see if the reconciliation that had begun was real. One question Moore had long wanted to ask Edwards: "Do you ever think about my brother?" Edwards answered, "All the time," adding that he felt the early death of his son was payback for the murders. In fact, Edwards said he occasionally returned to the forest where the boys were beaten and wondered, "Why did I do that?"[3] Later, Moore and Ridgen were invited to go to church with Edwards in Bunkley. Moore participated in the Sunday School class Edwards taught, and the two sat together during the singing and preaching service. At Edwards's house, they picked peaches and walked through the garden. Edwards had been in his garden in 1964 when Klansmen came to tell him they had located Henry Dee in Meadville. He laid down his hoe and went with them. By that time, Thomas's brother had joined Dee in front of the Tastee Freeze trying to hitch a ride home.

Ridgen's filming over the years included Thomas Moore's confrontations with Seale and Edwards, and eventually the conviction of one on the testimony of the other. "God did not give us the ability to forget," Thomas Moore told me in 2012. "But we can forgive. I've been a different person ever since."[4]

And there with him was David Ridgen, his camera rolling. We worked together on the Morris murder and other cases, and I have found him to be one of the most generous men I have ever known. His work is an inspiration to any journalist who chases truth.

A few days after Ridgen contacted me in early March 2008, one of his main collaborators, Robert Rosenthal, called. Rosenthal had recently been named executive director of the Center for Investigative Reporting (CIR) in Berkeley, California. He had previously worked as managing editor of the *San Francisco Chronicle*. Rosenthal invited me to a meeting at the *Clarion-Ledger* in Jackson, Mississippi, at the office of investigative reporter Jerry Mitchell, a legend in the cold-case reporting field. Mitchell's stories over the decades have led to the arrests and convictions of Klansmen in several old cases, including the 1964 Neshoba County, Mississippi, murders of three civil rights workers. I had first talked to Mitchell in early 2007 when he was writing about James Ford Seale and the 1970 plane collision in Concordia Parish that only Seale survived. Among the five dead in the other plane was Dr. Charles Colvin, who had been Morris's attending physician in 1964.

John Fleming, then a reporter with the *Anniston Star* in Alabama, also attended the meeting. Fleming's reporting on the February 1965 killing of twenty-six-year-old voting rights activist Jimmie Lee Jackson led to the 2005 conviction of former Alabama state trooper James Bonard Fowler. The killing had been one of the inspirations for the Selma-to-Montgomery marches that led to the passage of the Voting Rights Act of 1965. The former cop told Fleming he shot Jackson in self-defense. Following Fleming's story, Fowler was indicted for murder by a state grand jury. He was sentenced in 2010 to six months in jail after pleading guilty to manslaughter.

Also at the Jackson meeting was Aynsley Vogel with Paperny Films in Vancouver. Her boss, David Paperny, was interested in joining the effort that would become known as the Civil Rights Cold Case Project, sponsored by CIR. The project would also involve Syracuse and other universities, as well as reporters, filmmakers, and researchers. Several participants in the program were asked by Harvard's *Nieman Reports* in 2011 to write about the project.

"Our unifying motivation," Rosenthal reported, "was storytelling, justice and even reconciliation. I wanted to create a project of an ambitious sweep that would tell all the untold stories of killers, victims and their families in ways that would tie together a shameful chapter in American history and link it in powerful arcs to today." Fleming went right to the point: "If we, as journalists, don't tell these forgotten stories, who will?" Ridgen wrote, "The investigative process that leads to the courtroom can be for long stretches a solitary and exhausting effort that feels as cold and bleak as the case itself. At such moments, advancing the case requires the precision and subtlety of a battering ram." Hank Klibanoff, now the James M. Cox Jr. Professor of Journalism at Emory University in Atlanta, was named managing editor of the project. He and Gene Roberts had coauthored *The Race Beat: The Press, the Civil Rights Struggle, and the Awakening of a Nation,* which won the 2007 Pulitzer Prize. Klibanoff noted in *Nieman Reports* that during "the past 40 years our nation, at the federal and state levels, has reaffirmed its disdain for three kinds of criminal behavior characteristic of the Klan: organized crime, terrorism and hate crimes. Not allowing these unprosecuted cases to vanish—or those who committed these crimes to die without pursuit—fulfills that intent to track down and prosecute haters and terrorists. These crimes are so egregious and they are so woven into the context of who we Americans are today that we're interested in telling the stories even when there is no living perpetrator."[5]

For a two-year period, Klibanoff edited almost every cold-case story I wrote for the *Concordia Sentinel*. I would e-mail him the article, and he would send it back. Sometimes he would return my original story with so many edits and questions that I considered setting fire to my computer. But once the changes were made, the improvement was obvious. I grew to welcome his edits because a better story would appear below my byline. His suggestions resulted in one of my favorite ledes: "Forty-four years have passed, but Leland Boyd can still recall the shock he felt as a 12 year old when he first saw the charred, smoking rubble of Frank Morris's shoe shop on the morning of December 10, 1964."[6]

As he wrote in *Nieman Reports*, Jerry Mitchell believes it is his "job as a reporter to assemble whatever evidence exists and put it out there so everyone can see it. By doing this I hope to reveal how the system failed to provide justice. A friend of mine who happens to be a terrific investigative reporter has a button that reads, 'I just catch 'em. I don't fry 'em.' That's how I feel. My job as a journalist is to expose the truth, as best as I can determine it by the evidence I find and the interviews I do. It's up to authorities whether they act on it or not."[7]

Ben Greenberg, a freelance reporter and blogger from Boston, also became a part of the CIR cold-case project. His late father, Paul A. Greenberg, was a special assistant to Dr. Martin Luther King Jr. during the civil rights movement. For years, Ben Greenberg investigated the 1964 murder of Clifton Walker in Woodville, Mississippi. When in 2007 the FBI reopened the Walker case, its efforts seemed sluggish and disjointed. Greenberg's reporting in 2012, published in the *Clarion-Ledger* and *USA Today*, revealed what the *Concordia Sentinel* had discovered in its probes into other cold cases—that the FBI's field agents were not given the time needed to comprehensively reinvestigate; thereby, through no fault of their own, the fieldwork was inconsistent. Agents still had their everyday work to do, and today's terrorist suspects will always have priority over aging Klan suspects. The DOJ should have appointed a task force of a handful of agents to work these cold cases full-time.

The third agent assigned to the Walker case since 2007 told Greenberg that the FBI depended on the public for assistance "because we have resources and personnel limitations." FBI headquarters in Washington countered that the constraints cited by the case agent didn't exist. Ironically, while the FBI courted collaboration with journalists, the bureau often discounted comments made by witnesses reporters interviewed, claiming, "Individuals may profess to the media that they have direct knowledge of events that they later acknowledge to law enforcement was hearsay, rumor or opinion."[8]

LOUISIANA STATE UNIVERSITY professor-in-residence Jay Shelledy called me in April 2009. He holds the Fred Jones Greer Chair in Media Business and Ethics at the LSU Manship School of Mass Communications in Baton Rouge. One of his previous newspaper jobs included the editorship of the *Salt Lake Tribune,* with a newsroom staff of 175. Shelledy asked me to talk to Manship students about my cold-case work. I brought Robert Lee III of Ferriday with me. Lee, who died in 2016, looked like a linebacker for a professional football team. For years, Lee introduced me into black communities from Ferriday to Fayette, Mississippi. Once, when we were en route to talk to a man I believed might have information on one of the killings, I asked Lee what we would do if the man refused to see us.

"Oh, he'll see us," Lee said. "He might not talk, but he'll see us."

I asked him what he meant. Lee laughed. "If I have to kick the door in, he'll see us."

Lee had suffered discrimination and racism throughout his life. His father and mother, the Rev. Robert E. Lee Jr. and Lavinia Lee, friends of Frank Morris, had managed to see all four of their boys grow to manhood on the same streets and roadways that were traversed by Deputy Frank DeLaughter. Like all black families in Ferriday, the Lees had lost several friends to suspicious deaths. Lee III had been a friend of Joseph Edwards, who rode Reverend Lee's school-bus in the years before he went missing on the Ferriday-Vidalia highway.

After the talk to students, Shelledy took us to lunch. Dean Jack Hamilton and Matt Barnidge, a graduate student who became the first LSU intern to work with me on the cold cases, joined us. Shelledy envisioned an ongoing cold-case project in which students would research, investigate, and write about the old murders. That summer, Ian Stanford, another LSU graduate student, joined Barnidge in courthouses from Concordia Parish to Amite County, Mississippi, tracking down records on SDG Klansmen. Barnidge also helped me investigate the Morville Lounge. The result was a series of *Sentinel* stories about the lounge's connection to the Klan, the Carlos Marcello mob, and the Concordia Parish Sheriff's Office.

After discussing my need for intern help and for FBI documents that could be obtained through the Freedom of Information Act, Dean Hamilton said, "We're going to help you." Subsequent deans Ralph Izard and Jerry Ceppos have supported Shelledy's growing cold-case program, which has included thirty-two team members. The *Concordia Sentinel* has by far been the major benefactor from the project.

During most fall and spring semesters since 2010, a team of LSU cold-case students has visited the National Archives in College Park, Maryland, to retrieve what at this writing has totaled more than 150,000 pages of FBI investigative documents involving more than three dozen cases. These were released following LSU's Freedom of Information requests. In early 2015, those documents were released through LSU's cold-case Web site. Now historians and journalists can view documents not seen since they were archived a half century ago.

On the Washington trips, the students have interviewed the ever-changing members of the FBI cold-case unit. In Ferriday, they have followed me across the foundation of Morris's shop as I retraced his path the night of the fire. I have told them about his trail of bloody footprints, and I have seen in their eyes that the inhumanity of that long-ago night upsets them and compels them to help pursue the case. But the highlight of every student visit was a pilgrimage to see Reverend Lee, who died in 2015. When he was a strapping young man of ninety-three, I told him that when he reached one hundred, I was going to write a feature about him for the front page. He laughed and said he thought that was a fine idea.

On August 26, 2013, more than four hundred family and friends turned out for Lee's one hundredth birthday. The *Sentinel* ran a front-page story.

"I love you all," Lee told the group that gathered to celebrate him.[9] He said the greatest accomplishment of his life was his family. Born a year after World War I began, he had watched the Klan carnage of the 1960s with faith that things would get better. Yet never once did he think he would live to see a black president. When Barack Obama was elected in 2008, he, like so many others, expressed joyfully the exact words fire-scarred Frank Morris expressed in shock from his hospital bed forty-four years earlier: "I just can't believe it!"

WHAT EVER HAPPENED TO JOSEPH EDWARDS?

JOSEPH EDWARDS is the only civil rights–era murder victim on the FBI's list whose body has yet to be found. Because of this, his sister, Julia Dobbins of Bridge City, Louisiana, has an emptiness that other cold-case victims' families don't have. She can't give her brother a proper family burial.

Another person haunted by Edwards's disappearance was Marge Baroni, a white activist from Natchez whose family was ostracized by the white community in the 1960s. In her uncompleted master's thesis, housed at the University of Mississippi Libraries Archives and Special Collections, Baroni wondered how many murdered bodies rest unseen beneath the earth's surface or have been swallowed for eternity by the Mississippi River: "There's a refrain that goes through my mind from time to time. I never really lose it . . . It's 'What ever happened to Joseph Edwards?'"

A major circumstance of the case was Edwards's reputation for flirting with white women. It was also rumored he pimped black women to white men at the Shamrock Motel, where he worked as a porter. Another rumor involved the drowning of a four-year-old white boy in the Shamrock pool. It was speculated, but never proven, that Edwards was having a sexual relationship with or pimping the boy's mother. What's most important is that, true or not, the Klan and the cops believed Edwards was involved with the woman.

In 2010, Tori Stilwell, a nineteen-year-old journalism student at the University of North Carolina, worked as a cold-case intern for the *Concordia Sentinel*. Stilwell located Robin, the sister of the boy who drowned in the Shamrock pool. Robin had been at the motel the day her brother died. So financially desperate was the family in 1964 that her mother had to turn a trick prior to the funeral to earn enough money to buy shoes for her dead child to be buried in. Her surviving children were placed in foster care. Robin was never told where her brother was buried but yearned to know. Through Robin, we also learned that her mother was still living in another southern state.

Stilwell and I met Robin in Meadville, Mississippi, during the summer of 2010. We led Robin and her husband a few miles out of town to a rural Franklin County cemetery to show her the grave of her brother. Robin expressed her joy through tears. I told Robin that Joseph Edwards had a sister whose brother could not be buried until his body was found. In a way, Joseph Edwards had played a role in Robin finding her long-lost brother.

The second Shamrock incident, the one that triggered the attack on Edwards, involved the allegation that he forced a kiss on Iona Perry. The Justice Department cited seven suspects when it closed the case in 2013. They included SDG Klansmen Red Glover, Kenneth Norman Head, and Homer Thomas "Buck" Horton. Only one FBI informant had named the three as suspects: Ferriday mechanic and Klan leader E. D. Morace. An eyewitness had seen a white Oldsmobile, with a flashing red light on the dash and two whip antennae on the rear, pull Edwards's Buick over on the Ferriday-Vidalia highway. Glover drove a white 1964 Oldsmobile, but it had no rear antennae. He did, however, as a member of the Vidalia Auxiliary Police Department, have access to a portable flashing red police light.

Suspect number four, Vidalia police chief Bud Spinks, drove the town's patrol car, a rental, which was also a white 1964 Oldsmobile. But this car had a red beacon light mounted on the top, which would eliminate it as the car described by the witness. Although the witness thought he had seen a 1964 model, he was not interviewed by the bureau until three years after the incident, and he seemed uncertain.

In addition to Spinks, the Justice Department cited three other law enforcement suspects, including probation officer James Goss. Goss was the only suspect to have openly expressed a tangible motive to harm Edwards because of the alleged kiss. With his attorney present, Goss gave the bureau a signed statement in 1967 acknowledging he was furious with Edwards over the matter and initially wanted to attack him with his fists. He claimed repeatedly, however, that he did not kill Edwards.

I located Goss's daughter, Kay, in October 2009, four months after her father's death. I later met her in Ruston, Louisiana, and we drove a short distance north to the Vienna Cemetery to see her father's fresh grave. She said her father had often claimed "those bastards"—deputies Frank DeLaughter and Bill Ogden, also suspects in Edwards's disappearance—had tried to pin the murder on him.

In 1967, James Goss pointed out to agents that Ferriday jailer and police officer Junior Harp, a close friend of DeLaughter's, also drove a late-model white Oldsmobile. In fact, Goss said he always suspected Harp had a hand in Edwards's disappearance, although he offered no specific reason. Harp had taken DeLaughter's job as Ferriday jailer when DeLaughter became a patrolman for the town, and the two were involved with deputies in the 1962 beating of two black men at the courthouse.

FBI records show that when Sheriff Noah Cross hired Harp in March 1965,

Harp sold his personal car—a white 1962 Oldsmobile—to the sheriff's office and drove it as his patrol car. The sheriff's office was equipped with red flashing emergency lights for mounting on the dash. Even as a Ferriday jailer, Harp had easy access to those lights.

Two separate stories emerged about the night of the disappearance. One, that Edwards was pursued by the Oldsmobile from Vidalia to Ferriday, and two, that Ogden pursued Edwards from Ferriday to Vidalia. Both chases ended at the same place: the bowling alley.

On the night he vanished, Edwards told a witness he had a date with a white woman at the Shamrock at 11 p.m. This date was likely a setup. Once he left the motel after midnight, a plan was put into motion. The white car in pursuit from Vidalia and Ogden's patrol car coming from Ferriday converged at the bowling alley. Ogden told a witness that Edwards jumped out of his car and ran up the levee, while DeLaughter chased Edwards on foot. Ogden took an entrance road just east of the bowling alley and drove up atop the levee.

This could have happened seconds before or after the witness drove by the white Olds parked in front of Edwards's Buick. The witness said he passed the two cars but that seconds later the Olds, occupied by the four or five men he saw at the scene, passed him and raced out of sight. A short distance from the bowling alley on the north—or right side—of the Ferriday-Vidalia highway is Tuminello Road, which connects with Fisherman Drive, which intersects with the levee road at the mouth of Lake Concordia, a mile distant from Ogden's location on the other end. If Edwards was running on the levee, the maneuvers by the two cars would have boxed him in. Ogden claimed Edwards got away. But did he?

On August 7, 2009, I received an e-mail from a woman in Texas. "I think I may know some information that may be useful to you," she wrote. I called her. The woman had recently read the *Concordia Sentinel*'s account of Ogden's story about his pursuit of Edwards. She had previously worked at a nursing home in Ferriday where Ogden resided until his death in 2004. The woman said Ogden, like other patients, suffered from dementia and hallucinations. She described an apparition that had long haunted Ogden. Attendants rushed to his room on many occasions as he cried for help. He would point to the corner of the room: "Don't you see that little nigger boy? He's got blood on him. He's after me. I ran over him with my car."[10]

Naturally, the story jolted me. I immediately recalled a 1967 FBI document in which SDG Klansman Jack Seale, by then an informant, recalled Louisiana

Klansmen discussing a story that Edwards was taken to the levee "possibly to whip him, and they over did it." Seale said he heard the perpetrators "rolled him [Edwards] down the levee, thinking he was dead or buried him in the levee." Had Ogden hit Edwards with the patrol car and sent him rolling down the levee?

For years, I couldn't advance the story. But by 2013, I had learned that the U.S. Department of Agriculture (USDA) Farm Service Agency kept on file aerial photographs relating to its various farm programs. The thought that a photograph would have been taken in July 1964 of Edwards's car parked by the bowling alley intrigued me. The possibility was slim, but it wouldn't be my first dead end. I was disappointed to find that there were no July 1964 photos available but excited that aerial shots had been compiled on October 7, 1964. I spent a couple of hours sifting through large (two feet, two inches square) pictures stacked in no specific order until I came across an aerial photo of the bowling alley. Two FSA workers were in the room, and one eyed the photo with me. "Looks like they're building up the berm over here," he said, pointing to the mouth of Lake Concordia in the top center of the photo, where on the west side of the levee tons of dirt were being added to build up the levee berm, part of a larger project. Just to the north on the east side of the levee was a huge excavation pit with big equipment loading and hauling dirt to the berm. I thought about two things: first, that three weeks before Edwards went missing the White Knights in Neshoba County, Mississippi, had shot the three civil rights workers and buried their bodies in an earthen dam; and second, what Seale had claimed the Louisiana Klansmen had said of Edwards: "Buried him in the levee."

FBI agent John Pfeifer, whose investigations sent DeLaughter and Cross to jail for racketeering in the 1970s, believed that if Ogden had run over Edwards, the deputies would not have taken the injured man to the hospital. They would have finished him off and disposed of the body as quickly as possible before daylight. Quick disposal by water seems unlikely because of the darkness.[11]

At this writing, new information is being investigated on the possible location of Edwards's body. Discovering his body would enable his sister to give him a proper burial, and the remains might also offer forensic details about his death. Many questions remain. Did the killers leave behind a piece of evidence at the burial site? During a 1965 SDG wrecking crew project in Natchez—the vandalism of a black man's car in search of weapons—a Klansman left his initialed cigarette lighter at the crime scene but retrieved it in the nick of time. Perhaps somebody made a similar mistake during the Edwards killing.

WHO KILLED FRANK MORRIS?

FOR YEARS I have studied a photograph of Frank Morris and his employees standing in front of his shoe shop. Morris appears confident, his arms folded over his apron and his visor pulled down on his forehead just above his eyebrows. I wondered and wondered: Who would want this man dead?

In 1964, the FBI probe pointed at Frank DeLaughter and other police officers, but there was no evidence to support the suspicions. In 1967, E. L. McDaniel, DeLaughter's friend and fellow Klansman, pointed the FBI in the direction of four SDG Klansmen. These men were reportedly upset with Morris for allegedly flirting with white women and for permitting interracial sexual liaisons between white women and black men in the back of his shoe shop. For years, I asked people about those allegations, but never once did I find anyone who confirmed them. In 2011, an eighty-three-year-old white woman who didn't identify herself called to tell me she had read many of the stories in the *Concordia Sentinel* about Klan allegations against Morris.

"I was one of the women that carried my shoes, my husband's shoes, and those of our boys to Frank Morris's shoe shop," she said. "I went there often. I never went inside. I drove in front of the shop and he brought candy for my boys and took my order. He was a nice, respectful man. He never flirted with me, and I wasn't a bad-looking woman. He never flirted with the other women I knew."[12]

In 1967, O. C. "Coonie" Poissot told the bureau he was with DeLaughter the night before the arson and that the deputy was furious with Morris over a confrontation about shoes. DeLaughter indicated that he was going to teach Morris a lesson for being uppity to a white man. The argument came after Morris told DeLaughter he would have to pay in advance for repairs in the future. E. D. Morace told the same basic story in 1967 but specified that the two had argued over cowboy boots.

Poissot was identified by the FBI as an ex-convict and hoodlum, addicted to speed and a Klansman capable of violent acts. Poissot had a tattoo of a star on one ear lobe and a half moon on the other. He told June Latiolais of Louisiana that these were Klan symbols. Latiolais told me that she and her husband had known Poissot for years and that he despised blacks. Two of Poissot's daughters (by different mothers) described him as a man capable of great evil. One daughter, Jonene, grew to love him before his death in 1992, while the other, Shawnee, described her father as evil until his death. She also said he carried a silver dollar and once bragged about "killing a black man for the

Klan." These witnesses contacted me in 2010, and their stories inflamed my interest in Poissot because, by his own admission, he was the last person known to be with DeLaughter before the arson.

In June 2010, I called Bill Frasier, who had once been a deputy in Concordia Parish. Frasier was on a long list of current and former cops I wanted to ask about the Morris murder. In 1981, he had killed a black man he was transporting to the parish jail. Frasier claimed that en route the handcuffed suspect, arrested on a forgery warrant, pulled a knife and stabbed Frasier twice while he was driving. A struggle ensued, and Frasier said that in self-defense he drew his revolver and killed the suspect, shooting him six times. A Ferriday surgeon testified during a civil suit filed by the dead man's widow that one of the knife wounds was six to eight inches deep. A grand jury, after a ten-day session, cleared Frasier. In a civil trial, the jury ruled that the suspect was unlawfully arrested but that Frasier used necessary force in self-defense and that the suspect unlawfully assaulted him.

I asked Frasier if he knew anything about the Frank Morris murder. "As a matter of fact, I do," he said. Frasier said his ex-brother-in-law, Arthur Leonard Spencer of Rayville, Louisiana, had told him in the late 1960s that he had gone to Ferriday with another Klansman to burn down a shoe shop and was surprised when a black man came to the front. Spencer indicated that no one was supposed to be at the shop. Frasier said that Spencer's partner in crime was Coonie Poissot.

Brenda Rhodes, Frasier's sister and Spencer's ex-wife, told me she had known Poissot for years, having first met him in the 1960s at her mother's restaurant in a truck stop at Tallulah. Poissot, a trucker, was a customer. She had lost contact with him by the time she met and married Spencer. The two divorced, and the next time she saw Poissot was in Minden, Louisiana, in the early 1970s. After learning she had been married to Spencer, Poissot told her about the arson. Spencer's son, William "Boo" Spencer, said he had heard his father talk about the shoe shop fire all of his life.

In June 2010, I went unannounced to see Spencer. With me were filmmaker David Paperny of Canada and cameraman Dan McKinney, both part of the Center for Investigative Reporting Civil Rights Cold Case Project. Also in our van was Tori Stilwell, the *Concordia Sentinel*'s intern. As we headed to Spencer's, my cell phone rang. It was Rosa Williams, Morris's granddaughter.

"I just had an urge to call you," she said, "and let you know I'm praying for you." I didn't tell her until later where we were going.

As we drove to the end of a long lane through a cornfield to Spencer's house in rural Richland Parish, his wife with her children pulled out of the driveway and stopped as our two vehicles came abreast. I had already decided I was going to begin a conversation with Spencer by asking him if he knew Coonie Poissot. When Poissot's daughters called me, they said they were trying to fill in gaps in what they knew about his life and would be interested in contacting anyone who knew him. Mrs. Spencer, on her way to Wednesday night prayer meeting, said her husband would not be home for another hour, but she would call to let him know he had visitors. She wondered, "What do you want to talk to him about?" I said I wanted to talk to him about Coonie Poissot. She mouthed the word "Coonie" and said out loud she didn't know him.

After an hour, we came back. I knocked on the door, and Spencer came out wearing blue jeans and buttoning a denim long-sleeved shirt. He worked for a farm cooperative and drove trucks, tractors, and combines during the farming season. He was a big man, with dyed black hair. He sat on the porch swing, and I sat alone on the steps. I asked if Paperny and McKinney could film, he agreed, and a few minutes later they approached with their cameras.

He was clearly nervous but at the outset was adamant: "I don't know that Coonie fellow. A name like that I'd remember." His statement seemed incredible. Two of Spencer's children by Brenda Rhodes said Poissot was like a grandfather to them. When I told Spencer that Poissot was dead, he seemed to relax, but I could tell his mind was churning. He acknowledged having been in the Rayville Klan and that the Klan had wrecking crews.

"We might do a job for Ferriday and Ferriday do a job for us," Spencer said, but he insisted he had never heard of Frank Morris. He said he had attended ten to twelve Klan meetings and that while his uncle was a leader in the group, his father was passionately opposed to the Klan. Spencer said he was just a kid in December 1964, although he was one month shy of twenty-five. He grew increasingly suspicious and nervous. I attempted to give him my business card, and he read it but he wouldn't touch it. "For all I know you could be the FBI," he said. (Two days later, I wrote him a letter assuring him again that I wasn't with the FBI.)

"I've been around," he said. "I'm being straight up with you. I know it's more to this than what you're telling me. I'm not stupid."

When we departed, I reached out to shake Spencer's hand. He squeezed my hand so hard that I almost asked him to ease up. I believe he was warning me to be careful. The last thing he said to me before we left was, "That Coonie fellow. You say he's dead?"

A couple of days later, Spencer visited his son, "Boo," who had recently been released from prison. As Boo's wife, Edith, fried the two men pork chops for a late breakfast, Spencer joined Boo at the kitchen table and announced that the FBI (referring to me and my associates) had paid him a visit a couple of days earlier.

"Son, they got me," Spencer repeated. "They got me on that Frank Marcey [*sic*] fire. I'm the only one left."

When Boo and Edith Spencer told me this story, I couldn't figure out why they were using the last name of "Marcey." Then Boo told me, "That's the only name I ever heard. I figured when you first asked me about Frank Morris that you were talking about Frank Marcey."

There was something familiar about that name. Later, I studied one of the composition notebooks I have been filling since 2007. In one, I found a 2010 interview with the late Morris White, who for years was the Concordia Parish director of homeland security. White's father had been a businessman in Ferriday and knew Frank Morris well. In the interview, White had told me his father and other older businessmen always called Frank Morris by the nickname "Marcey."

Boo Spencer could not have made that up. I put together a scenario that made sense to me: DeLaughter, with Poissot in his patrol car the night before the arson, told him he wanted Morris's shop torched to teach the shoe repairman a lesson. Poissot was well connected with the Klans in Rayville and Tallulah and had told the FBI that he had joined SDG Klansmen for various wrecking crew projects in 1965, including one in Tallulah to burn down black activist Moses Williams's tire shop. Like Morris, Williams was a black businessman with an integrated clientele. Poissot said Morace and Red Glover were part of that wrecking crew, but at the last minute the fire attempt was aborted. Actually, the shop was destroyed by fire, and once again, Poissot placed himself at the scene of a crime. Bill Frasier and Brenda Rhodes also said that Poissot and Spencer had confided they committed the Tallulah arson. Moses Williams told me in 2010 that a five-gallon gas can had been found on the outside rear of his tire shop following the 1965 fire, just as in Ferriday a five-gallon gas can was found in the shoe shop rubble in 1964.

During the weeks ahead, I worked on the story. By the fall, I was ready to run with it. Bill Frasier said that he had told the FBI about Spencer in the summer of 2009, a year before he told me. If *time* was the new enemy, I wondered, what was the bureau waiting on? Initially, I had shared information with agents during the early months of the *Sentinel's* probe. But I noticed that when I asked for information, there was always a reason the request could not be granted. Hank Klibanoff, CIR's cold-case managing editor, reminded me firmly one day that it wasn't my job to feed the results of my work to the bureau and that my readers were my priority.

Even U.S. secretary of labor Thomas Perez, who in 2011 was the assistant attorney general for the Justice Department's Civil Rights Division, told me in an interview that when his department conducted investigations, "oftentimes, information flow is a one-way street. We ask people for information, we ask people to do things and we are not in a position to explain why we ask certain things. I certainly appreciate the fact that can be frustrating from the perspective of people like yourself and other interested parties, but we are concerned about pursuing the case and that is really the sole motivator for us as we have an active investigation and I can't get any more specific."[13]

THE TV NEWS PROGRAM *60 Minutes* showed an interest in jointly working on the Spencer story. The *Sentinel,* the CIR Cold Case managing team, and *60 Minutes* held several phone conferences to discuss the case. Associate producer Sumi Aggarwal of the news program came to Ferriday and interviewed Boo Spencer, Brenda Rhodes, and Bill Frasier. Beginning with associate producer Sam Hornblower in 2007, *60 Minutes* had investigated the Morris murder on and off and provided me with several hundred pages of FBI documents.

In October, a *60 Minutes* producer with our blessings told the FBI that we knew about Spencer. Cynthia Deitle, the head of the FBI's cold-case unit, over a series of phone calls and e-mails, asked the *Sentinel* to hold the story indefinitely, maintaining that it would jeopardize the case. By then, *60 Minutes* had decided it would instead pursue its investigation into the 1964 murder of Louis Allen in Liberty, Mississippi, seventy miles east of Ferriday.

One of the *Sentinel* family owners, Sam Hanna Jr., told Deitle that the newspaper intended to run the Spencer story unless the FBI provided a specific reason why publicizing the story would jeopardize the case. Deitle said she couldn't be specific. When Hanna said the story would run, he got a call from Justice Department lawyer Roy Austin, who asked that we hold the story until the end of December to give the FBI time to complete some interviews. For almost a year and a half, the bureau had known about Spencer but had not talked to him, nor did they know I had.

The Spencer story ran on January 11, 2011. It was a nerve-racking day. Ridgen followed me with his camera rolling, and Paperny and McKinney went to Rayville and filmed a KNOE-TV (CBS affiliate in Monroe) reporter going to Spencer's workplace to interview him. Joe Shapiro with National Public Radio was at the *Sentinel* office covering the story. Shapiro and I would later work together on the 1965 killing of Fayette, Mississippi, shoeshine man Johnny Queen. Together we would interview more than fifty local witnesses and would be shocked to learn that the FBI had interviewed fewer than five.

BBC Radio was in town for the Morris story. The Associated Press, the *New York Times,* CNN, and other media outlets gave coverage. In the days ahead, Jim Rainey of the *Los Angeles Times,* Mallary Tenore of Poynter, and many others would write lengthy stories on the case.

A month after the story ran, the Concordia Parish grand jury convened to investigate the Morris and Joseph Edwards cases. A $10,000 reward had been offered by the FBI for information leading to the arrest and conviction of Morris's killers. To my knowledge, this was the largest reward offered in any cold case following the FBI's 2007 announcement of its initiative. It was also the only case since that time that resulted in a grand jury. Concordia Parish district attorney Brad Burget named Justice Department lawyer Patricia Sumner as an assistant district attorney so she could oversee a state grand jury. Burget named one of his assistants, David Opperman, to help with the case, but the Justice Department didn't share much with the DA's office.

On the day the grand jury convened, February 8, 2011, E. L. McDaniel died. He had been a key informant in the Morris case. (I had called McDaniel, who had suffered a stroke, more than once in the preceding years. He said he couldn't remember his Klan days.) Father August Thompson called to say he had been subpoenaed to testify. A brother of an SDG Klansman called to ask me if the matter concerned the Frank Morris case. I told him it did. The calls kept coming, even from grand jurors.

A total of three separate grand jury panels—each serving an average of six months—listened to testimony for more than a year, but nothing happened. In May 2013, Leonard Spencer died at the age of seventy-three. I believe the Justice Department did Concordia Parish a disservice by not having a grand jury summary report published even if the jurors drew no conclusions.

Janis McDonald and Paula Johnson of the Syracuse University College of Law Cold Case Justice Initiative said Congress should hold oversight hearings to investigate why the Justice Department had failed to fully implement the mandates of the Emmett Till Act.

"There is no excuse for the delay by the Justice Department in bringing Spencer before a jury of his peers," they told the *Sentinel* in a statement. "They have known for four years about evidence brought forward of his admissions to family members that he participated in the arson and cruel death of Mr. Morris. A jury should be the ones to decide on the credibility of the evidence. Now he is dead. This sluggish type of investigation by federal law enforcement is emblematic of their approach to many of the cases of unsolved civil rights killings."[14]

In its letter of closure on the Morris case, the Justice Department mentioned that two witnesses had failed a polygraph test. Rhodes and Frasier called me in the fall of 2011 to tell me they had voluntarily taken polygraphs and were told they had failed. That the Justice Department mentioned two witnesses failed a polygraph in its closure letter infuriated me. The informants it had relied on from 1964 to 1967 were not given polygraphs, and few would have passed. In fact, the bureau had caught one of its top informants, E. D. Morace, in a lie. A Natchez man, beaten by the SDG in 1966 for speaking out against the Klan, pointed to a photograph of Morace as one of the men who had beaten him. Morace told the bureau it was mistaken identity.

In 2013, Dan Berry and Campbell Robertson of the *New York Times* came to Ferriday. They co-wrote with Robbie Brown the paper's lead front-page story on March 13: "When Cold Cases Stay Cold." LSU's Jay Shelledy provided the reporters with background and a photograph of Wharlest Jackson's bombed-out pickup.

"This part of the South is haunted by unanswered questions," the reporters wrote. "F.B.I. agents soon swarmed the area, infiltrating the Silver Dollar Group and forcing an end to its campaign of terror, though without any arrests. The children of Mr. Jackson do not expect the cold-case initiative to change the cold absence of resolution and have come to see the government's initiative as worse than nothing."

SILVER DOLLAR GROUP leader Red Glover died of a brain tumor in 1984 at the age of sixty-two. In August 2009, his stepson James Watts asked me during an interview why Glover hadn't been arrested if he had killed Wharlest Jackson in 1967. I couldn't answer the question. Most investigators familiar with the Jackson case believe Glover acted alone in the murder. I share that opinion.

Glover may have given silver dollars to fifty-two men, but only fifteen comprised his inner core and were murder suspects. These SDG Klansmen linked to murders included seven mill workers, two farmers, two deputies, two mechanics, two truck drivers, and one self-employed sanitation worker. Many served in the military, some in World War II. I link the SDG to eight murders. Their methods included arson (Frank Morris), a beating (Earl Hodges), a bombing (Wharlest Jackson), two shootings (Clifton Walker and Ben Chester White), and two drownings (Henry Dee and Charles Moore) that followed beatings. White, Dee, and Moore were picked up by their killers during daylight hours. White was killed at dusk; Walker, Dee, and Moore after dark. Joseph Edwards was stopped by the flashing light of a police car in the middle of the night. He did one thing the others couldn't—he ran in an attempt to escape. Where he ended up is still a mystery.

Much is written about Sam Bowers and the White Knights because they killed men who became civil rights martyrs. Everybody knows what Bowers did. He and other White Knights got caught and went to jail. Not the SDG. These devils walked away from their crimes free men, with the exception of James Ford Seale, who was convicted after living a full life and died four years after imprisonment.

Jerry Beatty of Ferriday, whose father operated the Gulf station at the main intersection in town where deputies hung out in the 1960s, said that when he was a child DeLaughter and Ogden, over coffee with Beatty's father, laughed about the Morris arson. Jerry Beatty said he heard the two confess their involvement.[15]

There was once a time when Frank DeLaughter would enter a bar in Concordia Parish and patrons would part like the Red Sea, but he died impoverished at the age of sixty-nine in 1996. He had often expressed fear of meeting his Maker, haunted by the things he had done. A Baptist preacher baptized him a few years before his death. Ex-cops have told me that DeLaughter slept with the windows of his house covered to keep ghosts from peeping in. It was said that even when he blocked his ears with his hands, he could still hear his victims scream.[16]

Ogden died in a nursing home in Ferriday in 2004 at age ninety. One preacher said he tried for years to bring Ogden into the light of God but feared the elderly former deputy was beyond redemption.[17]

IN 1977, AFTER GRADUATING with a journalism degree from Louisiana Tech University in Ruston, I worked at the *Hammond Daily Star* in southeastern Louisiana. Over the course of a few weeks, I did a series on a Klan group in Denham Springs thirty miles to the west near Baton Rouge. Klan leader Bill Wilkinson insisted the interview take place at midnight at his klavern hall outside Denham Springs. I was twenty-three years old and scared. When I knocked on the door, I heard a deep voice shout, "Enter!" At the top of the stairs were two behemoths. As I identified myself, Wilkinson appeared and invited me to his office on the second floor. His desk was filled with racist pamphlets, and at times he seemed to be trying to recruit me. The previous year he had stood outside President Jimmy Carter's home church in Plains, Georgia, to protest the president's recent suggestion that Southern Baptist churches be integrated. My interview with Wilkinson didn't amount to much. Years later, I was surprised to learn that he might have been an FBI informant at the time I interviewed him. And I was shocked when the British *Daily Mail* reported in the spring of 2015 that Wilkinson was living in his own $3 million resort in Belize.

Investigating half-century-old cases is not easy. To chase down old Klansmen and aging witnesses, and to find new ones, takes more than tenacity and skill. Something has to drive you. In 2008, I received a note from a female reader in Natchez. "Thank you, thank you," she wrote. "If all of the wicked hate crimes could be taken out of the secret places and stand in the light, this country could be healed! . . . One man can and does make a difference. Know that there are many of us who join you in your crusade for justice, if only by reading, weeping and praying."

I made a copy of the letter, folded it, and put it in my wallet. It's still there.

AT TIMES WHILE investigating this story, I found personal connections. The mother of James "Red" Lee, the man who hosted the SDG fish fry in 1965 and helped perfect the bomb that maimed George Metcalfe, taught me sixth-grade music. In the mid-1970s, some high school friends and I hauled hay for

J. D. Richardson, the owner of the Morville Lounge, who had recently completed his prison term. We unloaded the hay in the old lounge—once the home of pimps, prostitutes, and gamblers—before it was swept away by a Mississippi River flood. At that time, I didn't know who Richardson was.

Over the course of the years, I have read and heard and seen things I'll never forget.

I remember Wharlest Jackson's widow, Exerlena, sitting in a restaurant in Vidalia, recalling the "beautiful life" that ended when she heard the explosion that killed her husband. She died in 2009 at age seventy-two.

Who can not be haunted by Ben Chester White's final words, "Oh, Lord, what did I do to deserve this?" Or bomb survivor George Metcalfe's question about white people: "Why do they hate us so?"

I think about Earl Hodges, a troubled man who was trying to rebuild his relationship with his sons. A Klan member, he objected when his klavern wanted to whip a man for things he didn't do. The Klan also feared that Hodges would reveal KKK secrets to authorities, specifically about the Dee and Moore murders. These factors cost Hodges his life.

When I talk to Rosa Williams about her grandfather Frank Morris, I hear the voice of a twelve-year-old. When I talk to Wharlest Jackson Jr., the sound I hear is of a little boy longing for the arms of his father.

I will never lose sight of Julia Dobbins's anguished smile when she told stories about her mother, in the days and years after Joseph Edwards disappeared, asking almost everyone she saw, "Have you heard from Joe? What about Joe?"

The greatest message of hope comes from Franklin County, Mississippi, where Thomas Moore went to church with former White Knight Charles Edwards, the man who was part of the wrecking crew that killed Thomas's little brother. Edwards asked for forgiveness, and Thomas Moore forgave him.

There were men of great courage and honor who walked these Klan killing fields in the 1960s. FBI agents John Pfeifer and Billy Bob Williams faced death every day. These two men, who died while I was writing this book, gave me so much of their time and insight for one simple reason: They wanted these old cases solved. I will never understand why the bureau ignored them during its most recent investigations, and I am troubled by the silence of civil rights groups concerning the government's poor execution of its promises in 2007 to reinvestigate.

IN 1967, AN AGING Klansman decided to speak frankly with two FBI agents about the state of race relations. Justice for blacks, he said, was decades away. White people in the Natchez area, the Klansman reported, claimed not to "condone violence against Negroes," yet "this has been an accepted fact of life in the South." Generations would pass, he thought, "before this fact [would] drastically change."[18] Maybe change has arrived. Almost a half century later in 2015, Natchez and Adams County voters elected an African American sheriff over two white candidates, including the incumbent, making the victor the first black man to hold the office since Reconstruction.

The cases I have discussed in this book were cases that should have been investigated by local officials. For the past fifty years, every law enforcement official or lawyer—male or female, black or white—in every town, parish, or county where these murders occurred took an oath to enforce the law. Yet the vast majority didn't lift a finger to solve these crimes. In most of these murders, the federal government had no jurisdiction, but without the FBI and Department of Justice nothing would have been done.

Every community and every citizen bears the ultimate responsibility of justice, including me and including you. After half a century, who is to blame for the failure of justice in cases like these?

We all are.

AFTERWORD

AS I WRITE THIS, only a week has passed since three of my undergraduate students made a startling discovery in a rural Georgia county that holds secrets about a 1948 racially motivated murder that went unpunished.

Along with a dozen classmates, these students—a New Yorker, a San Franciscan, and an Atlantan—had been taking my Georgia Civil Rights Cold Cases class at Emory University in Atlanta, where they studied the life, death, and times of Isaiah Nixon. Mr. Nixon, an African American farmer, was shot dead at age twenty-eight in front of his wife and children because he voted in the Democratic Party primary in 1948.

First by phone, then in person in our classroom, the students had interviewed Mr. Nixon's daughter, who recalled in vivid and brutal detail watching two white men fire multiple shots into her father's body while her mother screamed, "Fall, Isaiah! Fall!" The students had found information on the now-deceased brothers who killed Mr. Nixon, on the long-dead sheriff (an uncle of the brothers) who may have protected the killers, on the all-white primary that Georgia fought to preserve even after the U.S. Supreme Court struck it down, on the all-white jury system that Georgia managed to continue after the high court barred it, on the roles of the NAACP and the black press in helping the Nixon family, and on the white supremacist demagoguery that Gene and Herman Talmadge—father and son, both governors, both U.S. senators—spewed to turn the state's citizens against one another.

The students also had learned that my inspiration for this project and the course was Stanley Nelson, the extraordinary editor of the *Concordia Sentinel,* the weekly newspaper (circulation 4,700) in Ferriday, Louisiana. The students had met Stanley at the beginning of the fall 2015 semester and couldn't get enough of him. They surrounded him, peppered him with questions about his work, and came away star-struck and pumped to model his methods in taking on the Isaiah Nixon case.

As editor, Stanley headed up a three-person newsroom. He ran the news coverage; wrote the local history column; covered the drainage commission, the police jury, and politicians; chased down press releases; typed up local crime reports; and spent the rest of his time knocking on doors just to see what was happening behind them. He was able to crack difficult cold cases only by working most nights and weekends.

I had had the privilege of working closely with Stanley for several years while he investigated the unsolved, unpunished, racially motivated murders of Frank Morris, Wharlest Jackson, and Joe Edwards on both sides of the Mississippi River, in the Ferriday-Vidalia-Natchez area. Week after week, sometimes six or seven times a week, Stanley—holding some revealing document—would open our telephone conversations by saying, "I think I found something. Tell me what you think."

I was so impressed that I joined LSU journalism professor Jay Shelledy in nominating Stanley for a Pulitzer Prize. You can count the number of weekly newspapers that have become finalists for a Pulitzer Prize on one hand; the number that have won would not take more than a couple of fingers. Stanley was chosen as a finalist, one of the three best entries in the United States in local reporting in 2011. The prize went to the *Chicago Sun-Times* for a project by a team of three reporters—a team as large as Stanley's entire newsroom!

That same year, with thirty-five years of newspaper reporting and editing behind me, I embarked on creating the Georgia Civil Rights Cold Cases Project (coldcases.emory.edu) at Emory University. Most, maybe all, of the perpetrators of the horrific cases in Georgia were long since dead, so I had no expectations that our students' work would lead to criminal prosecutions. But the historian's role continues long after the prosecutor's ends. My mission was to teach history animated by primary evidence; instead of focusing on the who-done-it, we would focus on why. We would apply Stanley's zeal, assiduous pursuit, and fair-minded thinking to an instructional setting where students would dig out primary documents to reveal truths that conventional southern history had ignored. What could be nobler than bringing Stanley's doggedness, his persistence, and his ethics to students willing to immerse themselves in the history of the Jim Crow South, students who would come away better understanding who we are today—and who we still could be—by understanding who we were?

All this was on my mind as I drove the students three hours south of Atlanta to Mt. Vernon, Georgia, parked outside the Montgomery County courthouse, and watched as they entered the court clerk's office. They showed great courtesy and deference (Stanley Nelson trademarks) as they met the clerk and requested materials from the 1948 trial that ended in the acquittal of the two men who admitted killing Mr. Nixon. They climbed ladders, stood on filing cabinets, and handed down small boxes containing fragile court documents and large, awkward, bound volumes of old broadsheet newspapers.

Their most important discovery was still ahead, twenty-five miles out of town, off a dirt road, in the African American cemetery where Isaiah Nixon was said to have been buried in an unmarked plot in 1948. The Nixon children, too young at the time of the killing to recall later where he was buried, as well as others interested in the Isaiah Nixon story, had looked for a headstone without success for nearly seven decades. A group had installed a memorial bench where they thought he might be buried. We were there mostly to pay our respects and to capture the atmosphere.

Our silence was broken when one of the students said, in a voice that carried over the flat terrain, "I found it." On her hands and knees, brushing away tree branches and leaves and digging her finger into muddy crevices that formed the letters of his name, the student indeed had discovered Isaiah Nixon's gravesite.

In her simple declaration, I heard an echo of Stanley's always-understated way of introducing big news: "I think I found something. Tell me what you think." It is in such ways that Stanley Nelson's mighty and essential work lives on.

—Hank Klibanoff
November 29, 2015
Atlanta, Georgia

APPENDIX
Biographies

SILVER DOLLAR GROUP MURDER VICTIMS

Clifton Walker, Woodville, Mississippi, February 28, 1964

Thirty-seven-year-old International Paper employee Clifton Walker was returning home from work when he was gunned down in the middle of the night on Poor House Road near Woodville, Mississippi. His body was discovered stretched across the front seat of his car. Evidence indicated Walker was reaching for his gun stored in the glove compartment when he was caught in a crossfire. The sister-in-law of Douglas Byrd, the top Mississippi Original Knights leader in 1963 before he became a White Knight in 1964, told MHSP investigators that Walker made a pass at her in late 1963, an allegation that would have become widely known in Klan circles, especially at IP, where Tommie Lee Jones, Thore L. Torgersen, and James L. Scarborough were among Walker's coworkers. All three were members of Red Glover's wrecking crews in 1963 and 1964. Klan informant E. D. Morace implicated Glover, Jones, Torgersen, and James Frederick "Red" Lee in the Walker shooting, but for reasons unclear, the FBI never followed that lead.

Henry Hezekiah Dee, Davis Island, Mississippi, May 2, 1964
Charles Moore, Davis Island, Mississippi, May 2, 1964

Dee and Moore, both nineteen, were kidnapped by Klansmen in Meadville, Mississippi, in the middle of the day, taken to the Homochitto National Forest, and beaten with bean sticks. Later, they were bound, tossed into the trunk of Ernest Parker's car, driven by Parker and brothers Jack and James Ford Seale to an old channel of the Mississippi River, and drowned. The Bunkley klavern of White Knights, led by the Seales' father, Clyde, believed Dee was a gun-running black militant. Moore had by coincidence joined Dee on the highway to hitch a ride home when James Ford Seale abducted the two young men. Murder charges were filed against Seale and Charles Edwards in 1964 but later dropped. In 2007, Edwards, who was implicated in the beatings but not in the drownings, was granted immunity and testified against Seale, who was convicted and later died in federal prison. The Dee-Moore murders were the only cases in which an SDG member was convicted.

Joseph Edwards, Concordia Parish, Louisiana, July 12, 1964

Edwards, twenty-five, disappeared after leaving the Shamrock Motel in Vidalia around midnight. A short time later, a witness driving on the Ferriday-Vidalia highway watched an old-model Buick, later identified as Edwards's, being pulled over by a white car with police antennae on the trunk and a flashing red light on the dash. FBI informant E. D. Morace implicated Red Glover, Kenneth Norman Head, and Homer Thomas "Buck" Horton in the murder of Edwards, while deputies Frank DeLaughter and Bill Ogden were implicated by other sources. Ogden told a preacher that after he and DeLaughter pulled Edwards over in front of the Dixie Lane Bowling Alley, Edwards jumped from his car and ran. Ogden, in his patrol car, and DeLaughter, on foot, chased Edwards up the Mississippi River levee, which paralleled the highway by the bowling alley. Ogden claimed Edwards got away. Another suspect was Vidalia police chief J. L. "Bud" Spinks. Louisiana probation officer James Goss was a suspect as well. He implicated Deputy Junior Harp, reporting that Harp's car was similar to the white one described by the witness. In 2009, a confidential source informed the *Concordia Sentinel* that before his death in 2004, Ogden, while in a nursing home, repeatedly summoned attendants to his room and in terror shouted, "Don't you see that little nigger boy? He's got blood on him. He's after me. I ran over him with my car." Edwards's body has never been found.

Frank Morris, Ferriday, Louisiana, December 10, 1964

Over three decades, the fifty-one-year-old Morris developed a loyal following of black and white customers at his shoe shop in Ferriday. In 1962, he had two run-ins with Junior Harp, the jailer at the Ferriday Police Department. Two FBI informants reported that Morris and Deputy Frank DeLaughter had intensely argued over payment involving a pair of cowboy boots hours before the arson. After midnight on December 10, 1964, Morris was awakened by breaking glass, and while confronting two men standing outside his shop—one holding a gasoline can and the other a shotgun—one threw a match inside the building, which erupted in flames. His body on fire, Morris nevertheless made his way out the back door and was quickly transported by two Ferriday police officers to the hospital. He died four days later. On his deathbed, Morris was interviewed by local authorities and the FBI. He is the only known Klan victim of the era to have physically described his attackers before his death. However, Morris said a dozen times he didn't know the men by name. After the fire, the Klan spread rumors that Morris had been allowing black men to use the back room of his shop to have sex with white women. In 1967, former Mississippi UKA grand dragon E. L. McDaniel implicated Tommie Lee Jones, Thore L. Torgersen, James Scarborough, and E. D. Morace in the arson. In 2010, the *Concordia Sentinel* found witnesses who said Coonie Poissot, who had died two decades earlier, and Arthur Leonard Spencer told them they had committed the arson but hadn't expected anyone to be in the shop. Poissot, an informant by 1967, told the FBI he was with DeLaughter hours before the arson and heard DeLaughter say he planned to teach Morris a lesson for being uppity, but claimed to know nothing about the arson. The *Sentinel* reported its findings in January 2011, and a month later the Justice Department convened a state grand jury in Concordia Parish, but no action was taken before Spencer died in 2013.

Earl Hodges, Eddiceton, Mississippi, August 15, 1965

Once a popular and skilled mechanic in Eddiceton, Mississippi, Hodges descended into alcoholism and womanizing, habits that cost him his marriage and separated him from his two sons. He was a member of the White Knights klavern in Franklin County, Mississippi, led by Clyde Seale. Following the Dee-Moore murders, Hodges had grown to despise Seale and once opposed one of his wrecking crew projects. Hodges soon dropped out of the Klan and, in the days before his murder, confided to others, including a preacher, his desire to become a better man and to make his sons proud of him again. Because of Hodges's opposition to the Klan and his heavy drinking, Seale and other Klansmen feared he would provide damning information to the FBI or to his brother-in-law, a member of the MHSP task force investigating the Klan. At a late-night meeting on August 15, 1965, Hodges, then forty-seven, was brutally beaten by Clyde Seale and Ernest Avants, who would take part in the Ben Chester White murder in 1966. Hodges's body was found at daylight at the foot of the garden behind his father's three-room shotgun house.

Ben Chester White, Adams County, Mississippi, June 10, 1966

White, a sixty-seven-year-old sharecropper and farm employee in rural Adams County, Mississippi, was lured into James Lloyd Jones's car and driven to the Pretty Creek Bridge, where Claude Fuller shot White seventeen times with an automatic rifle. Afterward, Ernest Avants shot White in the head with a shotgun. Fuller and Avants later set Jones's car on fire at another location. Jones confessed and implicated the other two men. Despite an airtight case, neither Jones nor Avants was convicted by Klan-infested juries, while Fuller was never tried. Impressed by the murder, Red Glover made Fuller a member of the SDG. In 2003, Avants, the only suspect still living, was convicted in federal court after it was discovered the crime had occurred on federal property. Avants died in prison the next year.

Wharlest Jackson, Natchez, Mississippi, February 27, 1967

In January 1967, Jackson, a thirty-six-year-old married father of five, became the first black man at the Armstrong Tire Plant promoted to a position previously held by white men only. Among his coworkers were Red Glover and James Frederick "Red" Lee, who in 1965 had planned the car bombing that seriously injured Jackson's good friend George Metcalfe. Metcalfe and Jackson were leaders of the reactivated Natchez NAACP. On his way home from work after an overtime shift ending at 8 p.m., Jackson died instantly when his truck exploded after he turned on his left blinker. The killing resulted in a massive FBI investigation that became known as WHARBOM. Hundreds of witnesses were interviewed by 180 agents. Additionally, WHARBOM included a second investigation into the Frank Morris murder and the first probe into the disappearance of Joseph Edwards. By 1970, the FBI had achieved one of its goals, "neutralizing" members of the Silver Dollar Group. While WHARBOM resulted in no murder convictions, it did bring about the conviction of Concordia Parish sheriff Noah Cross for his involvement in a mob-backed prostitution and gambling operation. Cross's deputy, Frank DeLaughter, was also convicted in the case as well as for police brutality in the beating of a prisoner. In the Jackson murder, many in law enforcement, including retired FBI agents, believe that Glover acted alone in the bombing.

CONCORDIA PARISH SHERIFF'S OFFICE

COWAN, Ike, Jr. (1926–1985). A veteran of World War II and the Korean conflict, Cowan spent an afternoon in 1966 spilling the beans on the nefarious operations of the Concordia Parish Sheriff's Office to FBI agent John Pfeifer. In particular, Cowan outlined how Sheriff Noah Cross collected protection money from gambling operators and pimps, with a primary focus on the Morville Lounge, operated by the Carlos Marcello mob. Pfeifer hoped to turn Cowan into an informant and attempted to convince him to testify in court against Frank DeLaughter, but Cowan considered the idea too risky and told Cross that the FBI was trying to pressure him into revealing the illegal operations of the sheriff's office. Cowan and other line deputies were called before federal grand juries and subpoenaed to testify in the federal trials of Cross and DeLaughter, but they all refused to utter one disparaging word against either defendant. Born in Concordia Parish, Louisiana. Died in Alexandria, Louisiana. Buried in Natchez, Mississippi.

CROSS, Noah Webster (1908–1976). Cross was elected to seven terms as sheriff of Concordia Parish beginning in 1941. His tenure ended in 1973, when he was imprisoned following his federal conviction in connection with a brothel and gambling den in Concordia Parish operated by the Carlos Marcello mob. While it is unclear if Cross was a member of the Silver Dollar Group, at least two of his deputies were. Cross held an honorary membership in the United Klans of America. The FBI considered Cross one of the most corrupt sheriffs in the South. Cross died in 1976 after serving briefly in federal prison. Never once did Cross investigate or assist in the investigations of the murder of Frank Morris or the disappearance of Joseph Edwards, crimes that involved the SDG and his deputies, who carried out the homicides in uniform and with the use of their patrol cars. Born in Concordia Parish, Louisiana. Buried in Natchez, Mississippi.

DeLAUGHTER, Frank Edward (1927–1996). DeLaughter worked as a fire-man, jailer, and radio dispatcher before becoming a police officer in Ferriday in 1962. As a fireman and later as a police officer, he killed at least two men under suspicious circumstances. While wearing a badge, DeLaughter oper-ated his own criminal ring and extorted goods and services from local busi-nesses, ranging from whiskey to shoe repair. Identified by the FBI as a mem-ber of the Silver Dollar Group, he was sworn into the United Klans of America in 1964 by E. L. McDaniel of Natchez, then grand dragon of the Mississippi UKA. DeLaughter participated in the 1964 disappearance/murder of Joseph Edwards and is believed to have masterminded Frank Morris's murder by ar-son. He also used local thugs to beat CORE workers in 1965. McDaniel recog-nized DeLaughter as a Klan dignitary at a UKA rally in Natchez in 1966, and he served as secretary of a Concordia UKA klavern. In the early 1970s, he was convicted in federal court for promoting prostitution at the mob-operated Morville Lounge, where he picked up protection money every week for de-livery to Sheriff Noah Cross. He was also convicted in federal court for police brutality in the savage beating of a white man who was believed to have stolen a slot machine motor from his employer, Blackie Drane. Following his release from federal prison after serving one year and a day, he was unemployed un-til 1976, when the Ferriday Town Council (which by then included a black al-derman) hired him as a dispatcher, returning him to the same environs where he had brutalized countless prisoners in previous years. Born in Brookhaven, Mississippi. Died in Ferriday, Louisiana. Buried in Natchez, Mississippi.

HARP, William Howell, Jr. (1930–2004). A police officer in Ferriday in the early 1960s who later became a Concordia Parish sheriff's deputy, Harp worked closely with Frank DeLaughter. In 1962, Harp had a run-in with Frank Morris and alleged that he made improper comments to Harp's wife. Harp ad-mitted to the FBI that he confronted Morris at the shoe shop afterward while dressed in his uniform and wearing a sidearm. Harp drove the town firetruck to the shoe shop on the night of the fire and later stood at Morris's bedside at the hospital while FBI agents questioned Morris about the arson. Harp drove a 1962 white Oldsmobile, similar to the one seen pulling over Joseph Edwards's Buick in 1964. A suspect in that case, James Goss, told the FBI he believed Harp was involved in Edwards's disappearance. Born in Concordia Parish, Louisiana. Died in Covington, Louisiana. Buried in Monterey (Con-cordia Parish), Louisiana.

OGDEN, William "Bill" Howard (1913–2004). A Concordia Parish deputy and identified by the FBI as a member of the Silver Dollar Group, Ogden was known to advise Klansmen when FBI agents asked questions about them. As Ogden struggled with a drunken bar patron in the early 1960s, his pistol reportedly discharged, killing another man sitting at the bar watching the fight. He was a suspect in the disappearance/murder of Joseph Edwards. Ogden told a preacher that he and Frank DeLaughter had stopped Edwards in front of the bowling alley, but the young black man abandoned his Buick and ran up the levee. Ogden said he followed in his patrol car but Edwards got away. In 2008, a source reported to the *Concordia Sentinel* that Ogden had hallucinations suggesting his guilt in the Edwards case while in his final years in a nursing home. Died in Ferriday, Louisiana. Born and buried in Liddieville (Franklin Parish), Louisiana.

SILVER DOLLAR GROUP MURDER SUSPECTS

FULLER, Claude (1922–1993). An employee at International Paper Company in Natchez, Fuller set fire to his car in 1963 in a failed attempt to collect insurance money and blame black men for the crime. He also hoped to make white Mississippians believe that armed gangs of blacks were roaming the countryside looking for whites to attack. By 1966, he had proven too violent and too mentally unstable even for the White Knights, who put him out of the group. Longing for a Klan home, he recruited four men into the Cottonmouth Moccasin Klan, a group he created. He lied to the group, claiming that he was authorized by Klan higher-ups to kill a local black man in order to lure Dr. Martin Luther King Jr. to Natchez, where Klansmen would then assassinate the civil rights leader. Fuller, James Lloyd Jones, and Ernest Avants picked up an aging African American named Ben Chester White. With Jones sitting in the driver's seat, Fuller shot the man seventeen times with an automatic carbine as White slumped over in the backseat. Avants shot White's corpse in the head with a shotgun, scattering flesh, blood, and brain matter throughout Jones's car. (Avants, who like Fuller had been kicked out of the White Knights, was believed to have been involved in the 1965 beating death of White Knight Earl Hodges of Franklin County, Mississippi.) In the White case, the three Klansmen left a trail of witnesses, but despite an airtight case, Jones was freed after a hung jury, Avants was acquitted, and Fuller was never tried. In 1967, Red Glover rewarded Fuller with a silver dollar and membership in the SDG. (In 2000, Avants, the only survivor of the three defendants, was charged in the murder by federal authorities because it had occurred in a national forest. He was convicted in 2003 and died in 2004.) Born in Alabama. Died in Adams County, Mississippi.

GLOVER, Raleigh Jackson (1922–1984). Glover learned to use explosives while serving in the U.S. Navy Seabees in World War II and Korea. As a Klan recruiter and investigator, Glover led several wrecking crew projects. In 1964, disgusted with traditional Klan groups and with politicians for their inability to stop integration, Glover started the Silver Dollar Group at the Shamrock Motel coffee shop in Vidalia. The group's mission was to fight integration by any means. He presented a silver dollar to each SDG recruit as a symbol of unity. Glover was the only SDG member never to admit his Klan affiliation to the FBI. To an informant, Glover implicated himself in the 1964 Clifton Walker murder four years after the fact. A suspect in the 1964 disappearance/murder of Joseph Edwards, he also masterminded the attempted murder by car bomb of Natchez NAACP president George Metcalfe in 1965. Authorities believe he acted alone in the 1967 car bomb murder of Natchez NAACP treasurer Wharlest Jackson. Born in St. Augustine County, Texas. Died in Natchez. Buried in Natchez.

HEAD, Kenneth Norman (1928–2004). Head served in the U.S. Marines in China at the end of World War II and later became the Exalted Cyclops of the Vidalia Original Knights klavern. A mechanic and electrician experienced in oil-field maintenance, Head also handled shaped electrical charges used to perforate well holes. A close friend of Red Glover, Head was involved in numerous wrecking crew projects and was a suspect in the murder of Joseph Edwards, the attempted murder of George Metcalfe, and the murder of Wharlest Jackson. Born in Natchez. Died in Bay St. Louis, Mississippi. Buried in Natchez.

HESTER, Elden Glen (1928–2004). An Armstrong Tire employee, Hester was given the nickname "Junk Man" by fellow SDG members because he stored explosives for Red Glover. A suspect in the murder of Wharlest Jackson, Hester was a member of the Franklin County, Mississippi, White Knights unit headed by Clyde Seale. Before the Jackson bombing, an FBI informant saw explosives in Hester's home outside Meadville. A short time after the bombing, another informant saw what was believed to be part of the same cache in an old farmhouse owned by Hester in Franklin Parish, Louisiana. Born, died, and buried in Franklin County, Mississippi.

HORTON, Homer Thomas (1935–1995). Nicknamed "Buck," Horton worked for Armstrong Tire before becoming a certified flight instructor and commercial pilot. He was elected as nighthawk in the Original Knights Klan unit in Vidalia in 1963 and was a suspect in the 1964 disappearance/murder of Joseph Edwards. Born in Brookhaven, Mississippi. Died in Jackson. Buried in Lincoln County, Mississippi.

JONES, Tommie Lee (1936–2007). The International Paper Company employee was involved in the Original Knights, White Knights, and United Klans of America. A close associate of Red Glover, he participated in a wrecking crew project as early as 1963, when he and other Klansmen beat a black man who later disappeared. The unauthorized act drew the ire of E. L. McDaniel, then head of White Knights projects in the region. When McDaniel and other Klan leaders admonished Jones, he was defiant, a stance that McDaniel never forgave. McDaniel later implicated Jones and three others in Frank Morris's murder. In early 1964, during a wrecking crew project, Jones was shot in the face by a black man the SDG was attempting to kidnap and kill. In 1965, Jones was arrested in Ferriday after hitting a black man in the head with the butt of a pistol. In 1967, Jones was incapacitated due to back surgery, thereby eliminating him as a physical participant in the car bombing of Wharlest Jackson, although one informant said Jones had indicated that Jackson should be killed. He acknowledged to the FBI his involvement in the beating of one black man, and the FBI believed it was close to turning him into an informant in 1967, but ultimately he hired a lawyer and quit talking. Jones died a few months after the FBI launched a new probe into the Morris murder in 2007; the bureau did not interview him prior to his death. Born in Gloster, Mississippi. Died in Natchez.

LEE, James Frederick (1933–1999). Son of a Baptist minister, Lee went by the nickname "Red." A veteran of the U.S. Army, the Armstrong Tire employee was a close associate of Red Glover and served as investigator for the

Black River Klan in Concordia Parish. In 1965, Lee hosted a fish fry at his Lismore home, where SDG Klansmen experimented with explosives two months prior to the car bombing of George Metcalfe. Lee and Sonny Taylor perfected the bomb that injured Metcalfe. He also was a suspect in the car bombing of Wharlest Jackson. Born in Orange, Texas. Died in Tennessee.

MORACE, E. D. (1926–1970). Morace was the investigator for the Original Knights unit in Ferriday and Clayton. A mechanic and part-time bouncer, he was described as the "head hatchet man" for the Ferriday Klan. By 1965, Morace was considered one of the FBI's most reliable informers, although a 1966 victim of a Klan beating identified him as one of his attackers. A suspect in the Frank Morris murder, Morace told the bureau that he investigated several Klan complaints about Morris. He discovered these charges to be untrue. Morace said that a short time before the arson, Morris and Frank DeLaughter had a heated argument over a pair of cowboy boots DeLaughter had ordered but refused to pay for. Morace was the lone informant to tell the bureau that Vidalia Klansman Kenneth Norman Head had implicated himself, Red Glover, and Buck Horton in the 1964 murder of Joseph Edwards. Morace also implicated Glover as the mastermind of the 1964 murder of Clifton Walker in Woodville, Mississippi. Born in Concordia Parish. Died in Ferriday. Buried near Sicily Island, Louisiana.

PARKER, Ernest Buchanan (1930–1996). One of the wealthiest Klansmen in the South, Parker was a self-employed farmer, oilman, and rancher, while also serving as Exalted Cyclops of the Morgantown White Knights klavern in Natchez. With his brother, Parker co-owned property on Parker's Island, more commonly known as Davis Island, in Warren County, Mississippi. There, Parker and brothers Jack and James Ford Seale drowned Henry Hezekiah Dee and Charles Moore. Parker died in a tractor accident at Davis Island. Born in Natchez. Buried in Natchez.

POISSOT, O. C. "Coonie" (1923–1992). In 1967, as an FBI informer, Poissot described his involvement in several wrecking crew projects with Red Glover and others. He also reported hearing Glover and Kenneth Norman Head confess to the car bombing of George Metcalfe. While riding with Frank DeLaughter in his police cruiser hours before the Frank Morris arson, Poissot claimed DeLaughter railed against the shoe repairman. The next night, the shoe shop was torched. Almost a half century later, following publication of an article on Poissot, by then dead, the *Concordia Sentinel* was contacted by two of Poissot's daughters. One daughter said that her father claimed to have killed a black man for the Klan and that he carried a silver dollar. Weeks later, the *Sentinel* interviewed a son, an ex-wife, and an ex-brother-in-law of Arthur Leonard Spencer, a former Klansman from Rayville, Louisiana. They said they had learned from Poissot and Spencer years earlier that the two had torched a shoe shop in Ferriday in the 1960s and that the fire had killed a black man, who wasn't supposed to be there. In an interview with the *Sentinel* in 2010, Spencer denied any knowledge of the Morris arson and denied having even heard the name "Coonie" Poissot, although two of Spencer's children claimed Poissot was like a grandfather to them. The *Sentinel's* story of the allegations against Spencer, printed in January 2011, was followed by three separate grand jury investigations, the first launched in February 2011. A federal prosecutor was named an assistant district attorney in Concordia Parish to handle the state grand jury probe. No charges or reports were issued before or after Spencer's death in 2013. Poissot, who was born in LaSalle Parish, Louisiana, had died two decades earlier in El Paso, Texas. He was cremated and his ashes scattered in the Franklin Mountains of west Texas.

SCARBOROUGH, James Lee (1921–1985). Scarborough was an International Paper Company employee who had served as a coxswain in the U.S. Navy during World War II. He was Exalted Cyclops of the Ferriday-Clayton Original Knights unit until ousted from the position in December 1965 on charges of divulging Klan secrets to Frank DeLaughter and Blackie Drane. Involved in several wrecking crew projects, Scarborough was a suspect in the Frank Morris arson murder and the attempted murder of George Metcalfe. Born, died, and buried in Union Parish, Louisiana.

SEALE, Clyde Wayne (1901–1983). A Bunkley farmer, considered the top White Knights Klan leader in Franklin County, Seale organized the attacks that resulted in the murders of Henry Hezekiah Dee, Charles Moore, and Earl Hodges. Seale's sons James Ford and Jack were feared by other Klansmen, as was he. Born, died, and buried in Franklin County, Mississippi.

SEALE, James Ford (1935–2011). Seale was the only SDG member convicted of murder (forty-three years after the crime); the original charges against

Seale and Charles Edwards were dropped a few months after the 1964 murders of Henry Hezekiah Dee and Charles Moore. In 1967, Seale acknowledged to the FBI that he was in the SDG and that he attended the 1965 fish fry gathering in Concordia Parish. However, he denied any crimes. He was believed to be involved in the murder of Earl Hodges. In the years to follow, while working as a crop duster, Seale crashed two planes in Concordia Parish, walking away from both crashes uninjured. The second, in 1970, resulted in the deaths of all five passengers in another aircraft that allegedly clipped the wing of Seale's plane over the Concordia Parish airport. Among the dead was Dr. Charles Colvin, who had been Frank Morris's attending physician in 1964. Seale was the only eyewitness and only survivor of the collision; there were no charges. On the testimony of Charles Edwards, Seale was convicted of the Dee-Moore murders in 2007 and sentenced to two life terms in federal prison. While in prison, Seale was shocked to learn about a report in the *Concordia Sentinel* that his brother, Jack Seale, had become an FBI informant in 1967. He had told Red Glover following the 1967 car bombing murder of Wharlest Jackson that Klansmen should remain forever silent, noting, "A man's mouth is his worst enemy." Not once did he open his to help resolve other SDG crimes and provide closure to the families of the victims. Born in Franklin County, Mississippi. Died in Terre Haute, Indiana. Buried in Franklin County, Mississippi.

SEALE, Myron Wayne (1927–1974). Considered one of the most violent Klansmen in Mississippi and Louisiana, Seale answered to the nickname "Jack." Best friend of UKA grand dragon E. L. McDaniel, Seale served as state nighthawk for the UKA. With a long police record dating back to his service in the U.S. Navy at the end of World War II, Seale was involved in the murders of Henry Hezekiah Dee and Charles Moore and also took part in numerous wrecking crew projects. A suspect in the 1964 bombing of Natchez mayor John Nosser's home, Seale was arrested but not convicted in the 1966 bombing of Oberlin Jewelers in Natchez. After his garbage disposal business failed and his utilities were disconnected due to nonpayment, he became an FBI informant in 1967. Born in Brookhaven, Mississippi. Buried in Natchez.

TAYLOR, James Horace (1929–1995). A Harrisonburg, Louisiana, logger and construction worker nicknamed "Sonny," Taylor became one of the FBI's most reliable informants in 1967, although he confessed to having planted the bomb that maimed George Metcalfe in 1965. Taylor said a Ferriday Klansman helped him plant the bomb but refused to identify the man. Taylor also told the FBI he helped Red Glover move a large cache of explosives from a Louisiana farmhouse not long after the 1967 car bombing of Wharlest Jackson. Taylor said he didn't know where Glover relocated the explosives. Taylor died in a nursing home in Wisner, Louisiana. Born and buried in Catahoula Parish, Louisiana.

TORGERSEN, Thore Lee (1923–2000). A U.S. Army veteran of World War II, Torgersen was employed by International Paper Company in Natchez. In 1967, during the WHARBOM probe, Torgersen informed the FBI of the June 1965 fish fry in Concordia Parish, Louisiana, where top Louisiana and Mississippi SDG members gathered for the first and only time. Klansmen experimented with explosives at the gathering, two months before George Metcalfe was seriously injured in a car bombing. Torgersen was a suspect in the 1964 Frank Morris murder. He ended all Klan ties during the WHARBOM probe. Born in Millville, Florida. Died and buried in Natchez.

NOTES

1. WHY FRANK?

1. Stanley Nelson, "Sewell, Walsworth Saw Morris Running," *Concordia Sentinel,* April 9, 2008, A1.

2. Kenneth Walsworth, interview by FBI Special Agents Donald R. Belmont and Donald McGorty, February 1, 1965, FBI Civil Unrest, Frank Morris file 157-HQ-2311, National Archives and Records Administration (NARA), Baltimore, MD.

3. John Pfeifer, interview by Stanley Nelson, April 2, 2011.

4. Stanley Nelson, "King Hotel in Ferriday was Klan Headquarters in Mid-1960s," *Concordia Sentinel,* March 2, 2011, A7.

5. Nicholas deB. Katzenback Testimony, *Hearings Before the Senate Select Committee to Study Governmental Operations With Respect to Intelligence Activities of the United States Senate,* 94th Cong., vol. 6, 1st Sess. (Washington, DC, 1975), 214.

6. Stanley Nelson, "Klan Recruitment Efforts Heavy," *Concordia Sentinel,* July 11, 2007, A1.

7. Stanley Nelson, "Bloody '64: Klan Suspected in Murders, Assaults, Bombings," *Concordia Sentinel,* July 2, 2008, A12.

8. Walsworth, interview by FBI.

9. Johnny Griffing, interview by FBI Special Agents Donald J. McGorty and Paul R. Lancaster, December 10, 1964, FBI Civil Unrest, Frank Morris file 157-HQ-2311, NARA.

10. Stanley Nelson, "Photos Captures Will Haney inside Club a Half-Century Ago," *Concordia Sentinel,* December 8, 2010, A11.

11. In 1950, Lewis's father Elmo, in his car with a loaded pistol, chased Jerry Lee's uncle Lee Calhoun through the streets over a property dispute. Elmo was charged with attempted murder. Ferriday's weekly newspaper, the *Concordia Sentinel,* predicted a "large court audience" before the matter was ultimately settled behind closed doors. "Ferriday Murder Trial Set Monday," *Concordia Sentinel,* April 28, 1950, A1.

12. James J. Simolke, interview by FBI Special Agents Thomas M. McGuinness Jr. and William Quackenbush, January 24, 1965, FBI Civil Unrest, Frank Morris file 157-HQ-2311, NARA.

13. Thomas Sidney Loftin, interview by FBI Special Agents Donald R. Belmont and Donald McGorty, January 25, 1965, FBI Civil Unrest, Frank Morris file 157-HQ-2311, NARA.

14. Nelson, "Sewell, Walsworth," A1.

15. Stanley Nelson, "Morris Seen as 'Human Torch' on Night of Shoe Shop Arson," *Concordia Sentinel,* April 13, 2011, A8.

16. Nelson, "Sewell, Walsworth," A1.

17. Ibid.

18. Nelson, "Human Torch," A8.

19. Dr. Charles Colvin, interview by FBI (agent name redacted), February 2, 1965, FBI Civil Unrest, Frank Morris file 157-HQ-2311, NARA.

20. Stanley Nelson, "Agent Sought 'Dying Declaration' from Morris," *Concordia Sentinel,* May 13, 2009, A2.

21. Ibid.

22. Stanley Nelson, "After 43 Years, Priest Still Wonders, 'Why Frank?'" *Concordia Sentinel,* May 16, 2007, A1.

23. Ibid.

24. Stanley Nelson, "James White Shot Klansman during Shootout in 1964," *Concordia Sentinel,* A10.

25. Stanley Nelson, "A Father's Grief: Who Killed Sullivan Morris' Son in 1964?" *Concordia Sentinel,* A9.

26. Rev. Robert Lee Jr., interview by Stanley Nelson, January 3, 2008.

27. Stanley Nelson, "Morris Knew His Attackers," *Concordia Sentinel,* June 6, 2007, A1.

28. Stanley Nelson, "The Morris Family Christmas Nightmare—1964," *Concordia Sentinel,* A1.

29. Nelson, "After 43 Years, Priest Still Wonders," A1.

30. Father August Thompson, interview by Stanley Nelson, April 29, 2012.

31. Ibid.

32. Rae Beatty, interview by Stanley Nelson, October 17, 2008.

33. Nelson, "Agent Sought 'Dying Declaration,'" A2.

34. Stanley Nelson, "Seale Blamed 1967 Election Loss on Jackson Bombing," *Concordia Sentinel,* October 28, 2009, A8.

35. Stanley Nelson, "Agent Sought 'Dying Declaration,'" *Concordia Sentinel,* May 13, 2009, A2.

36. John Doar and Dorothy Landsberg, "The Performance of the FBI in Investigating Violations of Federal Laws Protecting the Right to Vote—1960–1967," *Hearings Before The Select Committee To Study Governmental Operations With Respect To Intelligence Activities of the United States Senate,* 94th Cong., 1st Sess., vol. 6, Attachment 4, (Washington, DC, 1975), 949–950.

37. Statement of Cynthia Deitle, Chief of FBI Civil Rights Cold Case Unit, *Concordia Sentinel,* January 6, 2011, A1.

38. Nelson, "After 43 Years, Priest Still Wonders," A1.

2. THE KINGPIN, BIG FRANK DELAW, AND THE KLAN

1. United States of America v. J. D. Richardson (Monroe, LA, January 20–21, 1971), 204.

2. United States of America v. Noah Cross (Alexandria, LA, May 2, 1972), 254.

3. Ibid., 247.

4. Meg Casper, Press Secretary to Louisiana Secretary of State, interview by Stanley Nelson, May 6, 2013.

5. Hartwell Love campaign ad, *Concordia Sentinel,* February 6, 1948, 5.

6. "Teen Age Negro Youths Paroled after Three Years," *Natchez Democrat,* January 7, 1949, A1. "Cross, DeLaughter Indicted on 'Rackets' Counts," *Concordia Sentinel,* October 20, 1971, 1A.

7. "Sheriff Orders Slots, Gambling Devices Out by Wed. Evening," "Slot Machines, Other Gambling Called to Grand Jury's Attention," *Concordia Sentinel,* April 13, 1951, 1.

8. Robert Dabney Calhoun, *A History of Concordia Parish,* rpr. from *Louisiana Historical Quarterly,* January 1932, 12, 174.

9. Elaine Dundy, *Ferriday, Louisiana* (New York: Donald I. Fine, Inc., 1991), 58.

10. Noah Cross campaign ad, *Concordia Sentinel,* February 15, 1952, 3.

11. Michael Kurtz, "Political Corruption and Organized Crime in Louisiana: The FBI Files on Earl Long," *Louisiana Historical Association Quarterly* 29, no. 3 (Summer 1988): 243-49; Matt Barnidge, "Connected by Vice: The Longs, Marcello and Concordia," *Concordia Sentinel,* July 8, 2009, A1.

12. SAC New Orleans Memo to FBI Director, "General Organized Crime Conditions in the State of Louisiana, Vice Conditions and Political Corruption," May 29, 1939, Political Corruption and Organized Crime, Earl Kemp Long file 65-54154, National Archives and Records Administration (NARA), College Park, MD.

13. "The Mob," *Life Magazine,* September 1, 1967, 34–36.

14. John Pfeifer, interview by Stanley Nelson, April 2, 2011.

15. Ibid.

16. Lee Drane, interview by Stanley Nelson, January 6, 2010

17. "Industry Helps Concordia," *Concordia Sentinel,* August 16, 1967, A1.

18. "Jerry Lee Lewis Day," *Concordia Sentinel,* April 25, 1958, 1.

19. "Governor Faubus Thanks Concordia Donors in Drive," *Concordia Sentinel,* January 30, 1959, 1.

20. "Register Only Qualified Voters Urges Sen. Rainach," *Concordia Sentinel,* February 13, 1959, 1.

21. "Kingpin," *Concordia Sentinel,* December 11, 1959, 1.

22. David Neal, *Concordia Sentinel,* March 31, 1961, A1.

23. "Services Held for Former Mayor," *Concordia Sentinel,* April 27, 2001, A1.

24. Town of Ferriday, Minute Book, November 1954, Town Hall, Ferriday, Louisiana.

25. Ibid., June 12, 1956.

26. Frank DeLaughter Pardon Application, October 31, 1977, U.S. Probation Office, Western District of Louisiana, Shreveport.

27. *Natchez City Directory,* 1950–51.

28. Woodie Davis, interview by Stanley Nelson, March 2008.

29. "Negro Killed Here in Sunday Shooting," *Concordia Sentinel,* March 6, 1959, 1.

30. Stanley Nelson, "Witness Recalls DeLaughter Killing Unarmed Man in 1959," *Concordia Sentinel,* August 17, 2011, A8.

31. "Person Announces Candidacy for State Senator," *Concordia Sentinel,* August 28, 1959, 1.

32. Town of Ferriday Minute Book, April 12, 1960. Town Hall, Ferriday, Louisiana.

33. FBI Special Agent George A. Gunter, Report, August 7, 1962, FBI Civil Rights Division, Roy George Barlow file 44-1585, NARA.

34. Ibid.

35. Ibid.

36. Stanley Nelson, "Parish Justice, 1962: Accused at Angola 11 Days After Arrest," *Concordia Sentinel,* August 22, 2012, A12.

37. Ibid.

38. Ferriday Minute Book, August 13, 1963. John Pfeifer, interview by Stanley Nelson, April 2, 2011.

39. Rev. Robert Lee Jr., interview by Stanley Nelson, November 2008. John Pfeifer, interview by Stanley Nelson, April 2, 2011.

40. John Pfeifer, interview by Stanley Nelson, April 2, 2011.

41. "When Civil Rights and Social Action Became Personal," Rev. Granville Snyder Personal Recollections (unpublished), 2012. Copy in author's possession.

42. Teletype NO SAC to Director, January 29, 1965, FBI Civil Rights Division, Frank Morris file 157-2311, NARA.

43. Edward L. McDaniel, interview by Orley B. Caudill, University of Southern Mississippi Center for Oral History and Cultural Heritage, Hattiesburg, 1977.

44. "E. L. McDaniel Natchez Background," by FBI Special Agent Billy Bob Williams, November 5, 1964, FBI Civil Rights Division, E. L. McDaniel file 157-2156, NARA.

45. "E. L. McDaniel Los Angeles Background," by FBI Special Agent John C. O'Neill, December 16, 1964, FBI Civil Rights Division, E. L. McDaniel file 157-2156, NARA.

46. Edward L. McDaniel, interview by Caudill, 1977.

47. "Concordia Chapter K.K.K.," *Concordia Sentinel,* October 5, 1962, 1.

48. Edward L. McDaniel, interview by Caudill, 1977.

49. "The Present-Day Ku Klux Klan Movement," Committee on Un-American Activities, House of Representatives, 90th Cong., 2nd Sess., December 22, 1967 (Washington, DC: U.S. Government Printing Office, 1967), 2–3; William Joseph Simmons Statement, Testimony, "Hearings before The Committee on Rules, House of Representatives, on the Ku Klux Klan," 67th Cong., 1st Sess., October 13, 1921 (Washington, DC: Government Printing Office, 1921), 67–184.

50. Simmons Statement, Testimony, 67–184.

51. Ibid.

52. Royal Young Testimony, House UnAmerican Activities Committee, 89th Cong., Executive Sess., July 29, 1965 (Washington, DC: Alterson Reporting Co.), 211, 224, 299–300.

53. Ibid., 253, 271–73.

54. Royal V. Young Memo from Donald T. Appell Memo to the House UnAmerican Activities Committee on Royal V. Young Committee on Un-American Activities, House of Representatives, "Activities of the Ku Klux Klan Organizations in the United States," 89th Cong., 2nd Sess., July 20, 1965 (Washington, DC: Alterson Reporting Co., 1965).

55. Royal Young Testimony, House UnAmerican Activities Committee, 89th Cong., Executive Session, July 29, 1965, NARA, Washington, DC, 244–54.

56. "Dixie Town Is Tense after Employer Kills Four," *Baltimore Afro-American,* July 19, 1960, 6.

57. Mrs. Royal V. Young Comments to FBI Informant, January 29, 1964, FBI Civil Rights Division, Tommie Lee Jones file 157-3552, NARA, 1–8.

58. David Neal, "POWWOW," *Concordia Sentinel,* June 21, 1963, 1.

59. Royal Young Testimony, 257–62, 295.

60. Racial Informant Report to FBI, "OKKKK Split under Royal Young," April 15, 1964, FBI Civil Rights Division, E. L. McDaniel file 157-2151, vol. 1, NARA, 219, 222, 223.

61. Mrs. Royal V. Young Comments.

62. FBI Special Agents Clarence G. Prospere and Frank Ford, Ernest Gilbert Report, September 3, 1964, FBI Civil Rights Division, Ernest Parker file 157-3437, NARA, 6.

63. Banishment of Murray Martin, Grady Wilder, Douglas Byrd, E. L. McDaniel, and Ernest Gilbert, December 29, 1963, FBI Civil Rights Division, E. L. McDaniel file 157-2156, vol. 1, 243–44, NARA.

64. Vidalia Shamrock Meeting between Royal Young and Mississippi Klansmen by FBI Special Agent Earl Cox, January 11, 1964, FBI Civil Rights Division, E. L. McDaniel file 157-2156, vol. 1, 236–45, NARA.

3. ABDUCTIONS, WHIPPINGS, AND MURDER

1. James White, interview by FBI Special Agents John Willard Thomas and Robert E. Basham, August 23, 1967, FBI Civil Unrest, James White file 157-NO-9951, National Archives and Records Administration (NARA), College Park, MD.

2. Ibid.

3. Ibid.

4. Ibid.

5. Ibid.

6. Stanley Nelson, "Morris' Best Friend—James White—Shot Klansman During Shootout in 1964," *Concordia Sentinel*, March 25, 2010.

7. James White, interview by FBI, 1967.

8. James Allen Hinson, interview by FBI Special Agents Jack G. Wilson and David T. Daly, May 8, 1967, FBI Civil Unrest, Wharlest Jackson file 44-JN-2044, NARA.

9. Informant Report to FBI Special Agents Joseph G. Peggs and James A. Wooten, September 5, 1967, FBI Civil Unrest, James White file 157-NO-9951, NARA.

10. Ibid.

11. FBI Special Agent Donald J. McGorty Report, "Racial Matters," October 27, 1965, FBI Civil Unrest, Red Glover file 157-JN-2444, NARA.

12. Stanley Nelson, "SDG Leader 'Red' Glover was Lead Suspect in Wharlest Jackson Murder," *Concordia Sentinel*, September 3, 2009, A1.

13. FBI Correlation of Informant Reports, April 1, 1969, FBI Civil Unrest, Red Glover file 157-JN-2444, NARA.

14. J. T. Robinson, interview by FBI Special Agent Clarence Prospere, April 21, 1967, FBI Civil Unrest, Red Glover file 157-JN-2444, NARA.

15. Norris B. Fulgham, interview by FBI Special Agents George F. Benz and Charles A. Church, June 9, 1967, FBI Civil Unrest, Wharlest Jackson file 44-JN-2044, NARA.

16. J. T. Robinson, interview by FBI, 1967.

17. James White, interview by FBI, 1967.

18. Richard James, interview by FBI Special Agents William Wood and Brent W. Warberg, September 22, 1967, FBI Civil Unrest, James-Watkins file 44-NO-3364, NARA.

19. Ibid.

20. Mr. and Mrs. Nelson Flaherty, interviews by FBI Special Agent Ernest A. Serena, September 1967, FBI Civil Unrest, James-Watkins file 44-NO-3364, NARA.

21. Ibid.

22. Robert Watkins Report, FBI Chicago Division, September 18, 1967, FBI Civil Unrest, James-Watkins file 44-NO-3364, NARA.

23. FBI Teletype on Informant No. 1508, September 26, 1967, FBI Civil Unrest, James-Watkins file 44-NO-3364, NARA.

24. Sheriff Noah Cross, interview by FBI Special Agents Brent W. Warberg and William Wood, October 16, 1967, FBI Civil Unrest, James-Watkins file 44-NO-3364, NARA.

25. "Petition Seeks New Primary," *Concordia Sentinel*, December 20, 1963, 1.

26. James Hartwell Love v. Noah W. Cross Et Al. (Louisiana Third Circuit Court of Appeal, Lake Charles, LA, December 26, 1963).

27. "General Election, Adams County Results," *Natchez Democrat*, November 6, 1963.

28. FBI Special Agent Clarence G. Prospere, "Background History of the White Knights of the Ku Klux Klan of Mississippi," October 22, 1965, FBI Civil Unrest, White Knights file 157-HQ-1552, NARA.

29. Jack Nelson, "Sam Bowers, 43, Grim Bachelor, Under $50,000 Bonds," *Meridian Star*, July 30, 1968, A10.

30. Prospere, "Background History of the White Knights."

31. Ibid.

32. "Whitley—Alfred—Whipping of the Same," Adams County Sheriff's Office, Natchez, Mississippi, February 7, 1964, Mississippi Sovereignty Commission, Mississippi Department of Archives and History (MDAH) Digital Collections, Jackson.

33. Ibid.

34. "Negroes Describe Beatings to CRC: Officials Questioned About Prosecution," *Daily News*, February 18, 1965, A1.

35. Investigator John Sullivan, "A Discussion of Violence in Natchez, Mississippi, and Vicinity in Date, Order, Most of Which is Attributed to Klan Activities," House Un-American Activities Committee, July 30, 1965, NARA, Washington, DC, 3.

36. Ibid.

37. Ibid.

38. "Beating of Archie Curtis and Willie Jackson," Adams County Sheriff's Office, Deputies David Blough and Guy Smith, February 16, 1964, Mississippi Sovereignty Commission, MDAH Digital Collections.

39. A. V. Davis to Albert Jones, June 17, 1961, Mississippi Sovereignty Commission, MDAH Digital Collections.

40. Mary Curtis, interview by Stanley Nelson, August 18, 2009.

41. Sullivan, "A Discussion of Violence."

42. Stanley Nelson, "FBI Can't Disprove Self-Defense Claim in 1965 Fayette, Miss., Shooting," *Concordia Sentinel*, March 6, 2013, A1.

43. Investigator Rex Armistead, Mississippi Highway Safety Patrol, 1964, NARA, Washington, DC, 5.

44. *Natchez City Directory*, 1964.

45. MHSP Investigators D. B. Crockett and Ford O'Neal, "Clifton Walker Murder Report," March 2, 1964, NARA, Washington, DC, 4–6.

46. Dunbar Rowland, *Encyclopedia of Mississippi History*, 2 vols. (Madison, WI: S. A. Brant, 1907), 2:964–67.

47. Ibid., 1:611.

48. Ben Greenberg, "Decades after Slaying, Mississippi Family Seeks Justice," *Clarion-Ledger*, July 22, 2012.

49. Crockett and O'Neal, "Clifton Walker Murder Report," 4.

50. Mary G. Armstrong, "Memoirs of George Armstrong" (self-published, 1958), 369.

51. Crockett and O'Neal, "Clifton Walker Murder Report," 4.

52. Update on Clifton Walker Murder, October 20, 1964, MHSP, NARA, Washington, DC.

53. Crockett and O'Neal, "Clifton Walker Murder Report," 1–2.

54. Greenberg, "Decades after Slaying."

55. Crockett and O'Neal, "Clifton Walker Murder Report," 4–6.

56. Ibid., 1–4, 6.

57. Ibid., 2.

58. MHSP, "Continuation of Investigation of Murder Case, Wilkinson County, Miss., Victim, Clifton Walker, N/M," March 5, 1964, 4, MDAH.

59. Special Agent in Charge, New Orleans, Airtel to FBI Director, The White Knights of the Ku Klux Klan in Mississippi, March 7, 1964, 1, 24, FBI Civil Unrest, White Knights file 157-HQ-1552, NARA.

60. Silver Dollar Group and Minutemen Report by SAC, Alexandria, La., April 15, 1964, 4, FBI Civil Unrest, Silver Dollar Group file 157-HQ-4717, NARA.

4. SUPERIOR BY BLOOD

1. Thomas Moore and Thelma Collins v. Franklin County (U.S. District Court for the Southern District of Mississippi, Western Division, Jackson, Mississippi, August 5, 2008), 7.

2. David Ridgen, "Filmmaker David Ridgen Recounts Final Hours for Dee and Moore," *Concordia Sentinel*, October 22, 2009.

3. Moore and Collins v. Franklin County, 7.

4. Clyde Seale Testimony, Hearings Before the Committee on Un-American Activities (HUAC), U.S. House of Representatives, Washington, DC, January 1966, 2807–2812 (Washington, DC: U.S. Government Printing Office, 1966).

5. James Ford Seale Testimony, HUAC, 2807–2812 (Washington, DC: U.S. Government Printing Office, 1966).

6. "Ex-Minister Testifies He Saw Reputed Klansman Saw Off a Shotgun," *Picayune Item*, June 8, 2007.

7. Hollis Clay and Marilyn Posey, interviews by FBI Special Agents William D. Hoskins and Billy Bob Williams, September 11, 1965, FBI Civil Unrest, Earl Hodges file 157-JN-3830, National Archives and Records Administration (NARA), College Park, MD.

8. Moore and Collins v. Franklin County, 6–7.

9. Matt Saldana, "Day 5 Seale Trial: Profile of a Klansman," *Jackson Free Press*, June 6, 2007.

10. Ridgen, "Filmmaker David Ridgen Recounts Final Hours for Dee and Moore."

11. "James Ford Seale, Charles Marcus Edwards-Henry Hezekiah Dee-Victim, Charlie Eddie Moore-Victim," FBI Memo, January 12, 1965, 4–5, FBI Civil Unrest, James Ford Seale file 157-HQ-3676, NARA.

12. Ibid., 5.

13. Ridgen, "Filmmaker David Ridgen Recounts Final Hours for Dee and Moore."

14. United States v. James Ford Seale, Brief for the United States As Appellee, U.S. District Court of Appeals, Fifth District, New Orleans, Louisiana, March 14, 2008, 8.

15. Ibid.

16. "James Ford Seale, Charles Marcus Edwards," 2.

17. County Attorney Edwin E. Benoist Jr. Memo, Natchez, Mississippi, State of Mississippi vs. M. W. (Jack) Seale, Carrying Concealed Weapon, February 14, 1967.

18. FBI Special Agent Clarence C. Prospere, Ernest Buchanan Parker Report, October 28, 1966, FBI Civil Unrest, Ernest Parker file 157-HQ-3437, NARA.

19. "James Ford Seale, Charles Marcus Edwards," 2.

20. Link Cameron, interview by FBI Special Agents William F. Dukes and J. L. Martin, September 9, 1965, FBI Civil Unrest, Earl Hodges file 157-JN-3830, NARA.

21. Prior to that, the area was known as Davis Bend, a twenty-five-mile horseshoe-shaped turn in the Mississippi River twenty miles south of Vicksburg. In the years prior to the Civil War, Jefferson Davis and his brother Joseph owned the property. There, Jefferson Davis ran Brierfield, a 1,000-acre cotton plantation. The Mississippi changed course in 1867, cutting through the narrow neck of the bend and turning the Davis property into an island. While the island legally remains a part of Warren County, Mississippi, it is located on the Louisiana side of the river. Now an oxbow lake, the old channel—like other former old channels of the Mississippi—is often referred to as Old River. Marion Bragg, *Historic Names and Places on the Lower Mississippi River* (Vicksburg: Mississippi River Commission, 1977).

22. Fourth Davis Island Land Company, et al., v. Ernest B. Parker and Bobby Earl Parker (Supreme Court of Mississippi, January 16, 1985).

23. JN 30-R (Ernest Gilbert), interview by FBI Special Agent Clarence Prospere, September 14, 1964, FBI Civil Unrest, Ernest Parker file 157-HQ-3437, NARA.

24. U.S. v. James Ford Seale, 10.

25. "James Ford Seale, Charles Marcus Edwards," 1.

26. Ibid., 6.

27. Ibid.

28. U.S. v. James Ford Seale, 5.

29. "Two from Franklin County Are Charged in Murder of Town Men," *Natchez Democrat*, November 7, 1965, A1.

30. U.S. v. James Ford Seale, 69–70.

31. Special Agent in Charge, Jackson, Miss., Memo to FBI Director, "Henry Hezekiah Dee, Charles Eddie Moore, Miscellaneous," October 10, 1964, November 7, 1964, FBI Civil Unrest, James Ford Seale file 157-HQ-3676, NARA.

32. Ibid.

33. U.S. v. James Ford Seale, 47–48.

34. Ibid., 48.

35. MHSP Investigator Gwin Cole, Dee-Moore Murder Case Report, HUAC, November 6, 1964, 2, NARA, Washington, DC.

36. MHSP Investigator Gwin Cole, "Behavior of Mr. Bob McCain, Game Warden, State Games and Fish Commission, During the Search of Palmyra (Davis) Island," HUAC, November 9–10, 1964, NARA, Washington, DC.

37. "James Ford Seale, Charles Marcus Edwards," 6–8.

38. Frances Preston Mills, ed., *The History of the Descendants of the New Jersey Settlers of Adams County, Mississippi,* vol. 2 (Jackson, MS: self-published by "the society," 1981), 245.

39. Mary G. Armstrong, *Memoirs of George W. Armstrong* (self-published, 1958) 85–103.

40. Ibid., 372.

41. Ibid., 200.

42. Statement of Richard Joe Butler, Mississippi Highway Safety Patrol, HUAC, April 7, 1967, 1–15, NARA, Washington, DC.

43. MHSP Investigators D. B. Crockett, Ford O'Neal, George Woodard, "Shooting at Natchez, Mississippi, Victim: Richard Butler, N/M," HUAC, April 14, 1964, 1, NARA, Washington, DC.

44. Bill West, interview by Mississippi Highway Safety Patrol Investigator Gwin Cole, HUAC, November 5, 1964, NARA, Washington, DC.

45. Mrs. Haywood Benton Drane, re-interview by Mississippi Highway Safety Patrol Investigators Rex Armistead and H. T. Richardson, HUAC, October 10, 1964, NARA, Washington, DC.

46. John D. Sullivan to Donald T. Appell, Memo Concerning Sheriff Odell Anders, House HUAC, August 4, 1965, 1–3, NARA, Washington, DC.

47. FBI Special Agent Samuel N. Jennings, Informant Report to SAC, Jackson, MS, September 9, 1964, FBI Civil Unrest, White Knights file 157-HQ-1552, NARA.

48. Marvin McKinney Trial, FBI Special Agent in Charge, New Orleans, July 1, 1964, 1–2, FBI Civil Unrest, White Knights file 157-HQ-1552, NARA.

49. Stanley Nelson, "Gunshots in Morgantown Signaled Changes in Klan Membership," *Concordia Sentinel,* January 9, 2008, A1. Ernest Avants, interview by FBI Special Agents John Dennis Miller and Benjamin Graves, September 9, 1967, FBI Civil Unrest, Ernest Avants file 157-HQ-3701, NARA.

5. A GREAT STORM GATHERING

1. John Doar and Dorothy Landsberg, "The Performance of the FBI in Investigating Violations of Federal Laws Protecting the Right to Vote, 1960–67," Attachment 4, Select Committee to Study Governmental Operations with Respect to Intelligence Activities of the U.S. Senate Hearing, vol. 6 (Washington, DC: U.S. Printing Office, 1975), 888–991.

2. Ibid.

3. *The Klan Ledger,* May 10, 1964, FBI Civil Unrest, White Knights file 157-HQ-1552, National Archives and Records Administration (NARA), College Park, MD.

4. Joseph Alsop, "Murder by Night," *Washington Post,* June 17, 1964, A1.

5. Doar and Landsberg, "The Performance of the FBI," 935.

6. "Senator Long Sums up Civil Rights Bill," *Concordia Sentinel,* June 26, 1964, 2.

7. "May Be Publicity Hoax, Winstead Tells House," *Meridian Star,* June 25, 1964, A1.

8. Florence Mars, *Witness in Philadelphia* (Baton Rouge: LSU Press, 1977), 85.

9. "The Pow Wow," *Concordia Sentinel,* July 3, 1964, 1.

10. Adam Faircloth, *Race and Democracy: The Civil Rights Struggle in Louisiana, 1915–1972* (Atlanta: University of Georgia Press, 1995), 300–301.

11. Don Whitehead, *Attack on Terror: The FBI against the Ku Klux Klan in Mississippi* (New York: Funk and Wagnalls, 1970), 45.

12. Florence Mars, *Witness in Philadelphia,* 98–99.

13. Doar and Landsberg, "The Performance of the FBI," 888–89, 939. Jackson had been the site of an office in 1941 but had closed in 1946 due to a low caseload. Since that time, Mississippi cases had been split between division offices in Memphis and New Orleans. In 1964, before the Jackson office was reopened, there were thirteen resident agents in the state—six in northern Mississippi (Oxford, Clarksdale, Tupelo, Greenwood, Columbus, and Greenville) who reported to the field office in Memphis, and seven resident agents in southern Mississippi (Natchez, Biloxi, Gulfport, Hattiesburg, Laurel, Meridian, and Jackson) who reported to New Orleans. Some of the offices were two-person operations, while others were staffed with a lone agent.

14. Stanley Nelson, "1964 Case Closed: DOJ Identifies Seven Suspects; Location of Body Unknown," *Concordia Sentinel,* July 17, 2013, A1.

15. Ibid.

16. Paige Fitzgerald, Deputy Chief in Charge of the U.S. Department of Justice Cold Case Initiative, Notice to Close Joseph Edwards File, February 17, 2013, Civil Rights Division, Department of Justice, Washington, DC.

17. Ibid.

18. Stanley Nelson, "Cold Case Witnesses, Retired Agents Ignored by the FBI," *Concordia Sentinel,* June 6, 2012, A1.

19. Carl Ray Thompson, interview by Stanley Nelson, December 13, 2007.

20. W. T. Benson and John Dunlap, interviews by FBI Special Agents Merriman D. Diven and George F. Benz, August 23, 1967, FBI Civil Unrest, Joseph Edwards file 44-NO-2293, NARA.

21. Robert Wesley Easley and Dr. E. L. McAmis, interviews by FBI Special Agents Diven and Benz, August 23, 1967, FBI Civil Unrest, Joseph Edwards file 44-NO-2293, NARA.

22. Clara Dunlap, interview by FBI Special Agents Diven and Benz, September 8, 1967, FBI Civil Unrest, Joseph Edwards file 44-NO-2293, NARA.

23. Stanley Nelson, "Klansman's Son Recalls Shamrock, Silver Dollar Group and Joe Edwards," *Concordia Sentinel,* A7.

24. Stanley Nelson, "A Drowning, a Kiss Triggered Edwards Murder," *Concordia Sentinel,* May 5, 2010, A1.

25. FBI Special Agent George P. Gamblin, Silver Dollar Group Report, September 12, 1969, FBI Civil Unrest, Silver Dollars Group file 157-HQ-4717, NARA.

26. Ibid.

27. Ibid.

28. Stanley Nelson, "Witness Saw Edwards' Buick Pulled Over by Police," *Concordia Sentinel,* July 22, 2009, A8.

29. Nelson, "A Drowning, a Kiss," A1.

30. Ibid.

31. Ibid.

32. Ibid.

33. Nelson, "1964 Case Closed," A1.

34. Ibid.

35. Paige Fitzgerald, Notice to Close Joseph Edwards File.

36. Dewey White, interview by FBI Special Agent William E. Dent Jr., September 22, 1967, FBI Civil Unrest, Wharlest Jackson file 44-JN-2044, NARA.

37. MHSP Investigators Rex Armistead and H.A. Richardson, Informant Report on B. J. Pike, October 2, 1964, Hearings Before the Committee on Un-American Activities, U.S. House of Representatives, NARA, Washington, DC.

38. Nelson, "1964 Case Closed," A1.

39. Ibid.

40. Ibid.

41. Billy Bob Williams, interview by Stanley Nelson, January 25, 2014.

42. Patricia Sullivan, "Roy K. Moore, 94: FBI Agent Probed Civil Rights Killings," *Washington Post,* October 20, 2008.

43. Billy Bob Williams, interview by Stanley Nelson, January 25, 2014.

44. Ibid.

45. Doar and Landsberg, "The Performance of the FBI," 931–32.

46. Billy Bob Williams, interview by Stanley Nelson, January 25, 2014.

47. Doar and Landsberg, "The Performance of the FBI," 941, 943.

48. Jefferson College Records, January 22, 1949, through April 17, 1956, Jefferson College, Washington, Mississippi.

49. Billy Bob Williams, interview by Stanley Nelson, March 8, 2011.

50. Tommy Ferrell, interview by Stanley Nelson, October 10, 2013.

51. FBI Special Agent Clarence Prospere, White Knights Informant Report, February 17, 1964, FBI Civil Unrest, White Knights file 157-HQ-1552, NARA.

52. Billy Bob Williams, interview by Stanley Nelson, March 8, 2011.

53. Philip R. Manuel, Investigator, U.S. House of Representatives Committee of Un-American Activities, to Francis J. McNamara, Director, "Activity of the United Klans of America," Washington, DC, May 18, 1964, 1, NARA, Washington, DC.

54. FBI Special Agent Steve M. Callender, White Knights of the Ku Klux Klan of Mississippi Report, May 25, 1964, 2, FBI Civil Unrest, White Knights file 157-HQ-1552, NARA.

55. FBI Special Agent Clarence G. Prospere, Background History of WKKKKOM Report, October 22, 1965, 5, FBI Civil Unrest, White Knights file 157-HQ-1552, NARA.

56. Manuel, "Activity of United Klans of America," 1.

57. Stanley Nelson, "Deputy Seen with Stranger in Green Car on Night of Fire," *Concordia Sentinel,* March 10, 2010, A1.

6. A DECLARATION OF WAR

1. "Mayor Nosser Announces for Re-Election," *Natchez Democrat,* January 12, 1964, A1.

2. Tony Byrne, interview by Stanley Nelson, May 21, 2014.

3. "Former Police Chief Dies at Age 81," *Natchez Democrat,* February 20, 2007, A1.

4. Billy Bob Williams, interview by Bryan R. Holstein, February 13 and 16, 2007, Society of Former Special Agents of the FBI Inc., 2007.

5. Tony Byrne, interview by Nelson, May 21, 2014.

6. John Sullivan to Donald T. Appell, memo on Natchez Police Department Captain J. G. Wisner, U.S. House of Representatives Committee on Un-American Activities, Washington, DC, September 29, 1965, National Archives and Records Administration (NARA).

7. Adams County Sheriff Odell Anders, interview by FBI, October 23, 1964, FBI Civil Unrest, White Knights file 157-HQ-1552, NARA, College Park, MD.

8. John Sullivan to Donald T. Appell, memo on Mayor John Nosser, U.S. House of Representatives Committee on Un-American Activities, U.S. Government Printing Office, Washington, DC, December 18, 1965, NARA, Washington, DC.

9. Police Chief J. T. Robinson testimony, in *Justice in Jackson, Mississippi: Hearings Held in Jackson, Miss., February 16–20, 1965* (New York: Arno Press, 1971), 157–58.

10. Nicholas Von Hoffman, "Anti-Antebellum Natchez: How Things Do Change," *Chicago Sun-Times,* September 10, 1964, A1.

11. Ibid.

12. Bob Doyle, "Natchez Situation," U.S. House of Representatives Committee on House Un-American Activities, Washington, DC, December 11, 1965, NARA, Washington, DC.

13. Ibid.

14. Drew Pearson, "Threats, Courage in Miss.," *Tuscaloosa News,* November 10, 1965, A6.

15. Doyle, "Natchez Situation."

16. "My Problems: How Much Should a Family Knuckle Under," *Good Housekeeping,* June 1965, 62.

17. Doyle, "Natchez Situation."

18. John Sullivan, "A Discussion of Violence in Natchez, Miss., and Vicinity," U.S. House of Representatives Committee on Un-American Activities, July 30, 1965, 14, NARA, Washington, DC.

19. *A Report on Equal Rights Protection in the South* (Jackson, MS: U.S. Commission on Civil Rights, 1965), 20.

20. Stanley Nelson, "Five Possible Motives for 1964 Morris Murder," *Concordia Sentinel,* November 12, 2008, A8.

21. Sullivan, "A Discussion of Violence in Natchez, Miss.," 15–18.

22. "No Injuries as Blast Rocks Home of Mayor John Nosser," *Natchez Democrat,* September 26, 1964, A1.

23. "Mayor John Nosser Appeals to People," *Natchez Democrat,* September 27, 1964, A1.

24. "Klan Denies Any Part in Bombing," *Natchez Democrat,* September 27, 1964, A1.

25. Billy Bob Williams, interview by Holstein.

26. Billy Bob Williams, interview by Nelson, January 25, 2014.

27. Ibid.

28. Tony Byrne, interview by Nelson.

29. Billy Bob Williams, interview by Nelson.

30. Billy Bob Williams, interview by Holstein.

31. Ibid.

32. Stanley Nelson, "Bloody '64: Klan Suspected in Murders, Assaults, Bombings," *Concordia Sentinel,* September 2, 2008, A2.

33. "$5,000 Reward," *Natchez Democrat,* September 16, 1967, A1.

34. "State Workers Arrest Four Here in Year Old A-B," *Natchez Democrat,* October 23, 1964, A1.

35. "McKeithen Is Winner in Upset Election," *Natchez Democrat,* January 12, 1964, A1.

36. J. T. Robinson testimony, 157–59.

37. Billy Bob Williams, interview by Nelson.

38. Ernest Henry Avants, interview by FBI Special Agent Timothy Casey, October 23, 1964, and John Williams Barber by Special Agent Robin O. Cotton, October 24, 1964, FBI Civil Unrest, Ernest Avants file 157-HQ-3701, NARA.

39. Ibid. Also arrested were Frank Hyman Thurman (age twenty-nine) and James Kenneth Greer (thirty-one), both employees, along with the Avants, of International Paper, and milk route salesman John William Barber (age thirty-two).

40. "A Report on Equal Rights Protection in the South," 50–51.

41. List of Items Obtained from Home of M. W. (Jack) Seale, Adams County Sheriff's Office, Deputy David Blough for Sheriff Odell Anders, October 23, 1964, FBI Civil Unrest, Myron Wayne "Jack" Seale file 157-HQ-3769, NARA.

42. MHSP, Discovery of Dynamite by Sheriff Odell Anders, report, October 26, 1964, McCain Library and Archives, University of Southern Mississippi, Hattiesburg.

43. MHSP Investigator Ford O'Neal, Report to FBI Special Agents William F. Dukes and Thompson Berry Webb, October 20, 1964, FBI Civil Unrest, Ernest Parker file 157-HQ-3437, NARA.

44. "Arrest Ed Fuller in April Shooting," *Natchez Democrat,* October 27, 1964, A1.

45. "Whiskey Sales and Gambling in Natchez to Be Halted Tonight," *Natchez Democrat,* October 29, 1964, A1.

46. MHSP Investigator Gwin Cole Report, Natchez, November 13, 1964, Mississippi Sovereignty Commission, Mississippi Department of Archives and History (MDAH) Digital Collections, Jackson.

47. William T. "Billy" Ferrell to Governor Paul Johnson, Western Union telegram, December 28, 1964.

48. Gwin Cole Report, 1964.

49. John Sullivan to Donald T. Appell, memo on Paul Foster, U.S. House of Representatives Committee on House Un-American Activities, undated, NARA, Washington, DC; "Protest Action Highway Patrol," *Natchez Democrat,* November 1, 1964, A1.

50. Doyle, "Natchez Situation."

51. Dave Leip's Atlas of U.S. Presidential Elections, uselectionatlas.org.

52. Ibid.

7. "THE COLORED PEOPLE OF CONCORDIA PARISH"

1. Stanley Nelson, "Covering the Klan in the Natchez Region," *Concordia Sentinel,* July 25, 2007, A1.

2. Ibid.

3. Stanley Nelson, "FBI Agents Recall Klan Violence, Vices," *Concordia Sentinel,* May 28, 2008, A1.

4. John Herbers, "Burning of a Negro Arouses Louisiana," *New York Times,* December 24, 1964, A1.

5. John Howard Griffin, "Journal of a Trip South," *Ramparts,* Christmas 1963, 35–42.

6. Ibid.

7. Ibid.

8. Ibid.

9. *Louisiana in 1878, Report of the United States Senate Committee to Inquire into Alleged Frauds and Violence in the Elections of 1878, Concordia and Tensas Parishes* (Washington, DC: Government Printing Office, 1879), 1:169–378, 2:763–78.

10. John Roy Lynch, *Reminiscences of an Active Life: The Autobiography of John Roy Lynch* (Chicago: University of Chicago Press), 1970, 63.

11. Eric Foner, *Forever Free: The Story of Emancipation and Reconstruction"* (New York: Vintage, 2008), 160.

12. *Mississippi Slave Narratives: A Folk History of Slavery in Mississippi from Interviews with Former Slaves,* Federal Writers' Project, 1936–1938 (Applewood Books, published in cooperation with the Library of Congress), 34.

13. "White League Violence: The Political Murders in Tensas Parish," *New York Times,* January 9, 1879.

14. "Louisiana in 1878."

15. Robert Dabney Calhoun, "A History of Concordia Parish (1768–1931)," rpr. from *Louisiana Historical Quarterly,* January 1932, p. 143.

16. "White League Violence."

17. Herbers, "Burning of a Negro," A1.

18. Ibid.

19. Ibid.

20. Ibid.

21. Stanley Nelson, "Morris' Murder Reported from Texas to Connecticut," *Concordia Sentinel,* September 26, 2007, A1.

22. "FBI Reportedly Probing Louisiana Burning," *Victoria Advocate,* FBI Civil Unrest, Frank Morris file 157-HQ-2311, NARA; Herbers, "Burning of a Negro," A1.

23. Stanley Nelson, "A Father's Grief: Who Killed Sullivan Morris' Son in 1964?" *Concordia Sentinel,* October 12, 2011, A9.

24. Ibid.

25. Stanley Nelson, "Morris Was a 'Special Friend," *Concordia Sentinel,* June 13, 2007, A10.

26. Nelson, "A Father's Grief," A9.

27. Ibid.

28. George Wilson, interview by FBI Special Agents Donald J. McGorty, Elmer Litchfield and William Quackenbush, December 19, 1964, February 3, 1965, FBI Civil Unrest, Frank Morris file 157-HQ-2311, National Archives and Records Administration (NARA), College Park, MD.

29. Lloyd F. Love, interview by Special Agent Thomas McGuinness Jr., February 3, 1965, FBI Civil Unrest, Frank Morris file 157-HQ-2311, NARA.

30. "A Tribute to Mr. Pasternack," *Concordia Sentinel,* August 9, 1963, 5.

31. Love, interview by McGuinness.

32. Father August Thompson and Father John Gayer, interviews by FBI Special Agent Donald J. McGorty, December 16 and 19, 1964, FBI Civil Unrest, Frank Morris file 157-HQ-2311, NARA.

33. Stanley Nelson, "Morris Knew His Attackers," *Concordia Sentinel*, June 6, 2007, A1.

34. Burlington County, NJ, NAACP to U.S. Senator Clifford Case, December 21, 1964, FBI Civil Unrest, Frank Morris file 157-HQ-2311, NARA.

35. Al Rosen Memo, Civil Rights Division, U.S. Justice Department, January 21, 1965, FBI Civil Unrest, Frank Morris file 157-HQ-2311, NARA.

36. Della Mae Smith, interview by FBI Special Agents Thomas McGuinness Jr. and William Quackenbush, January 29, 1965, FBI Civil Unrest, Frank Morris file 157-HQ-2311, NARA.

37. Ibid.

38. George Sewell and Thomas Sidney Loftin Jr., interviews by Special Agents Donald R. Belmont, Donald J. McGorty and McInnis L. Ward, January 25, 1965, February 4, 1965, FBI Civil Unrest, Frank Morris file 157-HQ-2311, NARA.

39. Stanley Nelson, "Five Retired FBI Agents Still Unsure," *Concordia Sentinel*, November 4, 2009, A8.

40. Paige Fitzgerald, Frank Morris Case Closed Letter, undated (2014), U.S. Department of Justice.

41. Stanley Nelson, "Whose Finger Was Found in Shoe Shop Rubble?" *Concordia Sentinel*, July 4, 2012, A9.

42. Stanley Nelson, "Eyewitness Forced to Leave Ferriday," *Concordia Sentinel*, July 18, 2007, A1.

43. John Lee Jr., interview by FBI Special Agents Thomas McGuinness Jr. and William Quackenbush, February 2, 1965, FBI Civil Unrest, Frank Morris file 157-HQ-2311, NARA.

44. W. H. Harp Jr., interview by FBI Special Agents Donald Belmont and McInnis Ward, February 4, 1965, FBI Civil Unrest, Frank Morris file 157-HQ-2311, NARA.

45. Edna Brown, interview by FBI Special Agents Elmer B. Litchfield and William Quackenbush, February 14, 1965, FBI Civil Unrest, Frank Morris file 157-HQ-2311, NARA.

46. Girlfriend (name redacted), interview by FBI Special Agents Elmer B. Litchfield and William Quackenbush, February 1, 1965, Frank Morris Civil Unrest, Frank Morris file 157-HQ-2311, NARA.

47. Lee, interview by McGuinness and Quackenbush.

48. Agnes Scott, interview by FBI Special Agent Elmer B. Litchfield and William Quackenbush, February 9, 1965, FBI Civil Unrest, Frank Morris file 157-HQ-2311, NARA.

49. New Orleans Bureau to FBI Director, FBI Teletype, February 20, 1965, FBI Civil Unrest, Frank Morris file 157-HQ-2311, NARA.

50. Mildred Garner Statement to FBI Special Agents Clarence G. Prospere and William Dent Jr., April 7, 1964, FBI Racial Violence, George Sewell file 44-HQ-24043, NARA.

51. Mildred Garner Report by FBI Special Agent Clarence G. Prospere, May 20, 1964, FBI Racial Violence, George Sewell file 44-HQ-24043, NARA.

52. Harp, interview by Belmont and Ward.

53. Ibid.

54. Stanley Nelson, "Evidence Points to DeLaughter as Engineer of Morris Arson," *Concordia Sentinel*, November 30, 2011, A2.

55. Harp, interview by Belmont and Ward.

56. L. W. "Woodie" Davis, interview by FBI Special Agents Donald R. Belmont and McInnis Ward, February 5, 1965, FBI Civil Unrest, Frank Morris file 157-HQ-2311, NARA.

57. Smith, interview by McGuinness and Quackenbush.

58. Frank Morris, hospital interviews by FBI, December 16, 1964, FBI Civil Unrest, Frank Morris file 157-HQ-2311, NARA.

59. Frank DeLaughter, interview by FBI Special Agents Elmer B. Litchfield and William Quackenbush, February 5, 1965, FBI Civil Unrest, Frank Morris file 157-HQ-2311, NARA.

60. James K. Simolke, interview by FBI Special Agents Thomas A. McGuinness Jr. and William Quackenbush, January 29, 1965, FBI Civil Unrest, Frank Morris file 157-HQ-2311, NARA.

61. Harp, interview by Belmont and Ward.

62. Johnny Blunschi, interview by Stanley Nelson, July 3, 2013.

63. DeLaughter, interview by Litchfield and Quackenbush.

64. Ed Robinson, e-mail to Stanley Nelson, April 28, 2014.

65. W. C. Shoemaker, "Ex-Official Opposes Fed Police Force," *Daily News,* February 1, 1965, A1.

66. "The Colored People of Concordia Parish," letter to J. Edgar Hoover, April 10, 1965, FBI Civil Unrest, Frank Morris file 157-HQ-2311, NARA.

8. "WHY DO THEY HATE US SO?"

1. Jack D. L. Holmes, *Gayoso: The Life of a Spanish Governor in the Mississippi Valley, 1789–1799* (Baton Rouge: LSU Press, 1965), 124, 149–50.

2. John Pfeifer, interview by Stanley Nelson, April 8, 2011.

3. Stanley Nelson, "'Red' Glover Was Lead Suspect in Jackson Murder," *Concordia Sentinel,* September 2, 2009, A1.

4. FBI Special Agent Jack G. Wilson to Inspector Joseph Sullivan, May 31, 1967, FBI Civil Unrest, Red Glover file 157-JN-2444, National Archives and Records Administration (NARA), College Park, MD.

5. Nelson, "'Red' Glover," A1.

6. Ibid.

7. Betty Lou Watkins to SAC Roy K. Moore, FBI Steno, April 11, 1969, 21, FBI Civil Unrest, Red Glover file 157-JN-2444, NARA.

8. Nelson, "'Red' Glover," A1.

9. Stanley Nelson, "Klansmen 'Took Great Pride' in Refining Bombing Skills," *Concordia Sentinel,* January 21, 2009, A7.

10. FBI Special Agents James A. Wooten and Joseph G. Peggs, George Metcalfe Bombing Report, February 6, 1968, 1, FBI Civil Unrest, Wharlest Jackson file 44-JN-2044, NARA.

11. Jack Mitchell, e-mail to Stanley Nelson, 2013.

12. Ibid.

13. U.S. Census, 1940.

14. George Metcalfe, interview by FBI Special Agents Joseph J. Ryan and John M Callahan, February 28, 1967, FBI Civil Unrest, Wharlest Jackson file 44-JN-2044, NARA.

15. Stanley Nelson, "Bomb That Injured Metcalfe Made with Primer Cord," *Concordia Sentinel,* June 18, 2008, A1.

16. "NAACP Chapter Head Hurt by Bomb in Car," *Washington Post,* August 28, 1965, A8.

17. Wooten and Peggs, Metcalfe Bombing Report, 1.

18. Ibid., 2.

19. Ibid., 3.

20. George P. Rawick, ed., *The American Slave: A Composite Autobiography,* 19 vols. (Westport, CT: Greenwood, 1972-79), 5:236-246.

21. FBI Special Agents Benjamin F. Graves and Thomas Berry Webb, Informant #230-R Report, February 8, 1968, FBI Civil Unrest, Silver Dollar Group file 157-HQ-4717, NARA.

22. Informant JN T-3 Report to FBI, March 29, 1967, FBI Civil Unrest, Silver Dollar Group file 157-HQ-4717, NARA.

23. FBI New Orleans SDG Report, December 13, 1965, FBI Civil Unrest, Silver Dollar Group file 157-HQ-4717, NARA.

24. Stanley Nelson, "FBI Files Reveal Klansman Jack Seale Was Paid Informant," *Concordia Sentinel,* November 11, 2009, A8.

25. Joyce Windham Investigation, FBI Special Agent Frank B. Watts, October 11, 14, 1967, FBI Civil Unrest, Joseph Edwards file 44-NO-2293, NARA.

26. Kenneth Norman Head, interview by FBI Special Agents Aloysius J. McFall and Gilbert Arps, March 17, 1969, FBI Civil Unrest, Kenneth Norman Head file 157-HQ-3435, NARA.

27. FBI Special Agent John D. Brady, Report to New Orleans Division, April 5, 1967, 5, FBI Civil Unrest, Silver Dollar Group file 157-HQ-4717, NARA.

28. Ferriday Patrolman Kenneth McKnight, interview by FBI Special Agents William E. Dent and John D. Brady, March 29, 1967, FBI Civil Unrest, Tommie Lee Jones file 157-HQ-3552, NARA.

29. Ferriday Town Clerk Vernell Cooper, interview by FBI Special Agents William E. Dent and John D. Brady, March 29, 1967, FBI Civil Unrest, Tommie Lee Jones file 157-HQ-3552, NARA.

30. FBI Special Agent Don J. McGorty, James Fredrick Lee Report, November 19, 1965, 6-7, FBI Civil Unrest, James Frederick Lee file 157-HQ-4490, NARA.

31. Wooten and Peggs, Metcalfe Bombing Report, 3-4.

32. Nelson, "Bomb That Injured Metcalfe," A1.

33. Stanley Nelson, "Questions of Baptism and Faith Following Morris Murder," *Concordia Sentinel,* January 6, 2010, A10.

34. Nelson, "Bomb That Injured Metcalfe," A1.

35. "Natchez NAACP President Is Critically Hurt in Bombing," *Natchez Democrat,* August 27, 1965, A1.

36. Nelson, "Bomb That Injured Metcalfe," A1.

37. "FBI Agents Push Probe of Bombing," *Clarion-Ledger,* August 29, 1965, A1.

38. FBI Inspector Joseph A. Sullivan to Justice Department Assistant Director Alex Rosen, Thumbnail Sketch of Metcalfe Bombing, June 16, 1967, 5-6, FBI Civil Unrest, Wharlest Jackson file 44-JN-2044, NARA.

39. "Dixie Rights Leader Hurt by Auto Bomb," *New York Tribune,* August 28, 1965.

40. Rep. Charles C. Diggs, Michigan, "Southern Justice Is Segregated," *Congressional Record,* September 9, 1965.

41. "FBI Agents Pushing Probe of Bombing," *Clarion-Ledger,* August 29, 1965, A1.

42. "NAACP Chapter Head Hurt by Bomb in Car," *Washington Post,* August 28, 1965, A8.

43. "National Guardsmen in City As Aldermen Nix Demands," *Natchez Democrat,* September 3, 1965, A1.

44. Interview with Vic Crawford, by Stanley Nelson, April 13, 2009.

45. Wooten and Peggs, James Frederick Lee Report, 9–10.

46. James Lee, interviews by FBI, August 11, September 3, and September 11, 1965, FBI Civil Unrest, James Frederick Lee file 157-HQ-4490, NARA.

47. "Over 100 Arrested in Natchez March," Associated Press, October 4, 1965.

48. "Nobody Turn Me 'Round," *Time Magazine,* October 15, 1965; Marge Baroni Collection, Archives & Special Collections, J.D. Williams Library, University of Mississippi.

49. "Negro Natchez Boycott Hurts White Merchants," *Jet,* November 11, 1965.

50. "Negroes End Boycott at Natchez as City Agrees to Most of Their Demands," *Wall Street Journal,* December 6, 1965, A6.

9. "CRIPPLED JOHNNY" AND THE ALCOHOLIC MECHANIC

1. FBI Special Agent Samuel N. Jennings, United Klans of America Mississippi Klonvocation Report, June 7, 1965, 1–27, FBI Civil Unrest, E. L. McDaniel file 157-HQ-2156, National Archives and Records Administration (NARA), College Park, MD.

2. Ibid.

3. "The Present-Day Ku Klux Klan Movement Report," Committee on Un-American Activities, House of Representatives, 90th Cong., 1st Sess., December 11, 1967 (Washington, DC: U.S. Government Printing Office, 1967), 19, 29, 37, 45, 46, 50.

4. Ibid.

5. FBI Special Agent John C. McCurnin II, UKA Natchez Rally and March Report, October 30, 1965, FBI Civil Unrest, E. L. McDaniel file 157-HQ-2156, NARA.

6. Dunbar Rowland, *Encyclopedia of Mississippi History,* 2 vols. (Madison, WI: Selwyn Bryant, 1907), 1:700.

7. Stanley Nelson, "Self-Defense: FBI Says Self-Defense Claim Cannot Be Disproved in 1965 Fayette Slaying," *Concordia Sentinel,* March 6, 2013, A1; Joseph Shapiro, "Justice in the Segregated South: A New Look at an Old Killing," National Public Radio, May 3, 2013.

8. Ibid.

9. Ibid.

10. Ibid.

11. Jasper Burchfield, interview by FBI, February 18, 1965, NARA.

12. FBI Special Agent Clarence Prospere, White Knights Informant Report, February 21, 1964, FBI Civil Unrest, Whites Knights file 157-HQ-1552, NARA.

13. Nelson, *Concordia Sentinel,* and Shapiro, NPR.

14. Ibid.

15. Ibid.

16. Ibid.

17. Ibid.

18. Ibid.

19. Ibid.

20. Ibid.

21. Ibid.

22. Ibid.

23. John D. Sullivan to Donald J. Appell, House of Representatives Committee on Un-American Activities, September 21, 1965, NARA, Washington, DC.

24. Certificate of Death of Willie Earl Hodges, Coroner Dr. J. W. Hollingsworth, August 27, 1965, Mississippi State Board of Health, Office of Public Statistics, Jackson, Mississippi.

25. Stanley Nelson, "Seale, Avants Linked to 1965 Franklin County Murder," *Concordia Sentinel*, June 9, 2010, A1.

26. Neva Hodges, interview by FBI Special Agents Benjamin F. Graves and Reesie L. Timmons, September 11, 1965, FBI Civil Unrest, Earl Hodges file 157-HQ-3830, NARA.

27. Ibid.

28. Special Agents Clarence Prospere and Frank Ford, White Knights Informant Report, September 15, 1964, 11, 12, FBI Civil Unrest, White Knights file 157-HQ-1552, NARA.

29. MHSP Investigator Donald Butler, interview by FBI Special Agent William F. Dukes, August 20, 1965, FBI Civil Unrest, Earl Hodges file 157-HQ-3830, NARA.

30. Rax Marshall, interview by FBI Special Agents Graves and Timmons, September 11, 1965, FBI Civil Unrest, Earl Hodges file 157-HQ-3830, NARA.

31. Johnny Lee Cothren, interview by FBI Special Agents James A. Abbott and Robert F. Cooper Jr., September 12, 1965, FBI Civil Unrest, Earl Hodges file 157-HQ-3830, NARA.

32. Johnny Lee Cothren, interview by FBI Special Agents Graves and Timmons, September 7, 1965, FBI Civil Unrest, Earl Hodges file 157-HQ-3830, NARA.

33. Reverend W. H. Davis, interview by FBI Special Agents Graves and Timmons, September 13, 1965, FBI Civil Unrest, Earl Hodges file 157-HQ-3830, NARA.

34. Johnny Lee Cothren, interview by Graves and Timmons, September 7, 1965.

35. Mrs. J. C. (Lanette) Emfinger, interview by FBI Special Agents William D. Haskins and Thompson Berry Webb, September 9, 1965, FBI Civil Unrest, Earl Hodges file 157-HQ-3830, NARA.

36. Neva Hodges, interview by Graves and Timmons.

37. Rosia Roland Davis, interview by FBI Special Agents Graves and Timmons, September 11, 1965, FBI Civil Unrest, Earl Hodges file 157-HQ-3830, NARA.

38. Link Cameron, interview by FBI Special Agent William F. Dukes, September 20, 1965, FBI Civil Unrest, Earl Hodges file 157-HQ-3830, NARA.

39. Emfinger, interview by Haskins and Webb.

40. Warren H. Newman, interview by FBI Special Agents Graves and Timmons, September 2, 1965, FBI Civil Unrest, Earl Hodges file 157-HQ-3830, NARA.

41. Ibid.

42. Link Cameron, interview by Dukes.

43. Thomas L. Scott, interview by FBI Special Agents Graves and Timmons, September 11, 1965, FBI Civil Unrest, Earl Hodges file 157-HQ-3830, NARA.

44. William Campbell, interview by FBI Special Agents Graves and Timmons, September 7, 1965, FBI Civil Unrest, Earl Hodges file 157-HQ-3830, NARA.

45. William B. Watson, interview by FBI Special Agents Graves and Timmons, September 4, 1965, FBI Civil Unrest, Earl Hodges file 157 HQ 3830, NARA.

46. Wayne Hutto, interview by FBI Special Agent Edgar C. Fortenberry, September 8, 1965, FBI Civil Unrest, Earl Hodges file 157-HQ-3830, NARA.

47. Ibid.

48. Certificate of Death of Earl Hodges.

49. Butler, interview by Dukes.

50. FBI Special Agent William F. Dukes, report to SAC, Jackson, Miss., August 19, 1965, FBI Civil Unrest, Earl Hodges file 157-HQ-3830, NARA.

51. "The Present-Day Ku Klux Klan Movement," Committee on Un-American Activities, 19, 29, 37, 45, 46, 50, 90th Cong., 1st Sess. (Washington, DC: U.S. Government Printing Office, 1967).

52. Max Graves, interview by Stanley Nelson, June 26, 2013.

53. Jack Nelson, "White Knights Charge on Toward Extinction," *Los Angeles Times* News Service story in *Atlanta Journal,* July 30, 1968, 7B.

54. Max Graves, interview by Stanley Nelson; copy of Ed Benoist notes provided to Stanley Nelson by Graves.

55. Eugene Robert "Bob" Storey, interview by FBI Special Agents Reesie L. Timmons, David H. Phillips, and William C. Mearns, November 11, 1967, FBI Civil Unrest, Earl Hodges file 157-HQ-3830, NARA.

56. Helen Hodges Vernon, interview by Stanley Nelson, January 25, 2013.

57. Keith Hodges, interview by Stanley Nelson, January 19, 2013.

10. OUTLAW COUNTRY

1. Stanley Nelson, "1965 Concordia Lounge Arsons Linked to KKK/SDG," *Concordia Sentinel,* April 14, 2010, A10.

2. Stanley Nelson, "Preacher Tried to Change the Hearts of Klansmen," *Concordia Sentinel,* June 13, 2007, A1.

3. "Statement about the Ku Klux Klan," *Concordia Sentinel,* February 4, 1965, A1.

4. "Law and Order Urged by Parish Civic Clubs," *Concordia Sentinel,* February 18, 1965, A1.

5. Cornelia Jessey, "Contemporary Spirituality," *The Way International,* December 1977.

6. Ibid.

7. Father August Thompson, interviews by Stanley Nelson, January 29, March 11, 2011.

8. Jessey, "Contemporary Spirituality."

9. "CORE Official Twitty Beaten Up in Louisiana," *Tucson Daily Citizen,* December 30, 1965, A15.

10. Stanley Nelson, "Confrontation at Duncan Park," *Concordia Sentinel,* September 20, 2007, A1.

11. Father Thompson interviews.

12. Editorial, *Concordia Sentinel,* July 22, 1965, A1.

13. Stanley Nelson, "Justice Official Tagged Ferriday Outlaw Country," *Concordia Sentinel,* August 15, 2007, A1.

14. Ibid.

15. "Introducing the F.F.M.," FFM newsletter, August 15, 1965, 1, Father August Thompson personal collection.

16. Ibid.

17. *The Firey Cross,* September 23, 1965, Father August Thompson personal collection.

18. Robert "Buck" Lewis, interview by Stanley Nelson, August 6, 2014.

19. "Negro Gas Station Burned," CORE Press Release, New Orleans, December 19, 1965.

20. "Parish Negro Slain in Gunbattle with Local Law Officers," *Concordia Sentinel,* July 29, 1965, A1.

21. Lewis interview; Stanley Nelson, "Klansman Said Morris Warned; Duncan Recalls Deacons for Defense," *Concordia Sentinel,* February 13, 2008, A1.

22. Ibid.

23. Ibid.

24. Ibid.

25. Roy Reed, "His Home Bombed, Negro Is Arrested," *New York Times,* November 22, 1965, A25.

26. Stanley Nelson, "David Whatley's Trials: SDG Klansmen, Bombs and Ferriday High," *Concordia Sentinel,* September 29, 2010, A10.

27. "School Board Presents Plan to Desegregate," *Concordia Sentinel,* December 16, 1965, A1.

28. Nelson, "David Whatley's Trials," A10.

29. Ibid.

30. Ibid.

31. Ibid.

32. "Trio Faces Jail on Rights Charge," *Concordia Sentinel,* April 1, 1970, A1.

33. Ibid.; John Pfeifer, interview by Stanley Nelson, June 2, 2011.

34. "Three Local Men to Be Arraigned," *Concordia Sentinel,* November 11, 1965, A1.

35. "Witness Missing in Concordia Case," *Concordia Sentinel,* February 10, 1966, A1.

36. Stanley Nelson, "DeLaughter, Poissot Linked to Criminal Acts," *Concordia Sentinel,* March 23, 2011, A8.

37. Informant NO 1325-R, interview by FBI Special Agents William E. Dent Jr. and Joseph E. Peggs, April 18, 1965, FBI Civil Unrest, Wharlest Jackson file 157-JN-2044, National Archives and Records Administration (NARA), College Park, MD.

38. "Say Case Is Perfect in Mer Rouge Crime," *New York Times,* December 31, 1922, A18.

39. Ibid.

40. "The FBI Versus the Klan, Part 2: Trouble in the 1920s," April 29, 2010, www.fbi.gov/news/stories/2010/april/Klan2_042910/the-fbi-versus-the-klan-part2-trouble-in-the-1920s.

41. "Say Case Is Perfect," A18.

42. Informant Report by FBI, March 23, 1965, FBI Civil Unrest, Wharlest Jackson file 157-JN-2044, NARA.

43. John Pfeifer, interview by Stanley Nelson.

44. Informant NO 1325-R, interview by FBI, FBI Civil Unrest, Wharlest Jackson file 157-JN-2044, NARA.

45. John Pfeifer, interview by Stanley Nelson.

46. Lee King, interview by FBI Special Agents William E. Dent and Joseph G. Peggs, June 7, 1967, FBI Civil Unrest, Wharlest Jackson file 157-JN-2044, NARA.

47. Informant NO 1325-R, interview by FBI, FBI Civil Unrest, Wharlest Jackson file 157-JN-2044, NARA.

48. Ibid.

11. "OH, LORD, WHAT HAVE I DONE TO DESERVE THIS?"

1. "McKeithen Agrees to Meet with Delta Solons, Pastors on Parish Moral Problem," *Concordia Sentinel,* May 26, 1966, A1.

2. "Pastors Urge Governor to Padlock," *Concordia Sentinel,* August 4, 1966, A1.

3. Ibid.

4. "Governor Says Police Will Raid Again, but Prosecution Is Local," *Concordia Sentinel,* August 11, 1966, A1.

5. "Falkenheiner, Halcomb Clash for District Attorney Post; Three Other Races Saturday," *Concordia Sentinel,* September 22, 1966, A1.

6. "Halcomb Remains until New Term Begins for DA," *Concordia Sentinel,* September 29, 1966, A1.

7. John Pfeifer, interviews by Stanley Nelson, March 16, April 2, 2011.

8. Ibid.

9. Ibid.

10. Ted Gardner, interview by Stanley Nelson, May 16, 2012.

11. John Pfeifer, interviews by Stanley Nelson.

12. Ibid.; Ted Gardner, interview by Stanley Nelson.

13. John Blunschi, interview by Stanley Nelson, July 3, 2013.

14. John Pfeifer, interviews by Stanley Nelson.

15. Stanley Nelson, "Search for Klan Leader Led to Discovery of Morville Lounge," *Concordia Sentinel,* August 19, 2009, A1.

16. United States of America v. Noah W. Cross (U.S. District Court, Western District, Alexandria Division, May 1972).

17. Ibid.

18. United States of America v. J. D. Richardson Et Al. (U.S. District Court, Western District, Lake Charles Division, January 21–22, 1971).

19. Stanley Nelson, Matt Barnidge, and Ian Sanford, "Connected by Violence—the Mafia, Klan and Morville," *Concordia Sentinel,* July 15, 2009, A8.

20. Curt Hewitt, interview by FBI Special Agent John Pfeifer, April 30, 1971, document provided to Stanley Nelson by anonymous source.

21. John Pfeifer, interviews by Stanley Nelson.

22. Ibid.

23. Ibid.

24. Ibid.

25. Ibid.

26. FBI Special Agent John C. McCurnin II, UKA Rally on March 19, 1966, at Ferriday, La. Report, March 21, 1966, FBI Civil Unrest, E. L. McDaniel file 157-HQ-2156, National Archives and Records Administration (NARA), College Park, MD.

27. Ibid.

28. FBI Special Agent John C. McCurnin II, UKA Election Convention and Rally in Natchez, Miss., Report, May 16, 1966, FBI Civil Unrest, E. L. McDaniel file 157-HQ-2156, NARA.

29. Police Officer Kenneth McKnight, interview by FBI Special Agents William F. Dent and John D. Brady, March 29, 1967, FBI Civil Unrest, Tommie Lee Jones file 157-HQ-3552, NARA.

30. Mayor Woodie Davis, interview by Dent and Brady, March 29, 1967, FBI Civil Unrest, Tommie Lee Jones file 157-HQ-3552, NARA.

31. FBI Special Agent V. Walser Prospere, State Meeting at Natchez and Robert Shelton Investigation Report, September 21, 1966, FBI Civil Unrest, E.L. McDaniel file 157-HQ-2156, NARA.

32. FBI Special Agent John C. McCurnin II, Monroe Klansmen Visit Concordia Klansmen Report, May 9, 1967, FBI Civil Unrest, E. L. McDaniel file 157-HQ-2156, NARA.

33. FBI Special Agent John C. McCurnin II, UKA Election Convention and Rally in Natchez, Miss., Report, May 16, 1966, FBI Civil Unrest, E. L. McDaniel file 157-HQ-2156, NARA.

34. V. Walser Prospere, Natchez and Shelton Report.

35. Ibid.

36. Ibid.

37. Billy Bob Williams, interview by Stanley Nelson, November 8, 2009.

38. Charles Snodgrass to Col. T. B. Birdsong and Chief A. D. Morgan, Mississippi Department of Public Safety, Memo on HUAC, January 12, 1966, University of Southern Mississippi, McCain Library and Archives, Hattiesburg, Mississippi.

39. County Attorney Ed Benoist Files provided to author by Paul Benoist; Natchez Docket Book No. 338, 172, February 14, 1967.

40. FBI Special Agent Clarence Prospere, KKK Meeting at Morgantown, Natchez, Miss., Report, February 24, 1964, FBI Civil Unrest, White Knights file 157-HQ-1552, NARA.

41. Ed Benoist Files.

42. Charles E. Snodgrass, Mississippi Department of Public Safety, Explosion in Natchez Report, November 21, 1966, University of Southern Mississippi, McCain Library and Archives, Hattiesburg, Mississippi.

43. Ed Benoist files.

44. FBI Special Agent Samuel N. Jennings, White Knights of the KKK Report, September 15, 1964, 15, FBI Civil Unrest, White Knights file 157-HQ-1552, NARA.

45. Prospere, Klan Activity in Natchez Report, September 23, 1963.

46. James Lloyd Jones, statements to District Attorney L. L. Forman, June 16, July 15, 1966, in Ed Benoist files.

47. Ibid.

48. Ibid.

49. Ibid.

50. JN T1 Informant Report to FBI on Ernest Avants, May 18, 1965, FBI Civil Unrest, Ernest Avants files 157-HQ-3701, NARA.

51. James Lloyd Jones statements, in Ed Benoist files.

52. Ibid.

53. Ibid.

54. Ibid.

55. Ibid.

56. FBI SAC Roy K. Moore, Report to Assistant Director Al Rosen, June 16, 1966, FBI Civil Unrest, Ernest Avants file 157-HQ-3701, NARA.

57. Adams County Sheriff's Office Report, June 12, 1966. Copy in author's possession.

58. Dr. Leo J. Scanlon, Ben Chester White Autopsy Report, June 13, 1966, FBI Civil Unrest, Ernest Avants file 157-HQ-3701, NARA.

59. *Jet,* July 7, 1966, 15.

60. James Lloyd Jones statements, Ed Benoist files.

61. Ernest Avants, interview by FBI Special Agents Robert F. Boyle and Allen Kornblum, March 13, 1967, FBI Civil Unrest, Ernest Avants file 157-HQ-3701, NARA.

62. Update by County Attorney Ed Benoist to FBI, June 10, 1968, FBI Civil Unrest, Ernest Avants file 157-HQ-3701, NARA.

63. Update by District Attorney Lenox L. Forman to FBI, August 15, 1968, FBI Civil Unrest, Ernest Avants file 157-HQ-3701, NARA.

64. FBI Special Agent George P. Gamblin, Silver Dollar Group Report, August 13, 1968, FBI Civil Unrest, Silver Dollar Group file 157-HQ-4717.

12. CODE NAME: WHARBOM

1. Stanley Nelson, "New Info on Jackson Murder Came Too Late for Widow," *Concordia Sentinel,* August 27, 2009, 9A.

2. Ibid.

3. George Metcalfe, interview by FBI Special Agents Joseph J. Ryan and John M. McCallaghan, March 3, 1967, FBI Civil Unrest, Wharlest Jackson file 44-JN-2044, National Archives and Records Administration (NARA), College Park, MD.

4. Stanley S. Scott, "Natchez Bomber Strikes Again," *Crisis,* April 1967, 133.

5. Stanley Nelson, "New Info on Jackson Murder," 9A.

6. H. C. Golden, interview by FBI Special Agents Reesie L. Timmons and Lawrence J. Monroe, March 4, 1967, FBI Civil Unrest, Wharlest Jackson file 44-JN-2044, NARA.

7. Charles Evers, interview by FBI Special Agents James W. Awe and John L. Puddister, March 2, 1967, FBI Civil Unrest, Wharlest Jackson file 44-JN-2044, NARA.

8. Stanley Nelson, "New Info on Jackson Murder," 9A.

9. Ibid.

10. Ibid.

11. Chester Higgins, "Report On Bomb Killing of Miss. NAACP Leader," *Jet,* April 27, 1967, 16–24.

12. FBI Assistant Director Alex Rosen to FBI Deputy Director Cartha D. DeLoach, February 28, 1967, FBI Civil Unrest, Wharlest Jackson file 44-JN-2044, NARA.

13. FBI Special Agents James W. Awe and John L. Puddister, Crime Scene Report, March 2, 1967, FBI Civil Unrest, Wharlest Jackson file 44-JN-2044, NARA.

14. Dr. Leo J. Scanlon, Autopsy Report, March 2, 1967, FBI Civil Unrest, Wharlest Jackson file 44-JN-2044, NARA.

15. FBI Director to SAC Jackson, Teletype, March 3, 1967, FBI Civil Unrest, Wharlest Jackson file 44-JN-2044, NARA.

16. FBI Special Agents Charles Killion and Frederick P. Smith Jr., Explosives Report, March 2, 1967, FBI Civil Unrest, Wharlest Jackson file 44-JN-2044, NARA.

17. Higgins, "Report on Bomb Killing," 16–24.

18. H. P. Callahan to Mr. Mohr, Memo on WHARBOM Expense, November 18, 1967, FBI Civil Unrest, Wharlest Jackson file 44-JN-2044, NARA.

19. SAC Jackson to FBI Director, Urgent Teletype, February 28, 1967, FBI Civil Unrest, Wharlest Jackson file 44-JN-2044, NARA.

20. Informant No. 1325, interview by FBI, March 21, 1967, FBI Civil Unrest, Wharlest Jackson file 44-JN-2044, NARA.

21. FBI Special Agent Benjamin F. Graves to Inspector Joseph A. Sullivan, March 8, 1967, FBI Civil Unrest, Wharlest Jackson file 44-JN-2044, NARA.

22. Stanley Nelson, "Rayville Man Implicated in Arson That Killed Morris," *Concordia Sentinel*, January 12, 2011, A1.

23. Ibid.

24. Ibid.

25. O. C. Poissot, Statement to FBI Special Agents William E. Dent Jr. and Frank B. Watts, June 12, 1967, FBI Civil Unrest, Wharlest Jackson file 44-JN-2044, NARA.

26. Jim Ingram, interview by Stanley Nelson, October 13, 2008.

27. FBI Special Agent John Pfeifer, Report to SAC Jackson, March 4, 1967, FBI Civil Unrest, Wharlest Jackson file 44-JN-2044, NARA.

28. FBI Special Agent Aloysius J. McFall, Summary Report on James Horace Taylor Jr., June 7, 1967, FBI Civil Unrest, Wharlest Jackson file 44-JN-2044, NARA.

29. FBI Director to Inspector Joe Sullivan, Memo on Search Warrant, March 27, 1967, FBI Civil Unrest, Wharlest Jackson file 44-JN-2044, NARA.

30. Ibid.

31. Ibid.

32. FBI Special Agents Reesie L. Timmons and Benjamin F. Graves, Search of James Watts Attic, April 17, 1967, FBI Civil Unrest, Wharlest Jackson file 44-JN-2044, NARA.

33. Cherish Jean Nichols, interview by Stanley Nelson, April 10, 2014.

34. McFall, Summary Report.

35. FBI Assistant Director Alex Rosen to FBI Deputy Director Cartha D. DeLoach, Memo on Robert Luther Hart, March 20, 1967, FBI Civil Unrest, Wharlest Jackson file 44-JN-2044, NARA.

36. Red Glover, interviews by FBI Special Agents John Pfeifer and John Brady, March 4, 11, 1967, FBI Civil Unrest, Wharlest Jackson file 44-JN-2044, NARA.

37. Ibid.

38. Ibid.; John Pfeifer, interview by Stanley Nelson, April 8, 2011.

39. John Pfeifer, interview by Stanley Nelson, April 8, 2011.

40. Ibid.

41. Ibid.

42. Inspector Joseph Sullivan to FBI Assistant Director Alex Rosen, Memo on CS JN 229-R and Former CS JN 230-R, August 25, 1967, FBI Civil Unrest, Wharlest Jackson file 44-JN-2044, NARA.

43. Ibid.

44. Inspector Joseph Sullivan to FBI Assistant Director Alex Rosen, Memo on NO 1508-R, June 16, 1967, FBI Civil Unrest, Wharlest Jackson file 44-JN-2044, NARA.

45. Ibid.

46. Lennox Forman, interview by FBI Special Agent Reesie L. Timmons, September 20, 1967, FBI Civil Unrest, Wharlest Jackson file 44-JN-2044, NARA.

47. FBI Special Agent William E. Dent Jr., Report, September 20, 1967, FBI Civil Unrest, Wharlest Jackson file 44-JN-2044, NARA.

48. One informant who testified was paid $3,400 by the bureau, while another received $15,000. By the end of 1967, nine WHARBOM informants were paid $18,000 combined. SAC Jackson to FBI Director J. Edgar Hoover, Memo on WHARBOM Costs, December 9, 1967, FBI Civil Unrest, Wharlest Jackson file 44-JN-2044, NARA.

49. Pfeifer, interview by Stanley Nelson, 2011.

50. Ibid.

51. Noah Cross "Thank You" advertisement, *Concordia Sentinel,* December 20, 1967, 9A.

52. "McKeithen Asks for Recommendations to Determine Status of Clerk, Deputy," *Concordia Sentinel,* March 7, 1966, A1.

53. FBI Report on Concordia Parish, Louisiana, Sheriff's Election, November 4, 1967, FBI Civil Unrest, Wharlest Jackson file 44-JN-2044, NARA.

54. Pfeifer interview by Stanley Nelson, 2011.

55. United States v. Noah W. Cross (U.S. Federal Court, Alexandria, LA, May 1972).

56. Federal Grand Jury Proceedings, 1972, obtained by author from an anonymous source.

57. Pfeifer interview by Stanley Nelson, 2011.

58. United States v. Noah Cross (1972).

59. "Cross Takes Oath," *Concordia Sentinel,* July 5, 1972, A1.

EPILOGUE

1. Donald Washington, interview by Stanley Nelson, August 23, 2014.

2. Thomas Moore and David Ridgen, interviews by Stanley Nelson, February 17, 2012.

3. Ibid.

4. Ibid.

5. "Cold Case Reporting: Revisiting Racial Crimes," *Nieman Reports* 65, no. 3 (Fall 2011): 5–23.

6. Stanley Nelson, "Silver Dollar Sons: Klansman's Children Say Their Father Was Livid over Morris Murder," *Concordia Sentinel,* December 31, 2008, A7.

7. "Cold Case Reporting: Revisiting Racial Crimes."

8. Ben Greenberg, "Decades after Slaying, Mississippi Family Seeks Justice," *Clarion-Ledger,* July 22, 2012.

9. Stanley Nelson, "Rev. Lee Celebrates 100th," *Concordia Sentinel,* September 4, 2013, A1. Rev. Lee died in January 2014.

10. Anonymous source, interviews by Stanley Nelson, August 7, 2009, and November 20, 2012.

11. John Pfeifer, interview by Stanley Nelson, June 17, 2011.

12. Anonymous call to Stanley Nelson, February 16, 2012.

13. Thomas Perez, interview by Stanley Nelson, January 6, 2011.

14. Stanley Nelson, "Man Implicated in Frank Morris Arson Dies," *Concordia Sentinel,* May 22, 2013, A1.

15. Jerry Beatty, interview by Stanley Nelson, October 17, 2008.

16. Anonymous sources, interviews by Stanley Nelson, 2010 through 2013.

17. Anonymous source.

18. Cecil Mayo Peoples, interview by FBI Special Agents Thomas J. Connolly and Robert F. Boyle, March 27, 1967, FBI Civil Unrest, Wharlest Jackson file 44-JN-2044, NARA.

BIBLIOGRAPHY

PRIMARY SOURCES

ARCHIVAL DOCUMENTS

FBI Records
FBI Civil Unrest Archives, National Records and Archives Administration, College Park, MD

    Avants, Ernest. File 157-HQ-3701.

    Edwards, Joseph. File 44-NO-2293.

    Glover, Jackson. File 157-JN-2444.

    Head, Kenneth Norman. File 157-HQ-3435.

    Hodges, Earl. File 157-JN-3830.

    Jackson, Wharlest. File 44-JN-2044.

    Jones, Tommie Lee. File 157-HQ-3552.

    Lee, James Frederick. File 157-HQ-4490.

    McDaniel, E. L. File 157-HQ-2156.

    Morris, Frank. File 157-HQ-2311.

    Parker, Ernest. File 157-HQ-3437.

    Seale, James Ford. File 157-HQ-3769.

    Seale, Myron Wayne "Jack." File 157-HQ-3769.

    Silver Dollar Group. File 157-HQ-4717.

    Watkins, James. File 44-NO-3364.

    White, James. File 157-NO-9951.

    White Knights. File 157-HQ-1552.

House Un-American Activities Committee Records
Center for Legislative Archives, National Archives and Records Administration, Washington, DC

    Records of the U.S. House of Representatives. Record Group 233.

    Shamel, Charles E. Records of the House Un-American Activities Committee, 1945–1969/House Internal Security Committee, 1969–1976. July 1995.

Additional Government Records

McCain Library and Archives Digital Collections, University of Southern Mississippi, Hattiesburg

    Civil Rights Collection.

    Freedom Summer 1964 Collection.

Mississippi Department of Archives and History Digital Collections, Jackson, Miss.

    Series 2515: Mississippi State Sovereignty Commission Records.

COURT CASES

Thomas Moore and Thelma Collins v. Franklin County, August 5, 2008 (U.S. D.C. S.D. MS-WD).

United States v. J. D. Richardson, Monroe, LA, January 20–21, 1971.

United States v. James Ford Seale, March 14, 2008 (U.S. D.C. A 5th D).

United States v. Noah W. Cross, Alexandria, LA, May 2, 1972 (U.S. D.C. W. D. LA-A.D.).

INTERVIEWS AND PERSONAL CORRESPONDENCE

All interviews are with Stanley Nelson unless otherwise noted.

Beatty, Rae. Ferriday, LA, October 17, 2008.

Blunschi, John. Ferriday, LA, July 3, 2013.

Byrne, Tony. Natchez, MS, May 21, 2014.

Casper, Meg, Press Secretary, Louisiana Secretary of State. Phone interview, May 6, 2013.

Crawford, Vic. Natchez, MS, April 13, 2009.

Curtis, Mary. Natchez, MS, August 18, 2009.

Davis, Woodie. Ferriday, LA, March 2008.

Deitle, Cynthia. Statement to Chief of FBI Civil Rights Cold Case Unit, published in *Concordia Sentinel,* January 6, 2011.

Drane, Lee. Phone interview, January 6, 2010.

Ferrell, Tommy. Phone interview, October 10, 2013.

Fitzgerald, Paige, U.S. Department of Justice, to Rosa Williams. Frank Morris Case Closed Letter, 2014.

Gardner, Ted. Phone interview, May 16, 2012.

Graves, Max. Meadville, MS, June 26, 2013.

Hodges, Keith. Phone interview, January 19, 2013.

Ingram, Jim. Phone interview, October 13, 2008.

Lee, Rev. Robert, Jr. Ferriday, LA, January 3, November 12, 2008.

Lewis, Robert "Buck." Ferriday, LA, August 6, 2014.

Mitchell, Jack. Phone interview, 2013.

Nichols, Cherish Jean. Jonesville, LA, April 10, 2014.

Pfeifer, John. Phone interviews, March 16, April 2, April 8, June 2, 2011.

Robinson, Ed. E mail to Stanley Nelson, April 28, 2014.

Thompson, Carl Ray. Ferriday, LA, December 13, 2007.

Thompson, Father August. Pineville, LA, January 29, March 11, 2011, April 29, 2012.

Vernon, Helen Hodges. Phone interview, January 25, 2013.

Williams, Billy Bob. November 8, 2009, December 10, 2013, January 25, May 24, 2014.

———. Interview by Bryan R. Holstein, February 13, 16, 2007. Society of Former Special Agents of the FBI, Inc.

NEWSPAPERS

Atlanta Journal

Baltimore Afro-American

Chicago Sun-Times

Clarion-Ledger

Concordia Sentinel

Daily News

Jackson Free Press

Meridian Star

Natchez Democrat

New York Times

New York Tribune

Tuscaloosa News

Washington Post

OTHER PRIMARY SOURCES

Town of Ferriday. Minute Book. November 1954, April 1960, August 1963. Town Hall, Ferriday, La.

SECONDARY SOURCES

Armstrong, Mary G. *Memoirs of George W. Armstrong.* Self-published, 1958.

Bragg, Marion. *Historic Names and Places on the Lower Mississippi River.* Vicksburg, MS: Mississippi River Commission, 1977.

Calhoun, Robert Dabney. "A History of Concordia Parish (1768–1931)." Rpr. from *Louisiana Historical Quarterly,* January 1932.

Dundy, Elaine. *Ferriday, Louisiana.* New York: Donald I. Fine, 1991.

Faircloth, Adam. *Race and Democracy: The Civil Rights Struggle in Louisiana, 1915–1972.* Athens: University of Georgia Press, 1995.

Foner, Eric. *Forever Free: The Story of Emancipation and Reconstruction.* New York: Vintage, 2008.

Griffin, John Howard. "Journal of a Trip South." *Ramparts,* Christmas 1963.

Higgins, Chester. "Report on Bomb Killing of Miss. NAACP Leader." *Jet,* April 27, 1967, 16–24.

Holmes, Jack D. L. *Gayoso: The Life of a Spanish Governor in the Mississippi Valley, 1789–1799.* Baton Rouge: LSU Press, 1965.

"Introducing the F.F.M.," FFM newsletter, August 15, 1965, 1. Father August Thompson Personal collection.

Jessey, Cornelia. "Contemporary Spirituality." *The Way International,* December 1977.

Jet, July 7, 1966, 15.

Kurtz, Michael. "Political Corruption and Organized Crime in Louisiana: The FBI Files on Earl Long." *Louisiana Historical Association Quarterly* 29, no. 3 (Summer 1988): 229–52.

Lynch, John Roy. *Reminiscences of an Active Life: The Autobiography of John Roy Lynch.* Chicago: University of Chicago Press, 1970.

Mars, Florence. *Witness in Philadelphia.* Baton Rouge: LSU Press, 1977.

Mills, Frances Preston, ed. *The History of the Descendants of the New Jersey Settlers of Adams County, Mississippi.* Vol. 2. Jackson, MS: Hederman Bros., 1981.

"The Mob." *Life,* September 1, 1967.

"My Problems: How Much Should a Family Knuckle Under." *Good Housekeeping,* June 1965, 62.

"Negro Natchez Boycott Hurts White Merchants." *Jet,* November 11, 1965.

"Nobody Turn Me 'Round." *Time,* October 15, 1965.

Rowland, Dunbar. *Encyclopedia of Mississippi History.* 2 vols. Madison, WI: S. A. Brant, 1907.

Scott, Stanley S. "Natchez Bomber Strikes Again." *Crisis,* April 1967, 133.

Shapiro, Joseph. "Justice in the Segregated South: A New Look at an Old Killing." National Public Radio. Aired May 3, 2013.

Snyder, Granville. "When Civil Rights and Social Action Became Personal." Rev. Granville Snyder Personal Recollections (unpublished), 2012.

Whitehead, Don. *Attack on Terror: The FBI against the Ku Klux Klan in Mississippi.* New York: Funk and Wagnalls, 1970.

INDEX